CAMBRIDGE
UNIVERSITY PRESS

Modern Europe, 1750-1921

for Cambridge International AS Level History

COURSEBOOK

Graham Goodlad, Patrick Walsh-Atkins & Russell Williams

Series editor: Patrick Walsh-Atkins

CAMBRIDGE
UNIVERSITY PRESS

University Printing House, Cambridge CB2 8BS, United Kingdom

One Liberty Plaza, 20th Floor, New York, NY 10006, USA

477 Williamstown Road, Port Melbourne, VIC 3207, Australia

4843/24, 2nd Floor, Ansari Road, Daryaganj, Delhi – 110002, India

79 Anson Road, #06–04/06, Singapore 079906

Cambridge University Press is part of the University of Cambridge.

It furthers the University's mission by disseminating knowledge in the pursuit of education, learning and research at the highest international levels of excellence.

Information on this title: www.cambridge.org/ 9781108733922

First published 2019

20 19 18 17 16 15 14 13 12 11 10 9 8 7 6 5 4 3 2 1

Printed in Malaysia by Vivar Printing

A catalogue record for this publication is available from the British Library

ISBN 978-1-108-73392-2 Paperback

Contents

How to use this book

This book contains a number of features to help you in your study.

Each chapter begins with a set of **Learning objectives** that briefly set out the points you should understand once you have completed the chapter.

Learning objectives

In this chapter you will:

- learn why so many of the preconditions needed for industrialisation were present in Britain in the middle of the 18th century
- find out why the manufacturing industry grew at a rapid rate in Britain in the late 18th century

Before you start activities are designed to activate the prior knowledge you need for each chapter.

Before you start

- Research the human and physical geography of France in the late 18th century.
- Was it a rich or a poor country?
- Why was France seen as the centre of European culture?

The **Timeline** provides a visual guide to the key events which happened during the years covered by the topic.

Timeline

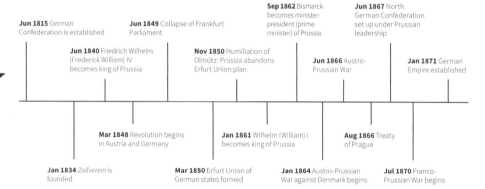

Jun 1815 German Confederation is established

Jun 1840 Friedrich Wilhelm (Frederick William) IV becomes king of Prussia

Jun 1849 Collapse of Frankfurt Parliament

Nov 1850 Humiliation of Olmütz: Prussia abandons Erfurt Union plan

Sep 1862 Bismarck becomes minister-president (prime minister) of Prussia

Jun 1866 Austro-Prussian War

Jun 1867 North German Confederation set up under Prussian leadership

Jan 1871 German Empire established

Mar 1848 Revolution begins in Austria and Germany

Jan 1861 Wilhelm (William) I becomes king of Prussia

Aug 1866 Treaty of Prague

Jan 1834 *Zollverein* is founded

Mar 1850 Erfurt Union of German states formed

Jan 1864 Austro-Prussian War against Denmark begins

Jul 1870 Franco-Prussian War begins

Each chapter contains multiple **Activities**. These are a mixture of individual and group tasks to help you develop your skills and practise applying your understanding of a topic

ACTIVITY 1.17

What was the principal reason for the success of the coup that brought Napoleon to power? How far was it down to the circumstances of 1799 or to his own skills?

Reflection boxes are included throughout the book so that you have the chance to think about how your skills are developing and how you can enhance your independent learning skills.

Reflection: How did you decide on a definition of a 'revolution'? In pairs, explain your method to each other. How are your methods different? Would you change your method for defining a 'revolution' following your discussion?

Key terms are important terms in the topic you are learning. They are highlighted in black bold and defined where they first appear in the text.

 KEY TERM

Fallow: Of farm land, left unused for a year, in order to avoid soil exhaustion.

EDWIN CHADWICK (1800–90)

Trained originally as a lawyer, Chadwick was deeply concerned by the impact of industrialisation on the way many people lived and worked. He became a committed reformer. His detailed, highly scientific, investigations into both individual welfare and public health led to both the New Poor Law of 1834 and the Public Health Act of 1848.

Key Figure boxes highlight important historical figures that you need to remember.

KEY CONCEPT

Cause and consequence

Look back at the information in this chapter on living conditions in towns during this period. Were poor living conditions solely the consequence of large and rapid population growth in towns, or did other causes contribute? Make a list of as many such causes as you can that explain why urban living conditions for the working class were poor. In what ways can you link these reasons together?

Key Concepts boxes contain questions that help you develop a conceptual understanding of History, and how the different topics you study are connected.

Think Like a Historian boxes contain prompts and questions requiring that you apply your skills in evaluation and analysis. They go beyond the syllabus to help you understand how these skills apply in the real world.

●●● THINK LIKE A HISTORIAN

Look at two different sources on the downfall of a political leader or government in recent times. How does your study of the collapse of the tsarist regime and the Provisional Government help you to understand the failure of other kinds of government?

Summary

After working through this chapter, make sure you understand the following key points:

- why the problems and policies of Louis XVI reached crisis point in 1789 and why his management of this crisis led to revolutionary change in France
- how the failure to find consensus on how France should be governed after 1790 led to the execution of the king,

Each chapter ends with a summary, Exam-style questions and a Sample answer.

The **Summary** is a brief review of the main points in the chapter to help you revise.

v

Exam-Style Questions provide an opportunity to relate your learning to formal assessment and practise writing longer answers.

1   a   Read Sources C and D. Compare and contrast Sources C and D as evidence of Prussia's responsibility for the outbreak of war with France in 1870.

    b   Read all of the sources. 'Bismarck planned in advance to complete the process of German unification by means of a war with France.' How far do the sources support this view?

Sample answer

To what extent was the French crisis of 1789 caused by economic factors?

Economic factors played a very large role in both the longer-term causes of the French Revolution as well as the shorter-term causes. Although there were other factors, such as the summoning of the Estates General itself in 1788, which led to the actual crisis of 1789, underlying everything was the fact that the French government had run out of money and an important section of the French population was very hungry as a result of bad harvests. There was also a real lack of will on the part of the king and his court to make the necessary changes that might have led to a solution of the many problems which France faced.

This has a good focus and gives an answer to the 'extent' part of the question by suggesting that it played a 'very large' part. It also shows balance by considering other causes. Some reflection on what might be 'economic' causes would help.

The **Sample answer** to one of the exam-style questions is a realistic student response, annotated with explanations about what makes it successful and commentary on how it could be improved.

Further reading

Daunton, M.J. (1995). *Progress and Poverty: An Economic and Social History of Britain 1700–1850.* **Oxford: Oxford University Press.** (This covers in depth every aspect of society and the economy in the period studied.)

Evans, E. (2001). *The Forging of the Modern State: Early Industrial Britain 1783–1870.* **London: Routledge.** (This is particularly good on the politics of the period, especially on the 1832 Reform Act. Part Three covers topics including the Poor Law, factory reform and Chartism well.)

The **Further Reading** section suggests additional resources where you can explore the topic in more detail.

Introduction

Aims of the coursebook

Cambridge International AS Level History is a revised series of three books that offer complete and thorough coverage of the Cambridge International AS Level History syllabus (9489). Each book covers one of the three AS Level options in the Cambridge International syllabus for first examination in 2021. These books may also prove useful for students following other AS and A Level courses covering similar topics. Written in clear and accessible language, Cambridge International AS Level History Modern Europe, 1750–1921, enables students to gain the knowledge, understanding and skills to succeed in their AS Level course, and ultimately in further study and examination.

Syllabus

Students wishing to take just the AS Level take two separate papers at the end of a one-year course. If they wish to take the full A Level there are two possible routes. The first is to take the two AS papers at the end of the first year of the course and a further two A Level papers at the end of the following year. The second is to take the two AS papers as well as the two A Level papers at the end of a two-year course. For the full A Level, all four papers must be taken.

There are four topics available to be studied within the European option:

- France, 1774–1814
- The Industrial Revolution in Britain, 1750–1850
- Liberalism and nationalism in Germany, 1815–71
- The Russian Revolution, 1894–1921

The two AS Level papers are outlined below.

Paper 1

This is a source-based paper which lasts for one hour and 15 minutes and is based on one of the four topics listed above. Schools and colleges will be notified in advance which topic it will be. The paper will contain at least three sources and students will have to answer two questions on them. The questions will be based on one of the four key questions set out in the syllabus. **There is no choice of question**. Students are expected to have the ability to understand, evaluate and utilise those sources in their answers, as well as having sound knowledge of the topic. In the first question (a) students are required to consider the sources and answer a question based on one aspect of them. There is a particular emphasis on source comprehension and evaluation skills in this question, but contextual knowledge is important as well. In the second question (b) students must use the sources as well as their own knowledge and understanding to address how far the sources support a given statement. The relevant knowledge is provided in the appropriate chapter in this book.

Paper 2

This paper lasts for one hour and 45 minutes. It contains **three** questions, and students must answer **two** of them. There will be one question on each of the three topics which have **not** been examined for Paper 1. So for example, if the topic covered in Paper 1 is the Russian Revolution, Paper 2 will contain a question on each of the following three topics:

- France, 1774–1814
- The Industrial Revolution in Britain, 1750–1850
- Liberalism and nationalism in Germany, 1815–71

Each question has two parts: part (a) requires a causal explanation and part (b) requires analysis. All the questions will be based on one of the four key questions set out in the syllabus. The focus of this paper is on assessing the students' knowledge and understanding of the specified topics and their analytical skills. The syllabus makes it clear what specific skills are being assessed in each paper, and how marks are allocated.

Acknowledgements

The authors and publishers acknowledge the following sources of copyright material and are grateful for the permissions granted. While every effort has been made, it has not always been possible to identify the sources of all the material used, or to trace all copyright holders. If any omissions are brought to our notice, we will be happy to include the appropriate acknowledgements on reprinting.

Thanks to the following for permission to reproduce images:

Cover Image: Jonathan Smith/Getty Images

Chapter 1: Photo Josse/Leemage/GI; Photos.com/GI; Nastasic/GI; adoc-photos/GI; Universal History Archive/GI; DEA/G. DAGLI ORTI/GI; Christophel Fine Art/GI; Print Collector/GI; Christophel Fine Art/GI; Hulton Archive/GI; DEA/G. DAGLI ORTI/De Agostini/GI; ilbusca/GI; Fine Art Images/GI; John Parrot/GI; Photos.com/GI; Hulton Archive/GI; GraphicaArtis/GI; Peter Barritt/GI; **Chapter 2:** duncan1890/GI; Ann Ronan Pictures/GI; Print Collector/GI; Universal History Archive/GI; GraphicaArtis/GI; DEA/M. SEEMULLER/GI; The Print Collector/GI; Olaf Protze/GI; Underwood Archives/GI; SSPL/GI; Science & Society Picture Library/GI; Mansell/GI; An image 'The Great monster' from Republican/Library of Congress; Hulton Archive/GI; DEA/BIBLIOTECA AMBROSIANA/GI; **Chapter 3:** Panoramic Images/GI; Universal History Archive/GI; Mansell/GI; Hulton Archive/GI; ullstein bild Dtl./GI; ullstein bild Dtl./GI; traveler1116/GI; traveler1116/GI; Jeune/GI; DEA/BIBLIOTECA AMBROSIANA/GI; ullstein bild Dtl./GI; ullstein bild Dtl./GI; **Chapter 4:** AFP Contributor/GI; Photo 12/GI; Keystone/GI; Photo12/GI; Fine Art Images/GI; Fine Art Images/GI; ullstein bild Dtl./GI; Keystone/GI; TASS/GI; The Print Collector/GI; Sovfoto/GI; Universal History Archive/GI; TASS/GI; **Chapter 5:** Caiaimage/Sam Edwards/GI; Heritage Images/GI; Heritage Images/GI; Print Collector/GI.

Key: GI = Getty Images

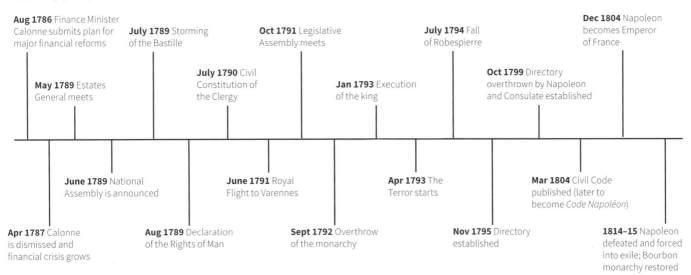

Chapter 1
France, 1774–1814

Learning objectives

In this chapter you will:

- understand why the Ancien Régime in France was unable to deal with the problems facing it in the 1780s
- learn why the attempt to bring financial reform to France in 1789 developed into a radical revolution
- analyse the various factors which affected the course of the revolution and determined its outcome
- understand how and why this revolution came to an end under the leadership of Napoleon, and assess his impact on France.

Timeline

Aug 1786 Finance Minister Calonne submits plan for major financial reforms

May 1789 Estates General meets

June 1789 National Assembly is announced

Apr 1787 Calonne is dismissed and financial crisis grows

July 1789 Storming of the Bastille

Aug 1789 Declaration of the Rights of Man

July 1790 Civil Constitution of the Clergy

Oct 1791 Legislative Assembly meets

June 1791 Royal Flight to Varennes

Sept 1792 Overthrow of the monarchy

Jan 1793 Execution of the king

Apr 1793 The Terror starts

July 1794 Fall of Robespierre

Nov 1795 Directory established

Oct 1799 Directory overthrown by Napoleon and Consulate established

Dec 1804 Napoleon becomes Emperor of France

Mar 1804 Civil Code published (later to become *Code Napoléon*)

1814–15 Napoleon defeated and forced into exile; Bourbon monarchy restored

Before you start

- Research the human and physical geography of France in the late 18th century.
- Was it a rich or a poor country?
- Why was France seen as the centre of European culture?
- Look at the countries surrounding France in 1789. What sort of relationship did France have with them? Was it always peaceful?

1.1 What were the causes and immediate outcomes of the 1789 revolution?

The Ancien Régime: problems and policies of Louis XVI

France in the late 18th century was ruled by an **absolute monarch**, Louis XVI. It was, however, a difficult country to govern. It had a population of about 27 million. There was significant regional difference across the country, along with a strong tradition for each part of France to deal with local issues in its own way. There were also different legal systems, which dated back for centuries. The regions had different systems of taxation and there were also customs barriers between some parts of France, meaning that trade could not move freely around the country. These conditions meant that, in practice, the king's orders were often ignored or proved too difficult to carry out.

KEY TERMS

Ancien Régime: Literally 'the old system of government', this describes how France was governed before 1789. It not only covers the government and administration, but also the structure of society and the role of the Church as well.

Absolute monarch: A king or queen who has complete power in a state. They can make laws and there are no constitutional limits to their power.

Real wages: Wages measured in terms of what they enable workers to buy, rather than the actual money received.

Social divisions in France

The vast majority – 80% – of the French population at this time were poor peasants. Agriculture was not highly developed and was inefficient. Peasants farmed tiny plots of land and their main aim was to grow enough food to survive. At the same time, they were heavily taxed by the government, their landlords and the Church. In addition, they had to maintain the roads for their landlords and their local community – work they were not paid for. Landlords had the right to hunt on the peasants' land. The peasants were also forced to use their landlords' wine presses and flour mills, at a high price.

There were only three good harvests between 1770 and 1789, and this resulted in rural poverty and hunger. The economy was simply unable to provide an adequate living for those who lived in the countryside, so many peasants were forced to move to the towns. This growing urban population, poor and unskilled, found there was little or no chance of quality employment. Unlike Britain, France had few factories making textiles, for example, to absorb this migration of workers. Meanwhile, the existing urban working class saw their wages decline as food prices rose. Bread usually formed about 75% of the French working-class diet. In normal times, a family would spend between 35 and 50% of its income on bread. After a bad harvest, when prices soared, fear of starvation took hold, and there was no money for heating and clothing. Increasing poverty, worsened by a decline in **real wages**, led to growing urban unrest, including bread riots. The police force had only limited numbers and found it difficult to maintain order.

A hungry, highly taxed lower class who were not represented by politicians, in both town and countryside, was an important factor in the events that followed. The distance between the rich and the poor was growing. The poor saw those they paid taxes to – the aristocracy and the Church in particular – enjoying lives of luxury, but peasants had no means of redressing their grievances. The legal system worked against them, and was, in fact, another means of control.

In French towns, the middle class was growing. Increasingly, these people were well educated and rich. By 1780, they owned around 20% of the land in France. They were involved in either commerce or industry, or in professions such as law and medicine. The vast majority of France's future revolutionary leaders came from this middle class; many of them had been lawyers. Some were increasingly involved in aspects of local government and administration, but became frustrated by their powerlessness. In addition to having no political power, it was not possible for them to join the top levels of government, the military and the judiciary system. Only the higher nobility could expect to take up those jobs. While people in the middle class were not as heavily taxed as the peasantry, they did pay some taxes, and naturally resented a system where they had no say in how their money was spent. Many traditional middle-class career posts such as judges and tax collectors, began to be passed from father to son, or could be bought for cash. Jobs were no longer decided by ability. As a result, money influenced local administration and the law. These educated and increasingly angry members of the middle class were to play a decisive role in the coming events.

The Church and the aristocracy

The Roman Catholic Church, with over 130 000 clergy, monks and nuns, was a very wealthy organisation. It owned 10% of the land across the country and paid no taxes. It controlled most of the education in France and also approved (or not) all publications. The Church was determined to maintain its control over as many aspects of French life as possible, and to keep hold of its wealth and benefits.

The most senior posts in the Church invariably went to members of the aristocracy, often totally inexperienced young men with little interest in performing their religious duties. As a result, many of the ordinary clergy from the lower classes – often hardworking and devout men determined to help their parishioners – could not progress to senior roles where they would be able to direct the Church towards carrying out what they considered to be its proper duties. Although the Church did not pay taxes, it did pay a contribution to the government. This contribution was paid, however, by the lower clergy and not the wealthy bishops. These factors led to a growing division between rich and poor within the clergy, the aristocrat and the commoner. This was one of the reasons why the Church was not able to present a united front to the revolutionary forces that later set out to destroy it.

The aristocracy dominated France. A tiny minority of the population owned around 30% of the land and most of the wealth. There were about 300 000 members of this elite group. They paid virtually no taxes. They were also exempt from things like **conscription** for the army and responsibility for road repairs. Instead, they enjoyed a range of benefits, often created centuries earlier, such as being able to hunt wherever they wished.

They dominated all the key posts at court and in the government, the Church, the judiciary and the army. One of the reasons why the French army often performed badly was because the officers were noblemen and promotion came through noble rank rather than through ability or experience.

French aristocrats tended to be hostile to those involved in trade and commerce. Unlike the British aristocracy during the same period, who were deeply involved in innovation in agriculture, industry and commerce, and who usually accepted their sons marrying the rich daughters of middle-class industrialists, the French aristocracy tended to remain a group apart. Generally, they did not wish to associate with the lower classes in such matters as industry and commerce.

As in the clergy, there was a division between the 'higher' and 'lower' aristocracy. The highest levels of this social class lived at Versailles, the court of the king of France near Paris. Here, in this vast and splendid palace, they had access to power, influence, and the top jobs and pensions awarded by the king. They lived in an isolated and privileged environment and were determined to keep it. A talent for court politics and intrigue was the key to the top jobs, and administrative ability often had little to do with success. The 'poorer' or 'lower' nobility, while anxious to retain their privileges, often resented the power and wealth of the 'higher' nobility at Versailles. The lower nobility, like the case of the lower clergy, were a reason why the nobility did not act together to defend their power during the years of the revolution.

 KEY TERM

Conscription: Compulsory enrolment into the army as a service to the state. Men had no choice in the matter and they had to be prepared to go and fight.

King Louis XVI and the *parlements*

The king was at the top of the social hierarchy. **Louis XVI** had been crowned in 1775, when he was young and inexperienced. He had a great sense of duty and many good intentions of ruling well. He inherited a system in which the king had absolute power, however, and he would have liked not just to keep, but to increase this power. His courtiers and ministers (they were usually the same thing) tended to be divided on the issue of the role of the monarch. Some wished to create an even more absolute monarch, in control of every part of French life, and to end the ability of local

3

parlements to block orders from Versailles and any local autonomy. Traditionally, laws made by the king could not be carried out unless they were published by the *parlements*, so these courts were in a position to delay or prevent the implementation of royal wishes. Only lawyers of noble rank could be members, and they were usually more interested in preserving their own privileges than anything else.

KEY TERM

Parlements: Judicial courts of appeal. There were 13 local *parlements* in France at this time, of which the one in Paris was the most powerful. They were not elected or representative bodies.

Some wished to go back to a system in which the king had to consult the aristocracy on matters of policy and administration, thus reducing his power. A few, influenced by the ideas of the Enlightenment (see 'Pressures for change') wanted to reform the whole system and make it both more efficient and more inclusive, eliminating its most obvious failings. For example, the king appointed intendants to administer the localities, called *departments*, in France. The intendants were royal agents and their job was to carry out royal wishes in their departments. They were often hated by local *parlements*, however, who did their best to ignore and resist them.

The divisions at court and within the aristocracy and clergy were often reflected when it came to local administration. There were bitter local rivalries, which made France a very difficult country to govern, and obviously in need of reform. These fundamental differences in outlook among the king's inner circle of courtiers made it difficult to find common ground when major decisions needed to be taken.

LOUIS XVI (1754–93)

King Louis XVI was deeply religious and was determined to rule well. He was, however, weak and indecisive, and reluctant to accept the reality of the situation he found himself in. His resistance to reform after 1789 and his obvious lack of sympathy for the changes of 1789–90 ultimately led to his execution in 1793.

ACTIVITY 1.1

Work with another student to identify the principal social, economic and political problems which faced Louis XVI when he came to the throne. Copy and complete the table to help you categorise the problems you have identified.

Social	Economic	Political

Which do you think were the most important? Why? What sort of strategy might he have adopted to deal with these problems?

Pressures for change (social, economic and political, including the Enlightenment)

The Enlightenment

In the 18th century France was home to some of the greatest thinkers and writers of the period. They became part of an intellectual and philosophical movement known as the 'Enlightenment', and they had a major influence on the whole revolutionary process in France. It can be difficult to assess the importance of abstract ideas on actual events, but it is known that many of the later revolutionary leaders, and Napoleon Bonaparte himself, were very well read and were influenced by the ideas of these thinkers.

Many of these writers did not just criticise what they saw happening in France; they also supported practical improvements. Some of the most important figures of the Enlightenment were:

- **Voltaire**, who was very critical of the role, wealth and influence of the Church, and attacked religious intolerance. He was also critical of the entire French legal system and its frequent miscarriages of justice.
- **Montesquieu**, who was critical of despotism and autocratic power. He wanted a system of checks and balances, where one part of a system of government, for example an elected parliament, could check the actions of ministers and the king. He was impressed by the British system, where parliament controlled law-making and could check the government. Montesquieu advocated the rule of law: that everyone should be equal before the law and subject to the law of the land.
- **Diderot**, author of an encyclopaedia of 'sciences, arts and crafts', who was determined to advance knowledge. He was a great advocate of independent thinking, and

was anxious to promote a critical and questioning attitude to everything.

- **Rousseau**, who argued for more education, was a great thinker who wrote about power and liberty. He proposed many ideas on how there could be both authority and freedom for men in the same society.
- **Quesnay**, who wrote on economics and argued against the constraints on the free production and movement of goods which existed at the time in France.

These men challenged established ideas, institutions and social structures. They encouraged argument and debate on a wide range of major public issues. They argued that there could be improvement in all areas of public life.

The writers wrote at a time when confidence in the French government was low. There was often famine and this led to riots. France in 1763 had just been humiliated in a major war with Britain and had lost most of its overseas empire, including Canada, to the victors. There was also little confidence in the young king crowned in 1775, and his Austrian wife, Marie Antoinette, was hated. Many of the future leaders who emerged during the revolution had read, thought about and debated the ideas of these great writers of the Enlightenment. When the Ancien Régime collapsed after 1789, it was these thinkers who provided ideas that led the way forward for the new governors of France.

The reaction of Louis XVI to attempts at reform
Political and economic factors

Social and ideological factors played a major part in the start of the revolution in 1789, but politics and economics also played a key role. In 1778, the decision was made to form an alliance with the colonists in America who were fighting for independence from Frances's old enemy, Britain. France declared war against Britain, determined to regain not only the colonies that it had lost to Britain in 1763, such as Canada, but also the prestige lost as a result of the many military defeats it had suffered in the war.

A-R-J Turgot, an admirer of François Quesnay, was the finance minister when Louis became king in 1775. He warned against any more involvement in wars, arguing that 'the first gunshot will drive the state to bankruptcy', but he was ignored. The king took advice instead from the Comte de Vergennes, his foreign minister, who was interested in France's (and his own) prestige, and did not worry about such matters as cost. The cautious Turgot was dismissed in 1776. He predicted correctly that the war would do little harm to Britain, and instead would prevent the vital financial reforms that France needed so badly, with the risk of national bankruptcy.

In 1777, a new finance minister was appointed. This was **Jacques Necker**. He was an unusual choice, as he was not a French aristocrat, but a middle-class banker of Swiss origin and also a Protestant. Naturally, this meant that many people at Louis's court disliked him, notably the queen. The appointment of an outsider like Necker indicates that there was a growing awareness that French state finances were in a dreadful state.

Necker was born in Switzerland and trained as a banker, and was finance minister three times: 1777–81, 1788–89 and 1789–90. Some historians argue that in his first tenure he caused many of the problems which faced France in later years. However, when he was recalled to office in 1788, he was seen as the man able to solve France's economic problems. He was, however, unable to provide either an accurate picture of the royal finances or solutions to the financial problems facing France. In 1789, he fatefully advised the king to call the Estates General.

JACQUES NECKER (1732–1804)

5

Necker promised to reform the financial system. Many people, unwisely as it turned out, had great confidence in him. He investigated and analysed France's finances, but he did not deliver reform. He funded the expensive war with Britain through borrowing at increasingly high interest rates. In 1781, he published – for the first time in France – a public account of the royal finances. However, in this report he claimed that these finances were in a good condition. They were not. He also hid the huge cost of the war with Britain. He was dismissed four months after the report was published. Government borrowing at high interest rates continued to increase.

The war with Britain came to an end in 1783. The United States became independent, but France gained nothing from the war except deeper **national debt**. There was now, however, an opportunity for financial reform and stability. With growing concern about the state of royal finances, another new finance minister, Charles de Calonne, was appointed in 1783. Initially, he declined to cut royal spending and simply borrowed more money to keep the government running, but he did start to plan important changes. He was aware that without change France would go bankrupt.

In 1786, with the cost of servicing the state's debts becoming too high, Calonne submitted a series of needed reforms to the king. He made three main proposals:

- Reform the system of taxation by increasing taxes for the wealthy.
- Stimulate the economy generally and encourage commerce and industry.
- Create confidence in France and its economy so it could borrow more money at lower rates of interest.

The king, prepared from time to time to take an interest in matters of finance, approved the plans. The decision was taken, in the light of growing public concern and interest in the economy, to submit these proposals to the **Assembly of Notables** in the hope of gaining support for the measures. This body, made up of nobles and clergy (only 10 of the 144 members were not nobles) then met for the first time since 1626.

KEY TERM

Assembly of Notables: A group of noblemen or senior members of the Church. The Assembly had been summoned by the king only four times in the past, to deal with emergencies. The Assembly had no authority – it could only consult, but not actually do anything. Calonne hoped that it would help him to gain some support for much-needed financial reform.

KEY TERM

National debt: The amount of money borrowed by a state or country, often at very high rates of interest.

Figure 1.1: France's economic problems before the revolution

Calonne was in an impossible position. He was disliked by the vast majority of the Notables. He had little serious support from the king and the rest of the government. Many of those in a position of influence chose to believe Necker's earlier statement that all was well with the royal finances. In addition, the expensive war was over, so they thought the crisis was also over. Calonne had no idea how to manage the Notables, and, in fact, there was no clarity on what the Notables' role was. Was it just consultative? Was the Assembly there just to support changes? Did it have any authority? Most Notables recognised a need for some reforms, but they wanted to make sure that they, and the class that they represented, did not suffer from those reforms.

The king was faced with an uncertain situation and tried to solve the problem by sacking Calonne in April 1787. Calonne was replaced by yet another finance minister, Etienne Brienne, who, as president of the Assembly of Notables was felt to have influence over its members. The king disliked and distrusted him, however, which meant that Brienne had limited royal support. When the Notables demanded an accurate account of the royal finances, the king refused and instead dismissed the Assembly. This caused great anxiety and protest among the educated public, and marked the start of the financial and political crisis that eventually led to the revolution itself.

The meeting and dismissal of the Notables showed:

- just how deep France's financial crisis was
- the many failings of the king and his court and government
- that the public had not been given a true picture of the state of the royal finances
- that there was real opposition in the country to the king and his government
- that the public demanded change and greater involvement in government.

The beginnings of widespread revolt

Brienne had to raise money so he increased taxes and borrowed more, but found it very difficult to persuade bankers to lend to a state which many felt was near breakdown.

Attempts to gain support for increased taxes from the *parlement* of Paris – the most powerful of the country's *parlements* – failed. The *parlement* refused to support tax increases until they were given an accurate picture of the royal accounts. The king refused again, seeing such demands as an attack on his royal powers, and banished the *parlement* members to the provinces. The people of

Paris were so angry at the king's action that both middle and lower classes, and huge crowds took to the streets in protest. This was the first sign of a potential alliance between the middle and lower classes against the king and the aristocracy.

The financial and political crisis continued throughout 1787 and 1788. The king recalled the Paris *parlement* and met with it in November 1787. He totally mismanaged it, having no grasp of why there was so much concern about the state's finances. The king undermined the ministers who were trying to negotiate and manage the *parlement* and, when the *parlement* refused to support the new taxes, the leaders of the 'opposition' were arrested and imprisoned in the Bastille, a royal fortress in Paris. The arrests resulted in countrywide protests, demonstrating the high level of public interest and support for reform.

Divisions were also emerging among the nobility and clergy over whether to support any change to their privileged and untaxed status, and it was clear too that the growing middle class was becoming increasingly alienated from the classes above.

The crisis worsened throughout 1788. There was widespread anger at the king's refusal to become involved in a civil war in the Netherlands. (The French felt the area was very much their sphere of interest and there was a risk of Austria increasing its power.) There was simply no money to pay for any intervention there. The lack of money, and the incompetence of the (noble) officer corps, meant that the army was viewed as potentially unreliable, even though it was the only way of keeping order in France. Thousands of pamphlets were by now being published throughout France, demanding social, economic and political change. The Paris *parlement* demanded complete constitutional change and was widely supported in this demand. By August 1788, it was clear that the state was virtually bankrupt and this was publicly admitted. However, Brienne, who was aware of the scale of the problem, and had some solutions, was dismissed by the king. This further reduced any confidence in the king and his court.

The tension and unrest was made worse by a series of hailstorms that summer which destroyed much of the harvest. Everyone knew that this would lead to a shortage of bread and higher prices. It would be a hard winter.

The king's solution was to recall Necker as finance minister. At his instigation, the decision was taken to summon the **Estates General**, which had not met since 1614, to solve France's problems.

Cahiers de doléances

Before the Estates General met, the districts of France were asked, as was customary, to put forward a list of issues they wanted the assembly to consider when it met. These lists were known as *cahiers de doléances*. In March 1789, the *cahier* from Dourdan, in northern France, contained the following, quite typical, demands.

The clergy – the First Estate – asked:

- to retain all the rights and privileges of the Roman Catholic Church
- to ban the practice of any other religion
- to give the Church complete control of all education
- to ban all publications attacking the Church and give the Church full control over all publications
- to retain freedom from taxation unless it decided to contribute
- that there should be a reform of the local legal system to ensure fairer justice for all
- that care should be taken to ensure adequate food supplies for all
- that landlords should be prevented from imposing high charges on peasants and hunting on their lands.

The nobility – the Second Estate – asked that:

- only the king should have power to make laws
- there should be no change in the system of taxation without consent of the Estates General
- the distinction between the three orders of the Estates General be strengthened
- the system of voting by Estates should remain
- care be taken to ensure the supply of grain
- fewer restrictions be placed on agriculture and industry
- there should be reform of the legal system.

The Third Estate – in theory the rest of the French people, but in practice the middle class – asked that:

- the national debt be paid off
- all taxes should be shared equally

- the system of compulsory work for a landlord be ended
- the administration of justice be reformed
- the *gabelle* (salt tax) be abolished
- the privilege of hunting be abolished
- the many regulations restricting trade be abolished
- there should be a school in every town
- the Church be reformed
- there should be local elections for local assemblies to deal with local issues.

ACTIVITY 1.3

Work with another student to study the list of issues from the three Estates. Where do you see agreement? Where do you see evidence that the Third Estate wanted something very different from the other two Estates? In the context of France in 1789, do you think these are very radical demands?

ACTIVITY 1.4

a Either on your own or in a pair, examine the actions, and prepare a defence of, the finance ministers who served Louis between 1774 and 1789.

b Analyse the image below. To what extent do you think this is an accurate representation of what was happening in France in 1789?

The three Estates weighed down by the National debt (France). 1789.

Figure 1.2: The opening assembly of the Estates General in Versailles, engraved by Isidore Stanislas Helman after a drawing by Charles Monnet, painter to Louis XVI. Published as part of a series of 1790 engravings titled: "Description abrégée des quinze estampes sur les principales journées de la Révolution" (Short description of fifteen prints on the main days of the Revolution). The engravings were republished as a single collection of 12 images in 1798.

The meeting of the Estates General

On 5 May 1789, for the first time since 1614, members of the Estates General of France gathered at the royal palace of Versailles. There was a background of large-scale and widespread social, economic and political unrest, as well as the prospect of national bankruptcy.

The Estates General was the nearest thing that France had to a national law-making and representative body, although its precise role had never been clearly determined. Louis XVI's immediate predecessors had not called it to meet as they saw it as a threat to their absolute power. Great hopes rested on the outcomes of this meeting, both on the part of the monarch and court on one side, and by the mass of the French people on the other. There had been immense interest in choosing its members, particularly from the middle class. Problems were to arise, however, as many of the aims were very conflicting.

The three Estates – the clergy, the nobility and the commoners – met in different parts of the palace, but each had an equal vote when it came to making decisions. The king and his ministers expected the First and Second Estates to support them if the Third Estate tried to make any radical changes.

The opening meetings did not go well either for the king or for those who desired reform. The king's main concern was to find a solution to his financial problems. Some of the educated middle class wanted a more extensive overhaul of government, politics, society and the economy. Some clergy and noblemen were prepared to accept a few of these major changes. Many more, unrepresented, people just wanted basic improvements to their lives, such as lower taxes, rents and bread prices.

The first two Estates refused to support any of the demands for reform made by the Third Estate. They were more concerned with protecting their privileges than in dealing with the real problems the country was facing. There was also the further complication that the First and Second Estates were divided among themselves over whether or not to cooperate with the Third Estate. Some clergy and noblemen were aware that, unless there was reform, the anger boiling up from below might have dangerous consequences. There was no clear leadership from the court and king on any issue.

On 17 June 1789, the Third Estate, tired of royal indecision and the selfish attitude of the other two Estates, made a

Figure 1.3: 'The Oath of the Tennis Court', ink drawing by Jacques-Louis David, 1790. David was a friend of Robespierre and was asked by the Society of Friends of the Constitution (later known as the Jacobin Club) to commemorate the Tennis Court Oath in a large painting. David became a deputy in the National Convention in 1793.

decisive move. The members agreed to change their name to the 'National Assembly'. By this action, they were saying that sovereignty, the supreme or final power within France, now lay with the people of France, represented by this Assembly. Sovereign power was no longer with the monarchy. The Assembly was, in effect, announcing that it was now in charge of France. It assumed control of the system of national taxation as an example of this newly acquired power. When the king tried to stop the Assembly by closing its meeting room, its members simply gathered in a nearby building, a covered tennis court. There, in what became known as the 'Tennis Court Oath', they decided to continue meeting until they had established a new, reformed constitution that would resolve their grievances. This was to be the first, critical, step on the road to revolution.

ACTIVITY 1.5

Look at Figures 1.2 and 1.3. How accurately do you think the artists conveyed the two events? How might the seating arrangements seen in Figure 1.2 explain why the Estates General failed? Why do you think the Figure 1.3 artist put the two clergymen at the very front of his painting? What value, if any, do you think images such as these have for a historian?

Tensions rise in France

In 1789, a series of events drove the process in an even more radical direction. In the countryside and towns, there was real hunger because of the poor harvest of the previous year, creating a tense situation. Although Necker warned him to be cautious, the king made some unhelpful decisions:

- He refused to give any power to the National Assembly and insisted that the Estates General continue to act in the way he expected, with the First and Second Estates outvoting the Third.
- He moved troops into both Paris and Versailles. This was seen by many as an attempt to stop any reforms by force.
- He dismissed Necker, whom many had felt was the one man capable of bringing in sensible reforms and solving France's economic problems. This resulted in even previously moderate members of all three Estates beginning to see that Louis himself was the problem. He would never reform French government unless he was forced to do so.

ACTIVITY 1.6

Working in a small group, discuss who or what you think was responsible for the crisis of 1789. Develop an argument for factors such as:

- The king
- The Ancien Régime as a whole
- Necker
- The Church and the Aristocracy
- The French economy
- Any others you can think of.

Remember to provide evidence to support your arguments.

List the main factors, place them in order of importance and add your reasons why you feel they are the most responsible.

Responses to Louis XVI's actions

The Storming of the Bastille

The turning point, when the reform movement became a revolution, occurred on 14 July 1789. The old royal fortress in Paris, the Bastille, was attacked by a Parisian mob who feared the reforms they hoped for were not going to happen. The Bastille was seen as a symbol of royal tyranny, although it actually contained few prisoners, troops or arms. During

the attack, the Bastille was destroyed and its governor killed. The event was highly significant, demonstrating the anger of the Paris working class and their determination to achieve change.

ACTIVITY 1.7

An extract from a French newspaper describing the fall of the Bastille, 14 July 1789

The fighting grew steadily more intense. The citizens had become hardened to gunfire. From all directions they clambered on to the roof of the Bastille or broke in to the rooms. As soon as an enemy appeared among the turrets or on the tower, he was fixed in the sights of a hundred guns and mown down in an instant. Meanwhile cannon fire was hurriedly directed against the inner drawbridge which it smashed. In vain did the cannon in the tower reply, for most people sheltered from it. People bravely faced death and every danger. Women, in their eagerness, helped us to the utmost, even the children ran here and there picking up bullets. And so the Bastille fell and the governor, de Launey, was captured. Blessed liberty has been at last introduced into this place of horrors, this frightful refuge of monstrous despotism. De Launey was struck by a thousand blows. His head was cut off and placed on the end of a spear with blood streaming down it. All the other officers were killed.

This glorious day must amaze our enemies and finally bring in for us, the people, the triumph of justice and liberty. In the evening there were great celebrations across Paris.

Source: Spielvogel, J. (1999). *Western Civilization: A Brief History.* Belmont: Wadsworth, p. 88

How does this source represent the views of the revolutionaries? Consider whether the source is written to communicate facts or to draw an emotional reaction from the reader. What is it about the language makes you think this?

Compare the source with the image in Figure 1.4. Relate the sources to what you know about the Bastille and the events of 14 July 1789. Consider whether the Storming of the Bastille was just a symbolic act that had limited impact.

Figure 1.4: *Prise de la Bastille* (Storming of the Bastille) by Jean-Pierre Houël, 1789. Houël was a famous painter and artist who was in Paris during the summer of 1789.

The Storming of the Bastille inspired an even greater breakdown of law and order throughout France, in what became known as the 'Great Fear' of the summer of 1789. There was a mass refusal to pay taxes. Grain shipments were attacked and the grain stolen. The homes of noblemen were looted and their owners attacked. Town leaders who opposed reform were killed. With the king still reluctant to act decisively, and many of his courtiers fleeing the court and the country, it was again the representatives of the Third Estate at Versailles who seized the initiative and acted.

The August Decrees

In what became known as the 'August Decrees', the Assembly did away with what was left of **feudalism** in France. It abolished:

- all the privileges of the nobles, such as their exemption from taxes
- the duties that a peasant owed to his noble landlord, such as paying taxes to him and having to work his land unpaid
- the *parlements* and their old-fashioned legal processes

- the provincial estates, which had been created in the Middle Ages and had largely fallen into disuse and radically reduced the status of the Roman Catholic Church in France.

 KEY TERM

Feudalism: A social system in medieval Europe, in which the nobility held lands from the Crown in exchange for military service, and the lower classes were tenants of the nobles, obliged to live on their lord's land and serve him with their labour and a share of their crops (or other taxes).

The Declaration of the Rights of Man and of the Citizen

Later in August 1789, the National Assembly passed what would come to be seen as one of the key statements of the whole revolutionary period – the Declaration of the Rights of Man and of the Citizen. The influence of several Enlightenment thinkers can be clearly seen in this famous document. The articles of the declaration established the principles on which the new system of government would be based.

Declaration of the Rights of Man and of the Citizen

*Approved by the National Assembly of France,
26 August 1789*

The representatives of the French people, organised as a National Assembly, believing that the ignorance, neglect, or contempt of the rights of man are the sole cause of public calamities and of the corruption of governments, have determined to set forth in a solemn declaration the natural, unalienable, and sacred rights of man, in order that this declaration, being constantly before all the members of the Social body, shall remind them continually of their rights and duties … Therefore the National Assembly recognises and proclaims, in the presence and under the auspices of the Supreme Being, the following rights of man and of the citizen:

Articles:

1   Men are born and remain free and equal in rights.

2   The aim of all political association is the preservation of the natural and imprescriptible rights of man. These rights are liberty, property, security, and resistance to oppression.

3   The principle of all sovereignty resides essentially in the nation. No body nor individual may exercise any authority which does not proceed directly from the nation.

4   Liberty consists in the freedom to do everything which injures no one else; hence the exercise of the natural rights of each man has no limits except those which assure to the other members of the society the enjoyment of the same rights. These limits can only be determined by law.

5   Law can only prohibit such actions as are hurtful to society. Nothing may be prevented which is not forbidden by law, and no one may be forced to do anything not provided for by law.

6   Law is the expression of the general will. Every citizen has a right to participate personally, or through his representative, in its foundation. It must be the same for all, whether it protects or punishes. All citizens, being equal in the eyes of the law.

7   No person shall be accused, arrested, or imprisoned except in the cases and according to the forms prescribed by law.

8   The law shall provide for such punishments only as are strictly and obviously necessary.

9   As all persons are held innocent until they shall have been declared guilty.

10   No one shall be disquieted on account of his opinions, including his religious views.

11   The free communication of ideas and opinions is one of the most precious of the rights of man. Every citizen may, accordingly, speak, write, and print with freedom, but shall be responsible for such abuses of this freedom as shall be defined by law.

12   The security of the rights of man and of the citizen requires public military forces. These forces are, therefore, established for the good of all and not for the personal advantage of those to whom they shall be intrusted.

13   A common contribution is essential for the maintenance of the public forces and for the cost of administration. This should be equitably distributed among all the citizens in proportion to their means.

14   All the citizens have a right to decide, either personally or by their representatives, as to the necessity of the public contribution; to grant this freely; to know to what uses it is put; and to fix the proportion, the mode of assessment and of collection and the duration of the taxes.

15   Society has the right to require of every public official an account of his administration.

16   A society in which the observance of the law is not assured, nor the separation of powers defined, has no constitution at all.

17   Since property is an inviolable and sacred right, no one shall be deprived thereof except where public necessity, legally determined, shall clearly demand it, and then only on condition that the owner shall have been previously and equitably indemnified.

ACTIVITY 1.8

In a pair or small group, look carefully at the Declaration of the Rights of Man. Summarise the key ideas in no more than 50 words. Where can you see the influence of Enlightenment thinkers? Which do you think was the most important principle, and why? Consider why the Assembly set out these principles before it started work on a new constitution.

ACTIVITY 1.9

Identify the principal differences between government under the Ancien Régime and those set out in the Decree below. You could set these out in a table.

In your opinion, how far do you think these changes represent a revolutionary change? Make a list of three reasons, with supporting examples as evidence, to justify your answer.

The Decree argued that:

- all power came essentially from the nation and should come only from the nation
- the French government was monarchical but there was no authority superior to the law; the king reigned only in the name of the law and was therefore under the law
- the National Assembly should be permanent and would be composed of a single chamber of members, elected by the people every two years
- the National Assembly had legislative power
- the king may veto a law
- no taxes of any kind could be raised except by the express permission of the National Assembly
- while executive power resided with the king, he could not make laws and would be under the law and accountable under the law
- justice would be administered only by courts established by law, following the principles of the constitution and according to the forms determined by law.

Reflection: How did you decide on a definition of a 'revolution'? In pairs, explain your method to each other. How are your methods different? Would you change your method for defining a 'revolution' following your discussion?

With these principles in mind, the Assembly then started to put its reform ideas into practice. The king and his courtiers continued to do nothing, so the Assembly acted. In October 1789, it decided on the principles on which government in France should be based. This was the Decree of the Fundamental Principles of Government and it shows the Assembly setting out their wishes for a new constitution for France.

The king was unwilling to accept this radical change to the system of government and limitation of his powers, but events soon forced him to change his mind. In October 1789, food prices started to rise and there was a serious shortage of bread in Paris. Rumours spread that troops known for their loyalty to the king had arrived at Versailles and were being lavishly entertained. Fears grew that these troops would be used to restore all royal power and abolish the National Assembly. Meanwhile, many cheap and radical newspapers in Paris demanded that the king should not close the Assembly and that he make changes to the way in which France was governed.

The women's march on Versailles

On the morning of 5 October, alarms sounded in Paris and crowds of women began to march from Paris to the royal palace at Versailles. Initially there were about 7000 and they had managed to obtain some weapons. They first invaded the National Assembly, which was still debating its reaction to the king's unwillingness to accept constitutional demands. To pacify this mob the Assembly sent some deputies and a number of women nominated by the marchers to the king, and they persuaded him to accept the August Decrees. Public anger and pressure had clearly worked.

This concession did not satisfy the women protesters, however, and with their numbers growing by the hour, they demanded that the king and the royal family returned with them to Paris. When the king did not reply immediately, the crowd simply broke into the palace and insisted on it. The king and his family were escorted by a crowd of 60 000 to Paris, where they remained, as one commentator said, 'more like prisoners than princes'. Force had won out. The Parisian crowd, more radical than was the case in the rest of France, was determined that there should be revolutionary change. The king had been forcibly removed to Paris, where radical influences were very strong, and the National Assembly would follow him. The fact that the decision-maker in France, the National Assembly, met in Paris from then on was profoundly significant and had a major influence on events.

KEY CONCEPT

Interpretations

While there is no disagreement about the main events which led to the outbreak of the revolution, many historians disagree over the reasons why a revolution broke out in France in 1789.

Was it caused by :

- poverty, leading to a revolt of the lower classes?
- prosperity, a growing middle class wanting to make more money?
- a national struggle for liberty or democracy or equality or justice?
- a criminal conspiracy against the old social order?

Historians often have very different reasons for what they write.

In the early 19th century, historians of the causes of the revolution were largely liberals who:

- argued that it was the natural part of the progress of a society, with the establishment of representative government
- felt the crimes of the aristocracy, the Church and an absolute monarchy made it inevitable.

While conservatives suggested that:

- it was a series of crimes by the lower and middle classes against society, the Church and the state which led naturally to the Terror and the killing of the king.

Later 19th-century historians suggested that:

- famine led to the king promising reform, raising high hopes, and then dashing them, which led to the anger of 1789 onwards.
- it was very politically and ideologically driven, some seeing it as a middle-class conspiracy
- it was a desire for equality, followed by a desire for democracy and then desire for national sovereignty that led to a republic.

Some 20th-century historians argued that:

- it was a struggle between classes rather than ideas or ideologies
- it was largely a clash between the middle class and the aristocracy and the Church over property

$\rightarrow$

KEY CONCEPT

- it was caused by a mix of prosperity and poverty: a more prosperous middle class wanting power and an urban working classes and peasantry wanting food and jobs; some argued that the urban working class were the driving force, others that the rural peasants were more important.

Source: Rude, George (1961). Adapted from *Interpretations of the French Revolution. Historical Pamphlet No. 47.*

Why do you think that historians put forward different reasons for the outbreak of the revolution? Why do you think these views changed over time? Which of the reasons do you think is the most reasonable? Why? Why have you chosen that reason over the others? Which do you think it the least acceptable reason? Why?

Much of the royal power and authority had now gone. France had been transformed, almost overnight, from a medieval, semi-feudal state into something quite different. No one yet new how different. The Ancien Régime was no more. It was a remarkable work of destruction. A new system of government and social order now had to be created, and there were many different ideas on what forms these might take. In dealing with one problem, the Assembly had created many more, and this, in turn, led to even greater instability.

1.2 Why were French governments unstable from 1790 to 1795?

There were various reasons for instability in France between 1790 and 1795. There was still a lack of agreement among decision-makers over who should govern the country and how it should be governed. This was further complicated by a deep antagonism between Paris and the many regions of France which resented domination by Paris. The serious social and economic problems discussed in the previous section continued, and, when war broke out against Austria in 1792, this worsened the situation as well as creating additional problems.

The period saw a very large number of radical changes in a very short period of time. These ranged from the abolition of the monarchy and aristocracy and vast religious changes to a new calendar with different names for the months.

15

One of the many changes brought in during the revolutionary period was the creation of a new calendar. The calendar started on 22 September 1792, the day after the acceptance of the new republican constitution for France. So, what had been 22 September 1792 became the first day of Year 1. There were still 12 months, but they were given new names, such as Prairial, Brumaire and Thermidor. Napoleon abolished this calendar and returned to the old system in 1805.

Revolutionary and counter-revolutionary groups: their views and aims

The destruction of the old system had taken place in theory, but two major problems remained in practice. The first was to get the king to accept the changes, and the second was whether the Assembly was capable of carrying out these great decisions. There had to be a new type of government created in France. Most members of the Third Estate agreed broadly on four important issues:

- France should still have a monarch, but it should not be an absolute monarchy. There had to be limits to royal power. Sovereignty now lay elsewhere and power had to be shared with the people.

Figure 1.5: *The Awakening of the Third Estate*. The aristocrat and the cleric on the left are showing fear at the sight of the member of the Third Estate on the right, breaking free from his chains and reaching for weapons. In the background is the Bastille and the head of its governor on a spike. How would you assess the reliability of this image in describing the events in France during 1789?

- Aristocratic and Church privileges should be abolished, and jobs should go to the most able candidates, not just to aristocrats.
- There should be a fair system of taxation.
- There should be proper accountability in government and a fairer system of justice.

However, no one had a clear plan of how this might be achieved. There were no obvious leaders and no real understanding of what the majority of the French people really wanted. Political life like this had not really existed in France before 1789 and members of the Assembly were inexperienced in making laws and deciding national policy. They were not helped by the many members of the nobility and clergy who were totally opposed to any change.

In the course of 1790, and in the absence of any leadership from the king or his ministers, the Assembly started the work of reconstruction and change. Their focus was on the four areas that had been of most concern to the majority of the French people before 1789:

- The unfair system of taxation
- The inefficient and corrupt system of local government, largely controlled by the aristocracy
- The out-of-date justice system
- The role, status and wealth of the Roman Catholic Church.

Many of the changes that the Assembly introduced in 1790 lasted for many years after the revolution. They did not, however, address many of the problems which concerned the poorest people in France, particularly the high price of food. This failing was to cause more instability.

The principal revolutionary groups

The representatives who met in the Assembly in 1790 were mostly men of property, often lawyers. Many were influenced by the ideas of the Enlightenment. They soon realised that an individual member of the Assembly could achieve little on his own, and the only way that decisions could be made and laws passed was by joining a group of like-minded Assembly members. These groups were known as 'clubs', and members would meet separately from the Assembly to discuss political matters. Three main groups emerged, like modern political parties, representing conservatives, moderate reformers and radical reformers within the Assembly.

The best known – and most influential – of these political clubs was the Jacobins. The group formed in 1789, was open to all citizens and had linked groups all across of France. It was powerful in Paris and had

strong connections with the Parisian working classes. The Jacobins were the most radical of the three groups, arguing strongly for the execution of the king and the end of the aristocracy and the Roman Catholic Church in France. This is evidenced in Figure 1.5, in which the aristocracy and the Church (represented by the priest) are shown to react in fear to a member of the working class. The Jacobins were largely responsible for **the Terror** in 1793–94.

The Feuillants, a group formed in 1791, was also known as the Society of the Friends of the Constitution. They were conservative, and sat on the right of the Assembly. They were strong supporters of a constitutional monarchy and opposed the decision to go to war with Austria in 1792. They were strong opponents of the much more radical Jacobins. Many of the Feuillants were executed by the Jacobins during the Terror.

The third club was the Girondins. They acquired this name as some of the members came from the Gironde region of France. This group was also formed in 1791. They were moderate republicans and voted in favour of the war with Austria in 1792. They were not as radical as the Jacobins and were not so concerned with political, social and economic equality. Some opposed the execution of the king and felt that the Paris 'mob' was too influential, wanting more consideration of the wishes of the people of all of France. Many Girondins would also be executed in the Terror.

KEY TERM

The Terror: The period of extreme violence in 1793–94 when thousands of French people were executed by guillotine, after a brief trial before revolutionary tribunals. Those executed were royalists, aristocrats, clergy or political opponents of the Jacobins.

Failures of the counter-revolutionary groups

Although many French people opposed both the revolution and the revolutionaries, and there were several attempts to restore the Bourbon monarchy to the throne of France, all were unsuccessful.

One reason for this was a lack of realism on the part of those who wished to restore the monarchy. Louis XVI, his wife and the rest of his courtiers simply failed to realise the depth of feeling in France against the system of government which existed before 1789. The king could not accept that there had to be major limits to his powers and that in future he would have to rule with the consent of his people. His heir, a sickly boy, died at the age of ten in 1795, two years after his father's execution. The next in line to the throne, the future Louis XVIII, issued the Declaration of Verona from his exile in Italy in the same year, insisting that the Ancien Régime, with the three separate Estates, should be restored. He failed to take advice that the majority of French people would never willingly give in to the former authority, whose power they had so resented.

In addition, bitter internal divisions weakened the royalists. Among the 40 000 **émigrés** who fled France there was no agreement about either their aims or how to achieve them. Some wanted a restoration of the former monarchy, with all powers and privileges returned to the nobles and clergy. Others felt that concessions had to be made and that there must be a constitutional monarchy which operated within limits. Some advocated killing all the revolutionaries; others argued for conciliation. Some of the émigrés refused to associate with others as they were not 'noble' enough. Like Louis XVI, they underestimated the loyalty of many to the revolution and assumed that if they returned to France, much of the population would rise up to support them.

KEY TERM

Émigrés: Members of the French population who left France during the first years of the Revolution and the Terror. The first *émigrés* were mostly members of the aristocracy, but members of the middle class also left France. In 1792 the National Convention banned *émigrés* from returning to France.

Opposition to the revolution within France was also badly divided and had different aims. Some activists were more anxious to restore the position of the Church than the king. Regions such as Brittany were willing to fight against the revolution, but their inhabitants would not go so far as to leave their homes and advance on Paris to overthrow it. Some people simply hated change and feared that different would mean worse.

As well as the divisions among supporters, the royalists lacked effective leadership. There was no charismatic figure with clear and realistic aims around whom all those who opposed the revolution could rally. Louis XVI was incompetent and mistrusted, and was sent to the guillotine in 1793. The young Louis XVII died in 1795. Louis XVIII had a talent for alienating people and no real leadership skills. It was only after the defeat of Napoleon and the invasion of France by his enemies for Louis XVIII to be placed on the throne in 1814.

The royalists also lacked effective foreign support. At different times, Austria, Prussia, the Netherlands and

Britain fought against revolutionary France, but none was able to defeat it. This was partly because France, despite initial difficulties caused by many of the officers becoming émigrés, proved still to have one of the best armies in Europe. Servicemen were now promoted on grounds of ability not of birth. In 1792, when Prussia and Austria invaded, they were driven back at the Battle of Valmy by the revolutionary army. It was a huge boost to revolutionary morale. As one invader wrote: 'The enemy has formidable artillery and their army is not as contemptible as we thought it would be. Nobody is coming over to join us as we had hoped and we have not noticed that opinions have changed in the territories we have invaded.' The French army proved superior to all, driving the Austrians out of the region that is now Belgium and then successfully invading Italy. Britain proved to be the most durable of opponents, but it had no strong army and was probably more interested in weakening France and seizing its remaining colonies than in putting a Bourbon back on the throne. The one major expedition against France – the Quiberon expedition in 1795, in which the British landed émigrés joined with local rebels – was smashed by General Hoche, and nearly 700 royalist supporters were shot.

Many people in France welcomed the gains of the revolution. This vital fact just did not seem to occur to those who wanted the monarchy to return. When Napoleon seized power after the end of the Directory (see 'Why was Napoleon Bonaparte able to overthrow the Directory in 1799?'), he took enormous care to ensure that privilege did not return and that equality before the law remained.

Finally, the Terror and the ruthless actions by the revolutionary armies deterred many from supporting the royalists. After 1793, many counter-revolutionaries were executed and their property was seized.

Until a monarch was prepared to understand that too many people in France stood against a return to the way the country had been governed before 1789, there would be no king for France.

The aims of the revolutionary groups: reform of taxation, local government, justice and the Church

To solve the immediate financial crisis, the Assembly decided to try two policies until a better and fairer system of taxation could be created. It would sell off the lands and valuables which had belonged to the Roman Catholic Church, and it issued a temporary paper currency called **assignats**. This worked reasonably well in the short term and brought some financial stability. A new system of income tax was also designed, so that the burden of taxation fell on those best able to pay: the rich. The hated taxes on consumption, such as the 'Gabelle', a tax on salt which the poor were particularly angry about, were abolished. A new tax on land, which, of course, fell on the owners of property, was introduced. These changes dealt with one of the greatest grievances which existed before 1789. There were no more tax exemptions for the rich. Taxation was to be based largely on wealth and property.

> **KEY TERM**
>
> **Assignats:** A new type of paper currency used instead of gold and silver coins and guaranteed by the government. The real value of this type of currency depended on people's confidence in it and their willingness to accept it as payment for goods or their labour.

Local government was also in need of reform. The old system, in large part established centuries earlier and inadequate for dealing with contemporary problems, was abolished. Eighty-three new departments (administrative areas) were created, designed to end the old regional differences, and they became the main links between Paris and the localities. Effective local government structures at all levels were set up, from big cities to small villages, with elections for key officials. This was a significant change to the way in which French people were governed, and has lasted pretty much the same to this day. The French people, however, were not yet used to having elections and this inexperience was to cause major problems.

The system of justice was totally changed too. Now it had to be open to everyone, free if necessary, and properly accountable. It would no longer be run in the interests of lawyers and the aristocracy. The local administrator of justice, as well as the keeper of law and order, the Justice of the Peace, was to be elected by the people. This was a popular and necessary measure.

Figure 1.6: A 500-livres *assignat.* What symbols of royal authority are included on the note? Why do you think this is, and what does this suggest about the National Assembly?

While initially no attempt was made to change religious beliefs, the Church became largely an agent of the state. Church lands, for example, were taken over by the state. Monasteries were abolished, the number of bishops reduced and the clergy came under state control. The king, reluctantly, agreed to this new Civil Constitution of the Clergy. There was a major split, however, over whether all the clergy should take a special oath agreeing to the changes in this Civil Constitution. For many in France, it was too radical a step and would lead to great divisions.

By the end of 1790, it appeared that the 'revolution' was over and that the greatest grievances of the French people had been dealt with. There were many signs of trouble to come, however, and political instability was to grow.

Many problems still faced French politicians. What, for example, should the role of the king be in the future? How much power should he have? Louis was reluctant to agree to the changes. Would he try to return to the hated days of the Ancien Régime? Few trusted him.

There was a bad harvest in the summer of 1790. Politicians were aware that this could well lead to hunger, particularly among the poor, and therefore more popular unrest, in the winter and spring of 1790–91. Dissent was not exclusive to the lower classes, however. There were growing numbers of nobles and clergy opposed to the changes and determined to keep their privileges.

There was also the issue of who should have the vote in elections for the Assembly in future. All men? Men of property only? Some radicals suggested that women might be given the vote. Meanwhile, there was a free and increasingly radical press arguing for more extreme measures. Censorship was gone.

ACTIVITY 1.10

Do you think the National Assembly can be seen as successful by the end of 1790? Either on your own, or in a pair, think about the criteria for 'success' in this context. How well do you think the Assembly met those criteria? What points can you put forward to argue that it did, and what points can you make to argue it did not? Have you given a clear answer to the issue of 'extent'? Is the reason why you have come to your conclusion clear?

What fundamental problems do you think France still faced at the end of 1790? Work with another student to identify them and put them in order of importance, together with your reasons.

Changes in government from 1790 to 1795

While many French citizens hoped that 1791 would bring stability and security to their country, this was not to be. A range of factors ensured that many further problems were to arise. People hoped that the new Constitution would solve all France's problems, but there was a lack of agreement among the French people on its terms. France was also faced by continuing poor harvests, erratic behaviour by the king, a growing counter-revolutionary movement and an increase in radicalism. All these issues led to further rapid political and social changes.

The Flight to Varennes

Two events now played a major part in the developing revolutionary process. The first was a notable action by the king. In June, Louis and his family tried to escape from France to the Austrian Netherlands to the north. They were captured by supporters of the revolution at the town of Varennes in northern France and returned under guard to Paris. There, the king effectively became a prisoner of the people. Naturally, his attempted flight increased suspicions that he was determined to oppose all the changes that had occurred and bring back the Ancien Régime. He was obviously, people believed, looking to gain support from the queen's Austrian family so that his own country could be invaded by foreigners who would destroy the revolution.

This flight and the king's capture led to many of the nobility – who became known as the 'émigrés' – escaping France and setting up centres of opposition abroad. They were seen as a real threat to the revolution. While there were some moderates in the Assembly who still felt they should try to negotiate with the king and keep him as a constitutional monarch, there was a growth in more radical views that the king should be killed, or at least deposed. The French people now had to make a decision. Antoine Barnave, a noted contributor to Assembly discussions who was later executed, asked: 'Are we going to finish the revolution or are we going to begin it afresh?'

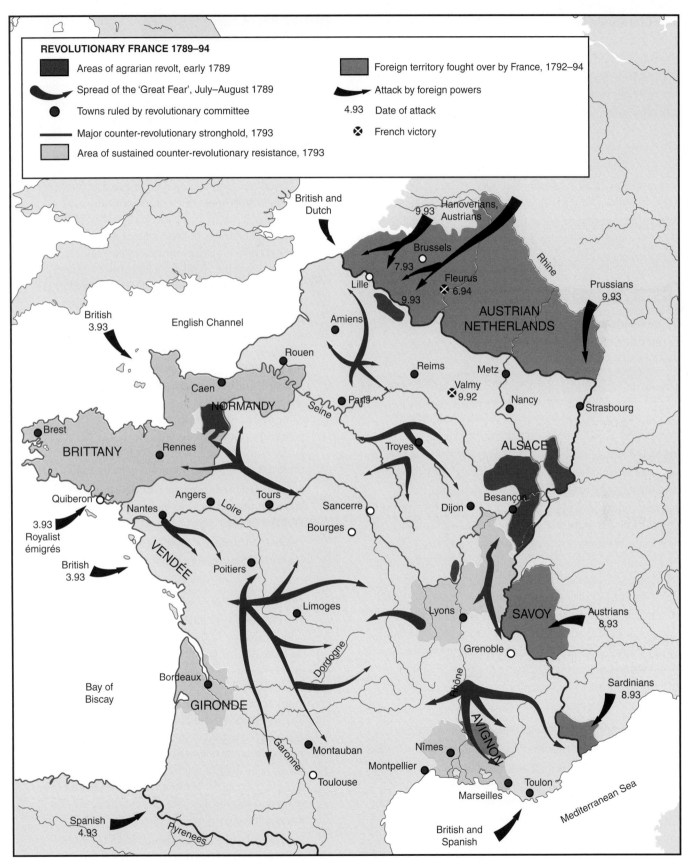

REVOLUTIONARY FRANCE 1789–94

- Areas of agrarian revolt, early 1789
- Spread of the 'Great Fear', July–August 1789
- Towns ruled by revolutionary committee
- Major counter-revolutionary stronghold, 1793
- Area of sustained counter-revolutionary resistance, 1793
- Foreign territory fought over by France, 1792–94
- Attack by foreign powers
- 4.93   Date of attack
- French victory

Figure 1.7: A map of France at the time of the revolution, highlighting the main areas of opposition to the revolution, and support for the royalists, such as the Vendée and Brittany.

The Champ de Mars

The Flight to Varennes was not the only thing to increase the tension and uncertainty in the country. A violent event in Paris in July worsened the atmosphere. There was a massacre in the Champs de Mars, a large green space near the centre of Paris. The **National Guard** fired upon a group of citizens trying to petition the Assembly to ensure that it dealt firmly with the king after his attempted escape. More than 50 people were killed. This was seen by many as a possible counter-revolutionary action and an attempt by the king to regain power. Several more radical Assembly members fled, and many people began to think that there had to be a more extreme solution to the problem of the king.

> **KEY TERM**
>
> **National Guard:** A largely middle-class militia, created in 1789 to act as a national police force. It was to play a vital role in trying to maintain law and order in France during the revolutionary period.

In September 1791, however, the National Assembly completed what it felt was its primary, and final, task. It created a new constitution for France. The king, reluctantly, agreed to it. This new constitution retained the monarchy and the king still had the right to veto new laws, but it transferred sovereignty and the right to make laws to the Legislative Assembly, which replaced the National Assembly. This was to be indirectly elected by the people of France, and two-thirds of the adult male population would now be allowed to participate in local and national elections. The constitution established the separation of powers, which meant that the Legislature (the Assembly), the Executive (the government) and the Judiciary (judges and the legal system) were largely independent of each other. This was designed to prevent tyranny in the future. The influence of Enlightenment judge and scholar Montesquieu (see 'Pressures for change', earlier) can be seen here.

This constitution made France into a constitutional monarchy and was a significant step towards democracy. It survived for only one year, however. Poor harvests ensured unrest would come. Many people disliked the oath that the clergy had to take agreeing to the Civil Constitution of the Clergy. The king was obviously mistrusted and there was a growing counter-revolutionary movement both in France and abroad with the émigrés. At the same time, many Assembly members felt that the revolution still had a long way to go and hoped to create a republic with no monarchy. Few really had any faith in this new system.

ACTIVITY 1.11

Few people had a clearer idea than the king himself of the situation in which France found herself: he was convinced that the ills of his kingdom were so glaring that they would correct themselves. He knew France was likely to have a civil war. He knew a foreign war would be useless. He felt the émigrés would become the object of hatred. He believed that only he could erect a barrier against all the misfortunes which must result from all these problems, he was convinced of this. He would help the moderates in the National Assembly against the popular revolutionary current. He would accept the changes he had already agreed to and he would deal with the foreign powers. He would accept reasonable proposals coming from Paris. He wanted his crossing of the frontier to prevent a civil war, to become a brake on treachery and stupidity. He was resolved that once the legitimate rights of royal authority had been restored, and the constitution, freely discussed, should have been approved by him, to proceed to Compiègne, to stay there for a long time, and thus gain respect for this fundamental law of the state, far from the disturbances of Paris, and remain there until the constitution was fully operational.

Source: Adapted from the Duc de Choiseul's 'Account of the Flight to Varennes, 20 June 1791'. Written in 1822

Quoted in Hardman, J. (ed.). (1981). *The French Revolution Sourcebook.* **London: Arnold, pp. 126–27**

The premier public servant abandons his post; he arms himself with a false passport; after having said, in writing to the foreign powers, that his most dangerous enemies are those who spread alleged doubts about the monarch's intentions. He breaks his word, he leaves the French a declaration, which if not criminal, is against the principles of our liberty. He must have been aware that his flight exposed the nation to the dangers of civil war. He suggests that he only wished to go to Malmedy, but I say he did not intend to make peaceful observations to the National Assembly, but he wished to support his own claims with arms and it was a conspiracy against liberty.

Source: Adapted from a speech from the Abbé Gregoire in the National Assembly's debate on whether to suspend the king, July 1791

→

ACTIVITY 1.11 (CONTINUED)

Quoted in Dwyer, P. and McPhee, P. (2002). *The French Revolution and Napoleon*. London: Routledge, pp. 52–53

In groups, compare and contrast the different views on Louis's reasons for the Flight to Varennes in the two sources. Which source could be seen as the most reliable, and why? What contextual knowledge can be used to explain why one of the sources might be more accurate than the other?

Foreign threats and the impact of war on France

As is so often the case, it was a combination of events which drove the revolution forward in the spring of 1792. During the winter of 1791–92 four issues arose that made more change likely:

- There was a real fear that Austria and Prussia, both major European powers ruled by absolute monarchs, would intervene to support Louis and destroy the revolution. The queen's brother was the emperor of Austria. Austria and Prussia had, in the Declaration of Pilnitz in 1791, made a public statement of support for Louis and opposition to the revolution.
- Many nobles feared for their lives and fled abroad. Once there, they appealed for help to restore what they regarded as law and order in France. Meanwhile, some of those who remained behind, including the queen, were in contact with influential friends and family abroad, seeking allies in the struggle to overturn the revolution.
- The harvest of 1791 had been poor. There was a shortage of bread, and prices of basic foods were rising. There were many hungry people in France.
- The refusal of some clergy to take the oath agreeing to the Civil Constitution of the Clergy was causing anger.

Radical and inexperienced members of the Assembly began to demand a war against Austria and Prussia, although neither country wished to actually invade France. These radicals hoped that war would force the king to take sides and either support the revolution enthusiastically, or abdicate or emigrate. They also hoped a war of 'liberation' would play a major part in ensuring the end of feudalism and absolutism in both France and Europe, and, perhaps strangely, that it would improve the economy.

Encouraged by popular opinion, and with the apparent support of the king, the Assembly declared war on Austria in April 1792. With France totally unprepared for such a war, and with many experienced officers having left the country, the campaign began with several military disasters against the Austrians. The war did, however, have a decisive effect on the progress of the revolution: it put many Frenchmen in the position of having to make up their minds who and what to fight for.

At the same time, many aristocrats and army officers deserted to the Austrian enemy. There was evidence that Marie Antoinette was doing all she could to help the Austrians. The king made it increasingly clear that he would like the enemy invasion to succeed, and his refusal to support the Assembly over the clergy's oath made it very clear where his sympathies lay. The war meant that sides had to be taken. It forced decisions on people and led to an alliance of the middle and working classes against the monarch and aristocrats.

The crisis came to a head in August 1792. In an event which became known as the *Journée*, or the September Massacres, there was an outbreak of violence in Paris, which was seen by many as a 'second revolution'. Frightened by advancing enemy armies, the hungry working class of Paris again took control of the city, and directed the National Guard to storm the Tuileries Palace where the king, his family and many courtiers lived. The National Guardsmen obeyed, killing several hundred of the royal defenders in the process. Further hundreds of the king's Swiss Guard (his own personal bodyguard), who had surrendered, were later massacred by the Parisians. With this serious bloodshed, power seemed to have passed from the Assembly to the Paris mob.

This proved to be a critical event in the revolutionary process. Following the *Journée*, the king and his family were arrested and imprisoned. The constitutional monarchy was at an end. France becoming a republic was only a matter of time. Some educated middle-class men assumed more leadership of the political process and united with the working class. The massacre of the Swiss Guard could be seen as the start of what became known as the Terror, as the killing of men simply on suspicion of royalist sympathies spread all over France. The Assembly dissolved itself and a new body, the National Convention, took its place.

The National Convention was elected by universal male suffrage: all French men, unless they were servants or

23

Figure 1.8: 20th June 1792: The people getting into the Château des Tuileries during the French Revolution. Original Artwork: Engraving by Conche Sons.

unemployed, were allowed to vote. It was the most democratic electoral system in Europe, although in fact fewer than 25% of those entitled to vote did so. The membership of the Convention was young and middle class; many were lawyers or businessmen. Some working – class men were elected, however. They were much more politically experienced than the men who had met at Versailles in 1789, and they were, above all, strongly influenced by the king's obvious hostility to reform and his links with France's enemy, Austria.

What had started as an attempt to solve France's problems had caused much greater ones, and political instability became a feature of France for the next seven years.

●●● THINK LIKE A HISTORIAN

Compromising on one's principles

Louis XVI had taken a solemn oath to uphold the Ancien Régime, with its absolutist principles, when he was crowned king of France. How justified would he have been if he had abandoned them both to save his own life and bring stability to France? Identify a leader from any walk of life, political or religious, who has made promises to get elected or represents a particular set of values, and has found it necessary to abandon those principle or promises. Make a case both defending and criticising that leader.

1793–95: Instability and terror

The two years of 1793–95 saw the greatest period of instability throughout the revolutionary process. At the end of 1792, the National Convention decided to abolish the monarchy and make France a republic. Louis XVI had been put on trial and condemned to death; he was executed in early 1793. His opposition to change, the distrust he generated, the fear that he was selling out to the Austrians, the background of war and the memory of the *Journée* all contributed to the feeling that the revolution would only survive if he was killed.

Louis's death solved little and in fact created even more problems. It also increased the number of enemies that the revolution had both in France and abroad. Chaos and instability descended on France for the next three years, caused by a variety of very different factors:

- France was at war throughout the period, and invasion was likely. War cost a considerable amount of money and required many men. Raising the money and getting men to fight caused further tensions, with many people hostile to the conscription necessary to keep the army going.
- France had been a monarchy for centuries. There were no men with experience of government , let alone democracy, among the revolutionaries. Many ordinary people doubted the right of the government to exist and govern France.

- Several provinces, especially the Vendée and Brittany, had opposed the death of the king, hated the attacks on the Church and resented having to take orders from Paris. Major cities such as Lyons and Marseilles also resented the dominance of Paris and its mob.
- There was a wide split within the Convention between those who wanted even more radical reform and those who did not.
- Serious hunger continued throughout France and there were regular food riots.
- A radical and uncensored press encouraged extreme ideas.
- The Paris mob, the **sans-culottes**, proved to be a major influence. They had demonstrated their powers in the *Journée*.

 KEY TERM

Sans-culottes: Working-class radicals in Paris and other French cities. They were named after the type of clothes usually worn by the urban working class, trousers rather than the expensive knee-breeches (culottes) which were the fashion among the rich.

ACTIVITY 1.12

One of the most stupid ideas that can come into the head of a politician is to believe that it makes sense for a nation to send armies against a foreign people to make them adopt its laws and its constitution. No one loves armed missionaries, and the first reaction that natural instincts and common sense gives is to see them as enemies and get rid of them. Movements which would be supported are those which are directed against real tyrants, like the American revolt against theEnglish or the events here of 14 July 1789. A foreign war, provoked and directed by a government in the sort of circumstances that we are in, is a nonsensical movement which will lead to the collapse of our state. Such a war will distract public opinion, create a diversion from the real fears of our nation and give the enemies of our liberty an advantage. War will mean our constitution will be subverted and is part of a conspiracy to destroy liberty in France.

Source: Adapted from Robespierre's speech in the Jacobin Club, 11 January 1792

Quoted in Beik. P. H. (ed.). (2000). *The French Revolution*. London: Palgrave, pp. 191–93

ACTIVITY 1.12 (CONTINUED)

What divides Robespierre and me is, 'What position should we take on the possibility of war?' If we are in danger, then while I think it is not necessary to attack, but we must defend ourselves. It is much better to fight in our enemy's country than in our own. We must carry the war beyond the Rhine. The émigrés have succeeded in collecting soldiers in Worms and Coblenz, and are both arming and providing them with supplies. The German princes have helped them. Therefore it is necessary that France uses its army to crush its impudent neighbours and prevent attacks. We know that the king and his court wants war and may have secret intentions against us. We know that we are correct in suspecting the king's government, but we must use a great military force to compel the Austrian emperor to recognise our new rights and deprive the émigrés of any support.

Adapted from Jacques-Pierre Brissot's speech in reply to Robespierre in the Jacobin Club, 20 January 1792. Quoted in Beik, P. H. (ibid.), pp. 197–98

Working in pairs, compare and contrast the views of Robespierre and Brissot on the possible outcomes of going to war. To help with your analysis you could set these out in a table.

Using your own knowledge, in the light of later events, which of the two had the most perceptive argument?

ACTIVITY 1.13

Accusations made against King Louis XVI at his trial in December 1792

Louis, the French people accuse you of having committed many crimes in order to establish your tyranny by destroying liberty in France.

You attacked the sovereignty of the people by suspending the assemblies of its representatives and by driving them by violence by their sessions.

You caused an army to march against the citizens of Paris and caused their blood to flow. You withdrew this army only when the capture of the Bastille and the general uprising showed you that the people were victorious.

→

25

ACTIVITY 1.13 (CONTINUED)

For a long time you contemplated flight and made your escape as far as Varennes with a false passport.

You apparently accepted the new Constitution. Your speeches announced a desire to maintain it, but you worked to overthrow it before it was achieved.

Your brothers, enemies of the state, have rallied the émigrés. They have raised regiments, borrowed money and formed alliances against us in your name.

You allowed the French nation to be disgraced in Germany, in Italy and in Spain.

You caused the blood of Frenchmen to flow.

Source: Hall, J. (ed.). (1951). *A Documentary Survey of the French Revolution.* **New York: Macmillan, pp. 386, 389, 391**

What crimes does this source accuse the king of committing? Looking back on what you have learned so far, how far do you agree that the king is guilty of them?

How does this source help you assess the significance of the death of the king in the history of the revolution? (Remember that 'significance' is not quite the same as 'importance'.)

The inexperienced politicians did their best, however. In early 1793, after the execution of the king, yet another new Constitution was written for France. With a single chamber in total control, executive power was passed to a Committee of Public Safety. This was a small group of ministers with substantial executive powers to deal with the many crises facing France. Their powers included control over the military and the judiciary. Against a background of civil war, soaring food prices, the fear of invasion by Britain and other European powers, and under pressure from the Paris mob, the Committee took radical action. A new law, the Law of Suspects, gave them sweeping powers to deal with opponents.

With the army dealing with the unrest in the Vendée and Brittany by brute force, the Law of Suspects was used to deal with opponents and suspected opponents of the revolution, as well as those suspected of hoarding food. Over 500 000 people were arrested and it is

estimated that about 16 000 were executed. The queen was the first to be killed, followed by nobles, priests and royalists. Over 10 000 died of ill treatment in prison and it is likely that about another 15 000 were killed without trial. More died when the army restored order in the provinces.

By the autumn of 1793, the worst of the fighting was over. Austria had been defeated, food prices started to drop, the government began to get control of the economy, the provinces had been calmed and heavy taxation of the rich was bringing in money. The revolution seemed secure and the Committee of Public Safety had shown that it could govern France. Two of the men emerging as leaders of the Committee – Georges Danton and **Maximilien Robespierre** – were anxious to bring stability to France. Danton was a Parisian lawyer who had strong connections with the working class in Paris. A Jacobin, a powerful speaker and a member of the Assembly, he was a strong advocate of the overthrow of the monarchy. Always a moderate, he opposed the extremes of the Terror, and, in the end, was executed for holding those views. Robespierre was to be an even more significant figure in the history of the French Revolution.

MAXIMILIEN ROBESPIERRE (1758–94)

Robespierre, a lawyer, was elected to the Estates General in 1789 as a member of the Third Estate. He was strongly critical of the monarchy, and was one of the first to suggest that the king should be put on trial and that France should become a republic. Robespierre has become inextricably linked to the period known as the 'Reign of Terror', in which thousands of people were executed for opposing the revolution. He was eventually arrested and executed in July 1794.

This law from June 1794 formally established the Reign of Terror:

- The Revolutionary Tribunal shall have a President and four Vice Presidents.
- The Revolutionary Tribunal is instituted to punish the enemies of the people.
- The enemies of the people are those who seek to destroy public liberty either by force or cunning and:
  - those who try to re-establish the monarchy
  - those who try to oppose the National Assembly in any way
  - those who have prevented the army's success or helped the enemies of the republic
  - those who have impeded the provisioning of Paris and profiteers
  - those who have spread false news and misled opinion
  - those who support the aristocracy and oppose the principles of the Republic.
- The penalty provided for all offences listed here is death.

Source: www.marxists.org/archive/jaures/1901/history/great-terror.htm

The cult of Robespierre

Robespierre saw himself as a man of high principles. He called for the replacement of Roman Catholicism with a 'Republic of Virtue', which emphasised duty, the need for all citizens to help each other, and a loyalty to democracy. Previous revolutionary leaders had limited the power of the Church, but few had attacked Christianity itself. Robespierre now introduced the Cult of the Supreme Being to replace the worship of the Christian God. He himself led one of the ceremonial processions to introduce the cult.

Robespierre remains a controversial historical figure. Some commentators believe that he saved the revolution from defeat at a critical time. Others criticise the dictatorial nature of his rule and the executions that took place under his leadership. On a personal level, Robespierre was also a man of contradictions. He was known as 'The Incorruptible' and was highly principled. He firmly believed that power belonged to the people and not to governments. He proved himself to be a ruthless politician, however, and would not tolerate rivals even among his fellow Jacobins, many of whom he sent to the guillotine.

Jacobin leader Maximilien Robespierre, in a speech explaining his 'Republic of Virtue'

We want a state of affairs where all unworthy and cruel passions are unknown, and all kind and generous passions are aroused by the laws. Ambition becomes the desire to deserve glory and to serve the fatherland. The citizen submits to the magistrate, the magistrate to the people and the people to justice. The fatherland guarantees the well-being of each individual, and where each individual enjoys with pride the prosperity and glory of the fatherland. Commerce is the source of public wealth and not only of the monstrous riches of a few people.

In our country we want to substitute morality for selfishness, honesty for honour, the rule of reason for the tyranny of tradition, the contempt of vice for the contempt of misfortune, love of glory instead of love of money, good people instead of the advantages of birth, a generous, powerful, happy people instead of despicable people – that is to say, all the virtues and all the miracles of the Republic for all the vices and all the absurdities of the monarchy.

What kind of government can realise these marvels? Only a democratic or republican government.

Source: Lyman, R. and Spitz, L. (1965). *Major Crises in Western Civilization*. Vol. 2. New York: Harcourt, Brace & World, pp. 71–72

27

The Reign of Terror was to last for a further two years. Robespierre was determined to remove the enemies of his version of the revolution from France. He had opponents and potential opponents, such as Danton, arrested and executed. Committees of Public Safety throughout France continued to use the guillotine. Many revolutionary figures felt that Robespierre was hoping to become a dictator with a police state, and that he would undo all the work of the revolution to date. Fearing the guillotine, deputies managed to get Robespierre arrested, and after a failed suicide attempt, he was executed along with 80 of his supporters. The revolution was starting to kill its own, and instability deepened.

While the death of Robespierre eased the Terror and resulted in the release of many prisoners, great divisions

Figure 1.9: *The Roll Call of the Last Victims of the Terror*, oil on canvas by Charles Louis-Lucien Muller, painted between 1845–1855.

remained within the government between the moderate Girondins and the Jacobins, the right and the left. The foreign threat had lifted after French military successes, but the harvest of 1794 was again very poor and there was another hard winter over 1794–95. Prices soared once more and those who had suffered under the Jacobin Terror of 1793–94 sought their revenge in what became known as the White Terror of 1794–95. The Jacobin Club was closed, and those linked with the earlier Reign of Terror were themselves hunted down, arrested and killed. (The 'white' part of the name came from the colour of the cockades that monarchists wore on their hats.)

By the time this period of terror had come to an end in 1795, Paris had run out of food and the mob had attacked the Convention again, demanding that power be transferred to the local communities in Paris. These groups also wanted greater democracy and radical measures, such as compulsory food searches and the death of those who had brought down Robespierre. This time the Convention did not respond to pressure. Its middle-class members were tired of what they saw as the excesses of the working class. They called in troops and arrested and executed the leaders of the *sans-culottes*. Following the illness and death of the ten-year-old uncrowned Louis XVII, his uncle, the Count of Provence was proclaimed King Louis XVIII. He, however, was in exile in Italy and there seemed little chance of a restoration of the Ancien Régime. Everyone now recognised that the Constitution of 1793 had failed, and it was time to try again to find a workable system of government for France.

ACTIVITY 1.14

Working in a group, assign individual members the following questions on the Terror. This will help to ensure full understanding of the topic. Each member should report to the group with their answers.

- What was the Terror?
- What caused it?
- Who led it?
- Who suffered most from it?
- What different perspectives are there on it? Could it be seen as a 'good' thing?
- Why did it end?
- Was it necessary?
- What were its implications?
- What were its consequences?
- How significant was it?
- Has it been given too much or too little coverage? How have sources such as those on pp 28, 29 and 30 helped you come to your conclusions?

Reflection: After each member of your group has spoken, decide which reason you think is the most important and why. Did you choose different reasons? Discuss how you chose the most important reason within your group. Would you change your answer after the discussion?

Economic problems

Issues affecting the economy were a major cause of the revolution. The bad harvest of 1788 and the following harsh winter, high food prices and an industrial recession were major background influences when the Estates General met in 1789. Many in France hoped that the various political and constitutional changes would lead to solutions for these crises. This did not happen. Political events continued to be strongly influenced by what was happening to the economy throughout the revolutionary period. The hungry Parisian *sans-culottes* played an important political role until at least 1795. In many cases, actions taken by the revolutionary assemblies only worsened the problems. The abolition of feudal dues in 1790–91 it led to a serious loss of income by aristocratic landowners. They retaliated by raising rents (this was still legal), which of course hit small farmers very hard and drove many into poverty. Industries which specialised in the luxury goods demanded by the aristocracy, such as the great silk industry in Lyons, suffered badly. There were major transfers of land as aristocratic

owners lost theirs and the extensive land holdings of the Church were nationalised. This caused upheaval in the countryside, but those who managed to get hold of this land now had a vested interest in the revolution. The growing reliance on paper money, the *assignats*, led to rapid inflation throughout the period.

War with Britain, which led to the British blockading all the major French ports, devastated France's overseas trade. The British navy, the most powerful in the world at the time, had warships permanently patrolling just outside French ports. They prevented merchant ships from leaving and captured those trying to enter. The great ports of Bordeaux and Marseilles were paralysed and there was mass unemployment there. At the same time, agriculture was disrupted by the army's demands for food and horses, and conscription caused a shortage of men to work the harvest. A need for solutions to these many economic problems was a major reason for the growing desire to bring to an end the instability caused by the revolution.

1.3 Why was Napoleon Bonaparte able to overthrow the Directory in 1799?

The aims and rule of the Directory

The death of Robespierre marked the end of the most bloodthirsty period of the revolution and the start of a move away from the extremism that had characterised Jacobin rule. The Convention drew up another constitution in August 1795. In order to balance power and avoid the dictatorship of one man or one group, a 'Directory' was established. This had two Councils: the Council of Five Hundred (with 500 elected members) proposed laws, while the Council of Ancients (with 250 members) accepted or rejected the proposed laws.

The country would be run by five 'directors', or senior ministers, who were selected by the Ancients from a list drawn up by the Five Hundred. They were responsible for choosing junior ministers, army leaders, tax collectors and other officials.

The first five directors were all supporters of the revolution and survivors of the Terror:

- Barras, who was initially the most dominant, was a former nobleman and an enthusiastic supporter of the revolution. He had been a key player in Robespierre's downfall.

- La Révellière-Lépeaux was a strong republican and opponent of the monarchy. He hated the Roman Catholic Church and was determined to prevent the Church from re-establishing any role in French society.
- Reubell, who was very knowledgeable on foreign affairs, was a more moderate republican than the others, but had voted for the execution of the king. He had been an opponent of Robespierre and disliked the extremism of the Jacobins.
- Le Tourneur was an engineer and military expert.
- Carnot, another member with a military background, was an opponent of Jacobin extremism and an able organiser.

Those who designed the new constitution aimed to restore stability and keep the most important achievements of the revolution. It was to be a middle way between the extremes of the Terror and the failings of the Ancien Régime.

The directors, and those who supported them, came from the middle class, which had gained from the revolution, acquiring land, status and, above all, political power. They had ended all the abuses of the Ancien Régime. Now these men wanted to make sure they did not lose what had been won at the cost of so much blood and hard work. Although they made money from their positions in the new government, claims that the directors were totally corrupt are probably exaggerated.

The reputation of, and opposition to, the Directory

The Directory faced considerable problems. The treasury was empty and the government was almost bankrupt. The war was expensive and people deeply resented the policy of conscription. Prices were rising, there was a shortage of currency and a barter economy developed. Although the Reign of Terror was over, factions still existed within France. Royalists, Jacobins and moderate republicans continued to fight for their own agendas. The press remained uncensored, so there was scope for monarchists and radicals to express extreme views. In fact, these internal divisions helped the Directory to survive, as the lack of cooperation between the many political groups meant that none was strong enough to challenge the new government.

Importantly, the Directory had the support of the army. If the royalists won back control of France, the war against Austria would end and many soldiers would be unemployed. The Directory also needed the army to put down uprisings by those who resisted the revolution. The government could not escape the opposition of the Jacobins and other radicals, who believed that members of the Directory had betrayed the revolution. Anger against the government increased after a severe winter in 1795–96 led to a shortage of food. Riots broke out and there were calls for the 1795 Constitution – by which the Directory ruled – to be abolished. The Directory called on the army to suppress the revolts, and the National Guard, formerly a focus of lower-class agitation, was re-formed to bring it under government control.

The Jacobins were not yet defeated, though, and in 1796 they launched a plot to overthrow the Directory and replace it with a 'Republic of Equals'. This was named the Babeuf Plot (after one of its leaders, Gracchus **Babeuf**) and was well organised. The rebels issued a newspaper to spread their ideas and gather support, and began stockpiling weapons in preparation for the fight ahead. Police spies uncovered the plot, however. The Jacobin leaders were arrested and Babeuf was executed.

Considered an extreme radical at the time, Babeuf was a brilliant agitator and journalist. He believed in the vote for all men and women and in the creation of a genuine democracy. He argued for the abolition of all private property and for equality for all. After the failed plot to overthrow the Directory, he was arrested and executed.

An extract from the 'Manifesto of the Equals', issued by the Jacobin plotters in 1796

People of France

Never before has a greater plan been conceived or carried out. Here and there a few men of genius, a few men, have spoken in a low and trembling voice. None have had the courage to tell you the whole truth.

The moment of great measures has arrived. Evil has reached its height: it covers the face of the Earth. In the name of politics, chaos has reigned for too many centuries. Let everything be set in order and take its proper place once again. Let the supporters of justice and happiness organise in the voice of equality. The moment has come to found a new republic the *REPUBLIC OF EQUALS*, a great home open to all men. The day of general restitution has arrived. Groaning families, come and sit at the common table set by nature for all its children.

Source: www.marxists.org/history/france/revolution/conspiracy-equals/1796/manifesto.htm

Elections, coups and the downfall of the Directory

Inspired by the failure of the Jacobins in 1796, the royalists put a great deal of effort into their campaign for the elections which were to be held in 1797, with some success. Helped by an uncensored press and an angry clergy from their pulpits, they mounted a determined attack against the Directory and the whole system of government it represented. They particularly emphasised the poor state of the economy and the failure of the Directory to deal with finance successfully. Fearing a royalist *coup d'état* which would lead to a restoration of the monarchy, the more radical directors acted swiftly. In what became known as the Coup of Fructidor, the Directors ignored the election results, suppressed royalists by force, imposed strict censorship on the press and removed the more moderate (potentially pro-royalist) directors. This left the more radical, pro-Jacobin element of the Directory in charge. The revolution might have been saved, but these actions only increased the feeling of insecurity and uncertainty in France and encouraged a growing feeling that stronger government was needed. The French, middle class, who had been the greatest beneficiaries of the

revolution to date, saw themselves, their position and their property threatened by royalist plots and radical revolts.

KEY TERM

Coup d'état: The sudden, and often violent, overthrow of government power by a group of citizens or military personnel.

Apart from the fact that its many enemies were badly divided, there were other reasons for the survival of the Directory until 1799. France was successful in war most of the time, gaining territory in Italy and finally making peace with Austria. The economy improved, helped by sensible taxation. Better harvests helped the directors to take firm control of food prices. They dealt wisely with the émigrés and opponents of the regime, but they also took care to punish those guilty of anti-Catholic extremes. They ensured effective local government and did their best to put the ideas of 1789 into practice, with no privileges for any class and a focus on equality. They also did their best to manage the frequent elections they were required to hold, which by 1797 were producing many council members hostile to the Directory, alongside those who hated the Jacobins and wanted a restoration of the monarchy.

While very much in control of France, however, the Directory was tolerated rather than loved. By 1799, several tactical choices and mistakes were costing them popularity:

- The directors' attempts to manage the elections so that favoured candidates won discredited the system.
- Their system of taxation, which fell mainly on property owners, upset this influential section of the population.
- During the military advance in Italy, Rome, the centre of the Catholic Church was captured, which offended the many Roman Catholics in France.
- An attempt by a young general, **Napoleon Bonaparte**, to invade Egypt had ended in disaster with the destruction of a French fleet and army.
- France found itself at war with Britain, Turkey, Russia and then Austria again.
- Both conscription and the forced loans needed to pay for the wars aroused anger.

While the Directory had survived earlier attempts to overthrow it, the event that became known as the Coup of Prairial proved its undoing. The Directory can to an end in 1799.

31

32

NAPOLEON BONAPARTE (1769–1821)

Napoleon was born in Corsica to a family of minor nobility of Italian origin. They had supported Corsican independence, and Napoleon himself didn't speak French until learning it in school. After military training on mainland France, he served as an artillery officer first under Louis XVI and then in the revolutionary armies, where the departure of the nobility opened up careers for men of talent. He was a general by the age of 24. Military success laid the basis for a political career. With the army as the only dependable basis of power in a country in political turmoil, he seized control in a coup, and later declared himself emperor. A series of military victories followed, as his armies wreaked havoc across Europe. However, a series of subsequent defeats saw him driven back into France and removed from power.

Successes and failures of the Directory

With the end of the Directory came the end of the revolutionary period. The Directory had always struggled to appear legitimate, in spite of the fact that it was sustained by elections. It had never really solved the issue of a working relationship between the Executive and the Legislature, and many people were reluctant to accept this form of democratic government. The wealthy minority were unhappy with the heavy taxation imposed on them by the majority. The forced loans and conscription required by war were unpopular. Few people liked the constitution, and it had given scope for both royalists and radicals to put forward their views, which added to a feeling of insecurity.

While the Directory had done a good job of creating a fairer and more efficient tax system, it was unable to convince many in France that it could manage the economy successfully. The Directory had to repudiate public debts at times. Key public services were neglected as money was needed to pay for the seemingly endless war. Bankers were reluctant to lend the government money and there was still substantial speculation in vital commodities such as wheat. Anxious to avoid the criticism of being too similar to the Ancien Régime, the Directory devolved power to the towns

and regions. In many cases, these did not have the means to keep control, so disorder grew. The Church retained strong loyalties in many rural areas and it preached disloyalty to the Directory. The inability to deal with this conflict between Church and state was a major weakness of the Directory. For many in France, religious faith was more important than support for the revolution.

So, the Directory faced attack from conservative elements such as the Church and aristocracy. It also came under pressure from the radicals. Some were inspired by Jacobin ideas. They had strong support among the urban working class, which had its own grievances. They wanted:

- a highly democratic form of government
- compulsory loans from the wealthy
- conscription for all, with no exemptions for the rich
- an end to the system of *assignats*, which they felt only led to speculation and benefited the rich.

Such demands represented a strong attack on the wealthy middle class and the Directory itself.

The lack of a strong, central and inspirational government capable of dealing with the problems and showing the French people a clear sense of direction was becoming obvious. The pressure was on to create a powerful and permanent Executive branch of government. The French people needed someone to blame for all that had gone wrong, and also an individual they could look to for leadership. They wanted the gains of the revolution as well as social, economic and political stability. Napoleon was able to sense this, and he capitalised on it.

While there had been military success, people were tired of war and its costs. Just before the Directory fell, in August 1799, the French army had been defeated by combined Austrian and Russian forces at the Battle of Novi in northern Italy. The French suffered well over 10 000 casualties, including the popular commander General Joubert.

The elections of 1798 showed how divided France was, with the Council of Five Hundred having both radicals and royalists elected. The new '500' attacked the Directors, accusing them of corruption and incompetence, which only added to the uncertainty. The time was ripe for another coup, particularly one which promised to bring the wars to a close, end the political uncertainty, retain the achievements of the revolution and, above all, bring stability to France.

A key figure in this 'Coup of 18 Brumaire' was actually one of the directors. **Abbé Sieyès**, had been involved in the making of constitutions since 1789. He aimed to create a new system of government which had firm control of the whole Executive process in France and reduced the role of any Legislature. He knew he had to seize power by a coup: trying to change everything legally would take too long and would probably fail. To take over, he needed an army and a reliable general – and he found just such a man in charge of troops in the Paris area, Napoleon Bonaparte.

ABBÉ EMMANUEL JOSEPH SIEYÈS (1748–1836)

Sieyès was a priest and a politician during the French Revolution. He criticised the privileges of the Church and the nobility, and supported the Third Estate in the 1789 Estates General. Sieyès disliked the 1795 Constitution and, at first, refused to serve in the Directory. He was so popular, however, that he eventually gave in to pressure and became a director. Despite this, he believed that the government was inefficient and self-serving, and he helped Napoleon come to power in 1799. He was made one of the three consuls, but resigned in protest when Napoleon declared himself emperor in 1804.

ACTIVITY 1.15

One has to give credit to the Directory as the first twenty months of their rule constitute a particularly remarkable period of administration. Five men, chosen in anger, came to power in the most unfavourable circumstances. Their offices did not even have tables to write on. Paper money was reduced to almost a thousandth of its previous value. There was insurrection in the Vendée, brigands everywhere and food supplies were critically short and France's armies were disorganised. In six months the Directory raised France from this terrible situation. Coin smoothly replaced paper money. Men lived in peace in the countryside, the brigands were gone, the army was successful and the liberty of the press was restored. Elections followed and one would have been able to say that France was now free. However, once

ACTIVITY 1.15 (CONTINUED)

they started to persecute over 100,00 individuals, such revolutionary measures spoiled their Constitution. The second half of the existence of that government, which lasted four years in all, was poor from every perspective.

Adapted from Mme de Stael's 'Considérations sur la Révolution Française'. She was Necker's daughter and lived throughout the revolutionary period.

Quoted in Dwyer, P. and McPhee, P. (2002). *The French Revolution and Napoleon*. London: Routledge, pp. 122–23

A great amount of anxiety caused by the financial situation prevails amongst the public. Investors are deeply worried by the coup of 18 Fructidor (4 September 1797). Violent grumblings can be heard about public poverty. The number of workers without employment in Paris has increased and it is the same in the provinces. The coming of winter raises real fear of its consequences. Rumours are rife that another coup is going to take place at any time. It is rumoured that the Directory will start to purge the Councils. There is the feeling that we have an aristocratic government and in the hands of men who are in no way republican and it may become a monarchy as in 1791. The only difference between the Constitution of 1791 and the Constitution of 1795 is that the execution of the laws is given to five men instead of one man. There are many fears about the political future, grumblings about financial matters and there is a real desire for peace.

A police report on the climate of fear in northern France, August 1797

Quoted in Dwyer P. and McPhee P. (above), pp. 126–27

Compare and contrast these two views of the Directory. Use a table like the one below to help you.

Reasons why the Directory lost support and popularity	
Source 1	Source 2

What do the sources suggest are the reasons why the Directory lost support and became unpopular? Which of the two sources do you think is the most useful to a historian, and why?

The military reputation and political ambitions of Napoleon Bonaparte

Napoleon had been born in Corsica, an island in the Mediterranean which was part of France. He was sent to a military academy in mainland France and trained as a soldier. He joined his first regiment in 1793, just as the revolution was reaching a critical phase. Always highly ambitious, demonstrating real military ability and showing considerable political awareness as well, he soon became noticed. With war declared against Austria in 1792, and with most of the senior, aristocratic, officers refusing to support the revolution or fleeing the country, the way was open for military men of ability and ambition from middle-class backgrounds, to rise to the top of the army.

Initially a supporter of Robespierre and the Jacobins, over time Napoleon distanced himself from them and carefully managed his support for the Directory in 1795. He played a very important role in suppressing counter-revolutionary forces that year, and in securing the Directory in office. His reward for this was to be put in command of the army of the interior while he was still in his twenties. From this key position he had great control over the future of the revolution. A year later, Napoleon was put in command of the French army in northern Italy. With these 30 000 poorly fed, badly paid, ill-equipped and demoralised men, he achieved astonishing success. Not only did he defeat the Austrian armies by his superb leadership, but he was left in control of the wealthiest and most productive part of Italy. As a result of his successes in Italy, and an attack on Austria itself, he managed to impose a peace treaty on Austria in 1798 which formally gave France much of northern Italy and territory in present-day Belgium. Napoleon became a national hero. Always conscious of the need to present himself in a favourable – revolutionary – light, he ran two newspapers. One was for his soldiers, to maintain their morale; the other was published in France to publicise his achievements on behalf of the country and the revolution, and to downplay royalist suggestions that he was aiming at personal dictatorship.

His invasion of Egypt in 1798 was less successful, however. The plan was to take over the country and, hopefully, begin to destroy British influence in the Middle East and, eventually, India. A British fleet and army drove Napoleon out, and he returned to France in 1799, cleverly managing to downplay the scale of his Egyptian defeat.

There was no limit to Napoleon's ambitions. In 1793, he had been just another junior officer leaving the military academy and joining his regiment for the first time. Five years later he was the successful senior commander of a victorious army which had defeated one of the major European powers and forced it to hand over vital territories. Napoleon was not a leading figure only in France, but also across Europe.

The weakness of the Directory in 1799 gave him the opportunity to rise from being just *a* leading figure to being *the* leading figure in France. He took every opportunity offered to him to rise as far as he could. Having been appointed to command all troops in the Paris area, a meeting with Sieyès gave Napoleon his opportunity to rise further. Sieyès thought that he could use Napoleon to further his own ends. Napoleon thought exactly the same about using Sieyès, but was careful to conceal it.

The coup of 1799

After careful planning, Sieyès and Napoleon, aided by Napoleon's brother, Lucien (president of the Assembly), and two other vital supporters – Fouché and Talleyrand – proceeded to seize power. Joseph Fouché (1759–1820) was an extreme Jacobin who had flourished during the unpredictable early years of the revolution. After the Reign of Terror, he survived Robespierre's fall, turning against him just in time. By 1800, Fouché was minister of police, in charge of an extensive policing system, but he kept his contacts with royalists. Charles Maurice de Talleyrand (1754–1838) was an aristocrat and had been a bishop before the revolution. After 1789, he supported the revolutionary governments in their Church reforms. He helped bring Napoleon to power and to form the Consulate. By 1813, however, Talleyrand had lost faith in Napoleon and instead worked for the restoration of the monarchy. When asked later what he had done during the French Revolution, Talleyrand replied: 'I survived.'

Any resistance, in the Assembly or elsewhere, was firmly, but not too violently, dealt with. The directors all resigned, and Napoleon's loyal troops ensured that the Parisian *sans-culottes* no longer decided the political future of France. Sieyès promised a new constitution,

Figure 1.10: 'The coup d'état of the 18th Brumaire (9th November) 1799'. 19th century. Artist: Unknown.

but in the meantime, France was to be governed by three consuls, who had considerable executive power. Napoleon took care to ensure that he was not just one of the consuls, but the 'first consul'. This allowed him to rapidly become the dominant force among them. He had taken another major step on his path to power in France. He had achieved this because he was an able leader, soldier, administrator and politician who had strong support from the army, Sieyès and his brother Lucien. He also recognised the great desire in France for stability and law and order, and the wish to keep many of the revolution's great reforms. Above all, he was immensely ambitious.

From a letter from Napoleon to Citizen D'Andigne, Paris, December 1799

I have been pleased at reading the letter from the fine citizens of the Western Departments supporting events in Paris. They show an attitude which does them honour and will be useful to France. Too much French blood has flowed during the past ten years and now enlightened men wish to create a government solely concerned to re-establish order, justice and true freedom. This government will gain the trust and respect of all Europe, and will also bring peace. Never again will revolutionary laws devastate the fair soil of France, the Revolution is over and consciences will be absolutely free and protection will be given equally to all citizens.

Source: Thompson, J. M. (ed.). (1934). *Napoleon Self-Revealed*. Boston: Houghton Mifflin, p. 70

ACTIVITY 1.16

Proclamation of 21 Brumaire, Year VIII (12 November 1799)

The Constitution of the Year III was dying. It could neither guarantee your rights, nor assure its own existence. Repeated assaults were robbing it irreparably of the people's respect. Malevolent, greedy factions were dividing up the republic. France was finally approaching the last stage of a general disorganization. Patriots have come together. All that could harm you has been set aside. All that could serve you, all that remained pure in the national representation has united under the banner of liberty. Frenchmen, the Republic, strengthened and restored to that rank in Europe which it should never have lost, will see the realization of its citizens' hopes and the fulfilment of its glorious destiny. Swear with us the oath we are taking to be faithful to the Republic, one and indivisible, founded on equality, liberty and the representative system.

Source: Consuls of the Republic. Bonaparte. Roger Ducos. Sieyés.

www.napoleon-series.org/research/government/legislation/c_proclamation.html

On my return to Paris, I found division among all the authorities and agreement on only one truth, that the Constitution was half destroyed and could no longer save liberty. Every faction came to me, confided their plans in me, and asked me for my support. I refused to be the man of one faction. A plan for the restoration of order by men seen as the defenders of liberty, equality and property was created and gave me the responsibility of organising the force necessary. I believed it my duty to my fellow citizens, to the soldiers perishing in our armies and for the national glory to accept their command. I then went to the Council of Five Hundred alone and unarmed; twenty assassins threw themselves on me and aimed at my chest…the grenadiers of the Legislative Body ran to put themselves between me and the assassins… they carried me out… cries of 'outlaw' were heard against me… the grenadiers had the hall evacuated.… The factions dispersed and fled. The majority, freed from these attacks, returned freely and peaceably to the meeting hall, heard the propositions for public safety, deliberated and prepared the resolution which is to become the new and provisional law of the republic.

Frenchmen, you will recognise in this conduct the zeal of a soldier of liberty, of a citizen devoted to the republic. Conservative and liberal idea have been restored to their rightful place by the disposal of rebels….

(Signed) Bonaparte

Source: Adapted from Napoleon's justification of the coup of Brumaire

Dwyer, P. and McPhee, P. (2002). *The French Revolution and Napoleon*. London: Routledge, pp. 137–39

Compare and contrast the reasons given in the two sources for the failure of the Directory. You could use a table to list your findings like the one used in Activity 1.15. In what ways do the two sources differ on the reasons why the French people should support the new system of government?

Reflection: Discuss your response to the two sources with another student. How did you decide on the usefulness of each source? Would you change your answer following your discussion?

1.4 What were Napoleon's domestic aims and achievements from 1799 to 1814?

When he became first consul in 1799, aged just 30, Napoleon had three broad aims. The first was to become, and then remain, the ruler of France. The second was to end the chaos of the revolutionary years. The third was to provide effective government in France, maintaining the best of the revolutionary gains while still keeping law and order. Napoleon felt that France needed firm government and an end to radicalism. He set out to create a middle way, avoiding both Jacobinism and the Terror on one side and the Ancien Régime with its privilege on the other. He would seek to offer France political stability, which would in turn create social and economic stability. In doing so, he removed some democratic freedoms, reducing elections both in number and political significance, thus ending the frequent changes in government.

If Sieyès had been more perceptive, and examined Napoleon's career before the end of 1799, he would have realised that Napoleon was much more than a good general. He had shown strong authoritarian, even dictatorial, tendencies in the management of his conquests in Italy and Egypt. Napoleon was a rational individual, strongly influenced by Enlightenment ideas and, above all, the idea of a strong unitary state with a powerful central authority. He was well aware that the ideals of 1789 were deeply rooted in France by 1799, and that any attempt to change them would be disastrous. He wanted to restore national unity and pride in France, as did the majority of French people, especially the middle class. He hated, as did many others, aspects of the Ancien Régime such as feudalism, inequality and religious intolerance, but he did not like democracy, and he was determined to break the power and influence of the *sans-culottes*. Again, this view was shared by many in the middle class.

ACTIVITY 1.17

What was the principal reason for the success of the coup that brought Napoleon to power ? How far was it down to the circumstances of 1799 or to his own skills?

Napoleon's initiatives as first consul

Napoleon proved exceptionally clever in the way he went from successful general to absolute ruler of France. One of his first acts as consul was to release from jail many émigrés

and radicals, as well as some priests. He hoped to create an atmosphere of both political and religious tolerance. His message was clear: if people obeyed the law, they would be free to live in peace. In 1802, there was a general **amnesty** for all émigrés. He created a strong government with his two fellow consuls, the former Jacobin radical Cambacérès and the old royalist sympathiser Lebrun, both known for their strong administrative skills. The time had come for reconciliation, not revenge.

Sieyès produced another new constitution, which established the Consulate, with its powerful Executive. This constitution, legitimised by a **plebiscite**, was a critical stage in Napoleon's rise to power in France:

- It placed the first consul (Napoleon) in the key decision-making role.
- The first consul appointed ministers.
- The first consul could initiate legislation.
- There was only a requirement for limited consultation in new legislation.
- There was no accountability.

KEY TERMS

Amnesty: A pardon for breaking any laws in the past.

Plebiscite: Like an election, a plebiscite is a popular vote. Instead of being called to choose a national assembly and a government, however, a plebiscite puts a question to voters about a specific issue and is almost always organised around a 'yes/no' decision. Essentially, it is another word for a referendum.

The 'nation' was still sovereign, but it was just not consulted. The concept of the need to elect rulers into power had been overlooked. Napoleon said: 'I alone represent the people.' The other two consuls provided some balance, but had little or no power. It was Napoleon, the first consul, who moved into the old royal palace in Paris, the Tuileries, in 1800.

Further steps on Napoleon's rise to power, making him; consul for life' (and being able to name his successor) and finally being declared emperor, were also confirmed by plebiscites.

Within weeks of becoming first consul, Napoleon stamped his authority on the new government. He was determined to prove that his coup was not another of a long list of ineffective coups, and that he was there to stay. In 1800, he showed the French people just what his regime was capable of.

Figure 1.11: *Napoleon Crossing the Alps*, oil painting by Jacques-Louis David, 1801. The King of Spain ordered the original version as a gift for Napoleon. Napoleon instructed the painter in how he should be portrayed, and ordered additional copies which he placed on public display at the Louvre Museum in 1801. How does the origin of the painting help to explain the message it contains about Napoleon's image?

Napoleon's authoritarian government

He set up new ministries, which he staffed himself, including the war ministry. All ministers reported directly to Napoleon. Along with this, he created a Council of State which consisted of all the principal ministers. It was a good balance politically and contained many able men who had taken different sides during the previous decade. Napoleon was good at spotting talent and using it. He also set up the Bank of France under a capable minister. This

was a vital step towards ending the financial problems that had contributed To chaos during the revolution. He also took great care to monitor the price of bread. Aware of harvest failings in 1800, Napoleon ordered that, despite this, food prices must be kept low in Paris in particular.

On the local government side, major structural reform was imposed on the provinces. Prefects, replacing the old intendants, were given considerable power and reported directly to Paris. Napoleon took considerable care to appoint able men (they were not elected). They were always sent to areas away from their birthplace, they had no connections. This was intended to avoid them helping their families or old friends. This process was an important step in the centralisation of power in France.

The regime quickly tackled the instruments of law and order. The police force, both local and central, was reformed by Fouché on Napoleon's orders. All police came firmly under state control. There was to be no more government by the *sans-culottes*. An elaborate system of spies and informers was set up to eliminate any enemies of the state. Mail could be censored as well. Minor rebellions broke out in Brittany and the west of France, but they were firmly dealt with. Armed force was used, followed by executions. 'Never since the time of Robespierre have laws been so severe,' one citizen reported, but, once an example had been set, conciliation followed.

The judiciary was also reformed. The central government appointed all judges, having checked their loyalty first. Repression by the government was made easier, but certain key gains of 1789 were kept, such as an insistence on equality before the law. Nonetheless, the interests of the state tended to dominate over those of the individual.

The majority of the newspapers in 1800 were radical Jacobin supporters, but serious censorship of the press would shut down over 60 (out of 73) in 1800 alone. Soon there were few alternative sources for news other than the official government newspaper, the *Moniteur*. Theatres were banned from putting on radical plays.

Napoleon reviewed all senior military appointments and ensured that only generals loyal to him remained in their posts. He also took great care to ensure soldiers were paid and fed, and he did his best to limit the unpopularity of conscription. While taking care to publicise that the unpopular war with Austria and Britain was not caused by him, Napoleon managed to defeat his enemies in two remarkable battles in the summer of 1800: Marengo and Hohenlinden. Both these military successes brought great prestige to France and possessions abroad. Napoleon, with his image carefully manipulated in the official press, was now a national hero. (The painting of Napoleon on this page is an example of how Napoleon used painting and images as propaganda).

What he had achieved in a matter of months was remarkable. By the end of 1800, Napoleon had established himself not only as the dominant figure in France, but also as an important player in European politics as a whole. He then turned to making peace so that he could consolidate his position in France and deal with the problems left over from the revolutionary period.

The inauguration of the empire

Napoleon's proclamation to the people of France on becoming emperor, 1804

The object of my dearest thoughts has always been the happiness of the French people and their glory the object of my labours. Called by Divine Providence and the Constitutions of the Republic to Imperial power, I see in this new order of things nothing but greater means of assuring national power and prosperity. I take comfort with confidence in the power aid of the Almighty God. He will inspire His Ministers to support me by all the means within their power. These Ministers of God will enlighten the people by wise instruction, preaching to them love of duty, obedience to the law and the practice of all the Christian and civil virtues. They will call the blessing of Heaven upon the nation and on the Supreme Head of the State.

Source: www.dkarpeles.com/napoleon/ proclamation-accession-as-emperor-may-18-1804/

By the time he became emperor, and had further successful military victories and conquests abroad, Napoleon had become increasingly authoritarian. Any legislative bodies were marginalised, censorship was tightened, and the press became highly enthusiastic about Napoleon and his policies. There was no more popular sovereignty – as he stated on one occasion: 'I am the representative of the people.' There was little or no serious opposition to his rule in France, however. He took great care to ensure that law and order were maintained, and that the country retained what the French people saw were the benefits of the revolution. He seems to have modelled himself on the 'enlightened despots' of the Ancien Régimes in Europe, where autocratic leaders ruled wisely.

Figure 1.12: The coronation of Napoleon (official title: *Consecration of the Emperor Napoleon I and Coronation of the Empress Josephine in the Cathedral of Notre-Dame de Paris on 2 December 1804*) by Jacques-Louis David, 1807. The painting was ordered by Napoleon after his coronation and was designed to show Napoleon's support from, and his support of, the Church.

●●● THINK LIKE A HISTORIAN

The freedom of the press

Napoleon censored the press and books after the excesses of the revolution. He argued that this would bring stability and security to France, which he felt was what the French people both wanted and needed. Look at the arguments that could be put forward for imposing restrictions on the mass media, the internet and social media. Then consider the case for allowing absolute freedom of expression. What restrictions do you feel might be reasonable to have on what you read, write or put on the internet or social media?

Napoleon made sure that middle-class aspirations were met, that property was secure (particularly property bought from the Church or émigrés) and that careers were open to talent, not just circumstances of birth. There was no longer a risk of a repeat alliance between the middle class, the peasants and the city workers, which had proved so dangerous in the early years of the revolution. He stabilised prices of basic foods and ensured regular supplies of all essentials. These policies, together with his great military victories and French expansion into Europe, ensured the loyalty of many and at least the tolerance of those who might oppose his regime. It was to take the combined armies of Britain, Prussia, Russia and Austria to unseat Napoleon from his throne and replace him with a Bourbon. The French people themselves were not going to overthrow him.

ACTIVITY 1.18

Compare the painting in Figure 1.12 with that in Figure 1.3, of the Tennis Court Oath, earlier in this chapter. What similarities and differences can you see between the two images? Looking back on what you have learned, how does Figure 1.12 help you to understand the changes that occurred in France in the period between the two paintings?

Nature and impact of reforms (legal, educational, social and financial)

As with almost every other aspect of Napoleon's career, his domestic policies have attracted considerable debate. Were the motives behind them just retention of power? Or was he a genuine heir to the revolution who wished to keep the French people free from the chains of the Ancien Régime? In his first years in power, there was a series of major domestic reforms which focused on four main areas:

- equality before the law
- religious freedom
- the protection of private property
- social, economic and political stability.

As we have seen, any clever politician in France wishing to retain power after the events of 1789–99 would have to do all he could in those four areas. At the same time, however, a genuine liberal, looking for a balance between the Ancien Régime and the excesses of the Terror and democracy, might well have the same objectives. France had not shaken off its tradition of authoritarian government and had taken a dislike to democracy and the radicalism and killings which seemed to go with it. The French people on the whole wanted a middle way, and Napoleon realised that if he delivered that, together with restoring the prestige of France abroad by military victories and acquisition of new territories, he could become the sole ruler of France and leave it safely to his heirs, just as the Bourbon monarchs had done in the past.

In 1801, Napoleon managed finally to end the wars with his European neighbours. He could now turn his attention to domestic matters.

The Concordat with the Roman Catholic Church

One issue that had divided France throughout the whole revolutionary period was what should happen to the Catholic Church. France had always been a strongly Roman Catholic country, with some tolerance for both Protestants and Jews. The Church and its members had been fiercely attacked in the early days of the revolution. There had been an attempt to 'dechristianise' France and many clergymen had been killed or had fled, while most of the Church's wealth and land was confiscated. In many parts of France, especially in the Vendée and Brittany, however, support for the Catholic Church had been an important reason for counter-revolutionary activity. Many deeply conservative people, especially in rural areas, wished to see the Catholicism restored to their lives and communities.

Napoleon knew that he had to compromise with the Church and bring to an end the bitterness which the revolutionary attacks on it had caused. Settling this issue would deprive the royalists of Church support, and it would also ease the fears of those who now owned the former Church property which had been sold off in the revolutionary years. Napoleon also had territorial ambitions in Belgium, south Germany and Italy, all strongly Roman Catholic countries. The Church could be a useful ally.

In 1801, Napoleon started secret discussions with the head of the Catholic Church, the Pope. Making a deal was not easy after such violence and appropriation. There was much bitterness there. On the whole, the French people wanted religious tolerance in France, but the Roman Catholic Church did not. In 1802, however, an agreement was reached and published. This agreement was known as the Concordat. Its terms were as follows:

- There was a formal reconciliation between the Roman Catholic Church and the French state.
- The Church formally recognised Napoleon's government as the legitimate government of France.
- Catholicism was officially recognised by Napoleon's government.
- The Church was free to organise public worship.
- The Church remained subordinate to the state. It retained some influence over primary education, but that was carefully monitored by the government. The state appointed the bishops and paid the clergy.
- The clergy had to take an oath agreeing to be loyal to the state.
- Church lands nationalised during the revolution remained with their new owners.
- Other religious groups, such as Protestants, were tolerated.
- Clergy were free to preach without penalty.

While this agreement was to cause problems later, it was a great achievement at the time. It ended what had been a major divisive issue in France throughout the revolutionary period. It was a necessary reform to ensure both the stability of the state and Napoleon's tenure of power, and was a practical solution to a real problem.

ACTIVITY 1.19

Napoleon's account of the internal situation of France – a statement which he laid before the legislative body, 31 December 1804

The internal situation of France is today as calm as it has ever been in the most peaceful periods. There is no agitation to disturb the public tranquillity, no suggestion of those crimes which recall the Revolution.

Experience has taught that a divided power in the state is impotent and at odds with itself. It is now clearly seen that for a great nation the only salvation lies in hereditary power. The First Consul has tried in vain to avoid this conclusion; but the public concern and the hopes of our enemies emphasized the importance of his task, and he realized that his death might ruin his whole work. Under such circumstances, and with such a pressure of public opinion, there was no alternative left to the First Consul. He resolved, therefore, to accept for himself the burden imposed by becoming Emperor.

After prolonged consideration by many, the French people, by a free and independent expression, then agreed that the imperial dignity should pass down in a direct line through the legitimate or adopted descendants of Napoleon Bonaparte.

The head of the Church, in order to give the French a striking proof of his paternal affection, consented to officiate at this ceremony. Napoleon pronounced the inviolable oath which assures the integrity of the empire, the security of property, the perpetuity of institutions, the respect for law, and the happiness of the nation.

The civil code has fulfilled the expectations of the public; all citizens are acquainted with it; it serves as their guide in their various transactions, and is everywhere lauded as a benefaction.

New schools are being opened, and inspectors have been appointed to see that the instruction does not degenerate into vain and sterile examinations. The *lycees* and the secondary schools are filling with youth eager for instruction.

Religion has resumed its sway, but exhibits itself only in acts of humanity. Adhering to a wise policy of toleration, the ministers of different sects who worship the same God do themselves honour by their mutual respect; and their rivalry confines itself to emulation in virtue. Such is our situation at home.

Source: Robinson, J. H. (ed.). (1906). *Readings in European History.* **Vol. 2. Boston: Ginn, pp. 491–94**

Working in pairs, carefully read Napoleon's account and answer the following questions:

Why did he make this statement?

What points does he make with this statement?

Why do you think he was keen to have the support of the Church?

Organise your thoughts by making notes for each question.

Legal reform: the *Code Napoléon*

Another major reform which was both necessary and ultimately very popular, was what became known as the Napoleonic Code.

The civil and criminal legal system in France in 1799 was a complex mess. Before 1789, there had been about 400 different legal systems in France. Regions and towns often had their own laws. The Church and some groups, such as merchants, had their own rules. Some nobles, for example, would be exempt from certain laws. The revolution had abolished many but not all of these old systems. Over 14 000 new laws had been passed by the various assemblies between 1789 and 1799, many of them now unnecessary and

discredited. The legal system in France needed radical reform if the new regime was to convince the French people that it could effectively govern the country.

Although most of the work reforming the legal system was done by others, Napoleon realised its importance, ensured it happened, and took credit for it after its success was proven. He later claimed it as one of his greatest achievements. It was an excellent compromise between liberalism and conservativism. Produced in stages between 1801 and 1806, and formally established in 1807, its main terms were:

- equality before the law
- freedom of religion

- freedom of conscience
- an end to feudalism
- the rule of law with the right to a proper trial and defence
- freedom to choose one's own profession.

The Code also introduced completely reformed systems of civil law, commercial law and criminal law, and brought in a new penal code. All laws were to be applied uniformly throughout France. The Code covered many areas of life, such as divorce, marriage, adoption, debts, loans and even gambling.

Critics at the time, and since, pointed out that the Code:

- favoured the middle class
- was biased in favour of owners of landed property and neglected the interests of industrial wealth
- tended to promote the interests of the state over that of the individual
- gave undue authority to the father/husband over women
- offered little to the poor or landless (there was no right to a livelihood)
- favoured the employer over the worker (workers' associations or trade unions were banned).

Nonetheless, most of the policies of the Code survived Napoleon's overthrow. Although radical in many ways for its time, it has since been criticised for not going further in its political and social reforms. It is important to see events in context, however, and the fact that – to take one modern criticism – the Code did not give women the vote was actually a fair reflection of what most French people wanted at the time.

With control of the press and publications, as well as an efficient and centrally controlled police force, any opposition to the Code was firmly dealt with. Fearing a royalist coup against him in 1804, for example, Napoleon ordered the capture and execution of the Duke of Enghien, who was related to the Bourbon monarchy. While this act angered many in Europe, it sent a clear message to potential opponents. The *Moniteur* newspaper, controlled by the government, always portrayed Napoleon in a favourable light and did much to influence opinion in France. Portraits of Napoleon, such as the one in Figure 1.10, always showed him in an heroic light. He was very much a pioneer of modern public relations techniques.

ACTIVITY 1.20

Identify points which can be used to praise and criticise the Napoleonic Code. Did it bring real benefits to France and its people?

Napoleon maintained that the Code was his greatest domestic achievement. List what you consider to be his other domestic achievements. Place them in order of importance, giving reasons for that order. Do you agree with his judgement?

Reflection: How did you decide the order of Napoleon's domestic achievements? Explain to another student how you made your choices. What criticisms of yours does your partner make? How would you defend your decisions? What criticisms could you make of their selection?

Financial and economic reform: banking and taxation

While the Code and the Concordat stand out as lasting reforms, Napoleon, particularly in the years before war began again in 1805, made many other efforts to end the problems that had faced the revolutionary leaders.

There were real improvements in the economy. In 1800, the Bank of France (with Napoleon and his family as shareholders) was formed to bring order and stability to the banking system and the French currency, and to bring an end to the problem of the *assignats*. He ended the forced loans and the cycle of inflation and deflation. He ensured that the state's debts were paid on time and, in 1802, there was a balanced state budget with income matching expenditure. With good administrators in the form of prefects chosen for their ability, a sensible and fair system of taxation was created. Good harvests also helped. Increasingly, Napoleon ensured that he gave the people no grounds to oppose him.

KEY CONCEPTS

Change and continuity: The Directory and Napoleon

Working in pairs, identify the principal changes that Napoleon brought to France in his domestic policies. Evaluate how fundamental they were. To what extent was France a very different country as a result of his rule? How different was Napoleon's rule to that of the Directory? Assess the degree of continuity between his rule and that of the Directory.

43

Napoleon had no wish to see a return to hereditary privilege, and the nobility remained abolished. He was well aware how much noble privilege had been despised by the French people. Instead, in 1802, he introduced a new 'reward' for service to the state, the *Legion d'honneur*. This was an award for real achievements which benefited the country, but it carried no special privileges.

Care was taken to ensure that the price of bread was strictly controlled so that there would be no return to the hunger-driven radicalism of the *sans-culottes* of the revolutionary period. Prefects were made to improve the quality of roads, which helped trade and communications (and also the rapid movement of troops). The long, straight, tree-lined boulevards of France today are a Napoleonic legacy. Once stable, the economy tended to be subordinated to Napoleon's other needs. There were some attempts to encourage manufacturing, and protective trade tariffs became French policy.

Educational reforms

Napoleon also brought in major changes in the system of education. While there had been attempts during the revolutionary period to improve it, much damage had also been done. The Church had been one of the main providers of education in France. Part of the Concordat had been the decision to leave the Church playing a large role in primary education (up to age 10), but Napoleon was very interested in secondary education, for boys aged 10 to 16.

In 1801, a report from the prefects on the poor state of education led to important developments in this area, in which Napoleon had a major influence. A state-controlled system of education for boys aged 10 to 16 was set up. The curriculum was controlled by the state and teachers were trained, paid and monitored by the central government. There was little emphasis on religion in the new curriculum. The focus was mainly on subjects such as French and mathematics, designed to produce a middle-class elite (and a non-revolutionary one) capable of administering France in the future. In addition, 30 *lycees* were created throughout France to provide advanced and specialist higher education for the future leaders of

France. A reformed university system, led by the 'Imperial University' was created in 1808.

On the whole, the poor were excluded from these reforms. Like many of the middle class, Napoleon felt that educating the poor was a waste of time and money. The army needed ordinary soldiers and farming needed simple labourers. Neither needed much education. Girls and women did not feature seriously in these reforms either. Nonetheless, was the case with many of Napoleon's domestic policies, this system of education was both popular and enduring.

So, with the return to war in 1805, and now the crowned and anointed emperor, the hereditary ruler of France was anxious to dominate Europe, and he focused less on domestic policy. The major reforms of Napoleon's first six years in office were firmly established. They had restored the stability that the French people longed for, and did much to ensure that Napoleon retained the loyalty and respect of the French people and remained firmly in power.

ACTIVITY 1.21

To help you reach a conclusion based on evidence, consider these two different views of Napoleon: a ruthless dictator who only wanted to stay in power, or a leader only wanting power so he could help the people of France. Copy the table and record your evidence.

Evidence to support the following views of Napoleon.	
"a ruthless dictator who only wanted to stay in power"	"a leader only wanting power to help the people of France"

Either working on your own or in a pair, find evidence to support both these views. Which view do you think is the fairest to Napoleon?

Exam-style questions

Source analysis questions

Read all four sources and then answer both parts of question 1.

SOURCE A

Memoir written by the royal princes to Louis XVI, December 1788

Sire, the state is in peril. A revolution is being prepared and it is being brought about by the stirring up of minds. Political writings have been published during the Assembly of Notables and the new political demands drawn up by the various provinces and cities. The disastrous growth of this terrible agitation means that opinions which would previously have been seen as treason, today seem reasonable and just to most men. These all prove that there is a new spirit of disobedience and scorn for the laws of the State.

Source: http://alphahistory.com/frenchrevolution/ the-memoir-of-the-princes-of-the-blood-1788/

SOURCE B

Pamphlet written by the Abbe Sieyès, 'What is the Third Estate?', January 1789

The nobility is a foreigner in our midst because of its civil and political privileges. All departments of the government have fallen into the hands of this noble caste that dominates the law, the Church and the army. As a result of their spirit of brotherhood, nobles always prefer each other to the rest of the nation. Their power is total; in every sense of the word, they reign in France It is not the king who reigns, but the aristocracy of the court, which is the head of the vast aristocracy which overruns every part of France. The aristocracy is fighting against reason, justice, the people and the king.

Source: http://pages.uoregon.edu/dluebke/ 301ModernEurope/Sieyes3dEstate.pdf

SOURCE C

List of demands sent in by a district of France before the meeting of the Estates General, March 1789

We beg the king to remove from the clergy the liberty of taxing itself and we wish it to be taxed in the same way as the Third Estate. We likewise wish that all nobles be taxed in the same way, and that all tax exemptions be removed. We do not wish to alter the position of the Estates in any way and the other privileges of the First and Second Estates could remain. There is a postmaster who farms many fields for which he is not made to pay any land tax because of his ancient office for which he does no work. He should be included in the taxes which the Third Estate have to pay. The Estates General should concern itself with the salt tax, which of course falls most heavily on those least able to pay. We would also request that attention be paid to the lack of equality before the law as there is evidence that men of noble rank are escaping justice unnecessarily.

Source: www.iupui.edu/~histwhs/H114.dir/H114. webreader/H114.read.ia.Cahier.html

SOURCE D

From the memoirs of a French aristocrat who became an émigré, written in 1823

The most striking of the country's troubles was the chaos in the finances, the result of years of extravagance at Court, as well as the vast expense of the American War of Independence which cost the state over 12 million livres. No one could think of any remedy. The worst of the abuses were the arbitrary system of taxation, the cost of collection and the irresponsible defence of privilege by the richest sections of society. This extended from the great and influential men of the kingdom, to the privileged orders, to the provinces and to the towns, so the burden of taxation fell on the least wealthy part of the nation.

Source: Marquis de Bouillé, Mémoires (Paris, Baudoin, 1823).

1 **a** Compare and contrast the attitudes towards the nobility in Sources B and C.

   b 'Anger over privilege was the principal cause of the French Revolution.' How far do the sources support this view?

Essay based questions

Answer both parts of the questions below.

2 **a** Explain why the Bastille was stormed.

   b To what extent was the French crisis of 1789 caused by economic factors?

3 **a** Explain why Napoleon was able to seize power in 1799.

   b 'The Directory did a good job in difficult circumstances.' How far do you agree?

Sample answer

To what extent was the French crisis of 1789 caused by economic factors?

Economic factors played a very large role in both the longer-term causes of the French Revolution as well as the shorter-term causes. Although there were other factors, such as the summoning of the Estates General itself in 1788, which led to the actual crisis of 1789, underlying everything was the fact that the French government had run out of money and an important section of the French population was very hungry as a result of bad harvests. There was also a real lack of will on the part of the king and his court to make the necessary changes that might have led to a solution of the many problems which France faced.

> This has a good focus and gives an answer to the 'extent' part of the question by suggesting that it played a 'very large' part. It also shows balance by considering other causes. Some reflection on what might be 'economic' causes would help.

The government's shortage of money went back to the 1770s, when the king and his foreign minister, Vergennes, decided to help the American colonies in their bid to become independent from France's old enemy, Britain. Although warned that the French economy was in no position to fight an expensive war, this advice was ignored. Most of the costs of the war were financed by borrowing money at very high rates of interest. When the war finally ended in 1783, France gained little except a very large

increase in its national debt and an increasing reluctance by lenders to lend any more money to the French government.

> This paragraph develops the point well. There is good supporting detail here, but there needs to be greater focus on developing the 'very large' point.

Another major problem was that the system of tax collection was inefficient and often corrupt. Much of the money which should have come in to the government simply got lost in the system. What was an even more important factor was that the two richest sections of the community, the aristocracy and the clergy, were largely exempt from taxation. The heaviest taxed sections of the population were the middle class and the working class. Many middle-class men disliked paying taxes when they had no involvement in how the money was spent, and they also disliked the fact that many men richer than them paid no taxes simply because they were noblemen. The working class resented the taxes that fell on essentials, such as salt, and also the fact that they often had to do unpaid work on the lands of the aristocracy. These economic factors meant that when the Estates General met in 1789, there were a lot of grievances connected to money.

> Again, this has a sound focus and good supporting detail, but needs to be more obviously related to the 'extent' part of the question.

Bad harvests led to their being real hunger in many parts of France, with prices rising and a shortage of the main diet of the working class – bread. No action was taken by the government or the king to deal with this, even though all could see the luxurious lifestyle of the king and his court at his great palace of Versailles. Every attempt at reforming the government's finances by a series of ministers like Necker, Calonne and Brienne after 1781 had failed. The king was reluctant to act and the aristocracy who surrounded him at court did not want their wealth to be taxed. Necker had attempted to give a true picture of France's finances in 1781, but failed to do so, and painted an over-optimistic picture of the country's finances, hiding the true crisis. It was the knowledge that France was heading for bankruptcy, unable to pay its debts and raise any more money to run the country, that led to the calling of the Estates General. This was to trigger the revolution.

This has good focus and depth, and demonstrates a good level of understanding. The comment at the end is a good, succinct way to end one paragraph and lead into another.

This is a very competent response, which, with a greater analytical focus could have been excellent. The final paragraph summarises the essay quite well, but needs to be more explicitly linked to the initial issues of 'extent'. The degree of knowledge and understanding shown is high, but to improve the essay, there should be more of an analytical focus. More debate on the 'extent' part of the question is needed, and clearer points made as to why economic factors played such a large part in the crisis.

However there were other factors which led from the meeting of the Estates General to the process becoming a revolution, the execution of the king and the end of the monarchy. The king would not compromise and accept that he had to become a constitutional monarch to survive. Many of the aristocracy and clergy would not give up their privileges and exemption from taxation. Many middle-class men strongly resented paying taxes and having no means of influencing how they were spent. They wanted political representation. Many were influenced by the ideas of the Enlightenment and wanted a much fairer and more just system of government. They wanted things like equality before the law and a much more efficient system of government.

This introduces other causative factors, but does not provide detail on why they were of less importance.

Overall it was economic factors which brought the crisis on and led to the calling of the Estates General. However it was other factors which then led to the actual revolution and the death of the king. Much better management of the Estates General by the king would have prevented further trouble. Many of the aristocracy and the clergy would not give up their privileges and events like the Storming of the Bastille and the Flight to Varennes made it even more revolutionary.

Summary

After working through this chapter, make sure you understand the following key points:

- why the problems and policies of Louis XVI reached crisis point in 1789 and why his management of this crisis led to revolutionary change in France
- how the failure to find consensus on how France should be governed after 1790 led to the execution of the king, serious political instability and the Reign of Terror
- how the attempt to provide stable government in France by the Directory came to an end with Napoleon's seizure of power
- an analysis of Napoleon's domestic rule in France and the methods he used to retain power.

Further reading

Martin, D. (2013). *The French Revolution*. London: Hodder. (There are three particularly useful chapters here: 1, on the 'Essentials' is a good overview and useful as a general guide; 4, on 'What sort of revolution' and 9, on the Directory are particularly valuable.)

Rees, D. (2015). *France in Revolution 1774–1815*. 5th Edition. London: Hodder. (The final two chapters on Napoleon's domestic policies and the impact of the revolution are particularly useful.)

Waller, S. (2002). *France in Revolution 1776–1830*. London: Heinemann. (The first section, aimed at AS students, is particularly good on the background to 1789 and the financial crisis. The second section, aimed more at A Level students, has many ideas which will assist in the development of analytical skills.)

Dwyer, P. (2014). *Citizen Emperor: Napoleon in Power 1799–1815*. London: Bloomsbury. (The first two chapters are excellent on Napoleon's domestic policies. The remainder of the book focuses on his foreign policy and wars.)

Doyle, W. (2018). *The Oxford History of the French Revolution*. 3rd Edition. Oxford: Oxford University Press. (This is probably the best scholarly study, with detailed coverage of the whole period from 1774 to 1802 and an excellent level of comment.)

If your school or college is a member of the UK's Historical Association, you can access a huge range of online material specifically designed for AS and A Level students, as well as revision guides. There are podcasts on a range of topics such as the origins of the French Revolution, the causes of the Terror, the impact the Terror had on the revolution and the rise of Napoleon. There are also a number of articles you can download, such as 'Causes of the French Revolution', 'Interpreting the Revolution' and 'Napoleon's Domestic Policies'.

Chapter 2
The Industrial Revolution in Britain, 1750–1850

Learning objectives

In this chapter you will:

- learn why so many of the preconditions needed for industrialisation were present in Britain in the middle of the 18th century
- find out why the manufacturing industry grew at a rapid rate in Britain in the late 18th century
- understand why rapid industrialisation led to great social and economic changes
- understand why industrialisation led to popular reaction as well as political and constitutional change.

Timeline

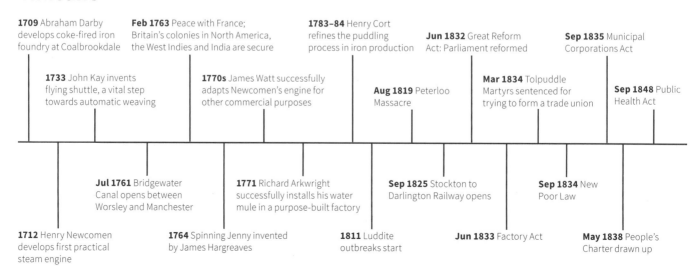

1709 Abraham Darby develops coke-fired iron foundry at Coalbrookdale

Feb 1763 Peace with France; Britain's colonies in North America, the West Indies and India are secure

1783–84 Henry Cort refines the puddling process in iron production

Jun 1832 Great Reform Act: Parliament reformed

Sep 1835 Municipal Corporations Act

1733 John Kay invents flying shuttle, a vital step towards automatic weaving

1770s James Watt successfully adapts Newcomen's engine for other commercial purposes

Aug 1819 Peterloo Massacre

Mar 1834 Tolpuddle Martyrs sentenced for trying to form a trade union

Sep 1848 Public Health Act

Jul 1761 Bridgewater Canal opens between Worsley and Manchester

1771 Richard Arkwright successfully installs his water mule in a purpose-built factory

Sep 1825 Stockton to Darlington Railway opens

Sep 1834 New Poor Law

1712 Henry Newcomen develops first practical steam engine

1764 Spinning Jenny invented by James Hargreaves

1811 Luddite outbreaks start

Jun 1833 Factory Act

May 1838 People's Charter drawn up

Before you start

- Find out the population of Britain in 1750, 1800 and 1850. What proportion lived in towns of more than 5000 people in 1750 and then in 1850? What proportion lived and worked in the countryside in 1750 and then in 1850?
- Find out where Britain had colonies in the middle of the 18th century.

2.1 What were the causes of the Industrial Revolution?

The agricultural revolution

Between about 1780 and 1850, Britain became the first industrialised nation in the world. Large parts of Britain, especially the north-west of England and the English Midlands, developed major manufacturing industries. Before this, these areas had been open fields and farms. These new industries employed many thousands of people, and the goods they made were transported all over the world. New forms of transport were developed to bring in the raw materials needed and to export the finished products.

In 1750, clothing was made by hand in the homes of agricultural workers who created a couple of metres of cloth a week. By 1850, huge steam-powered machines in factories produced thousands of metres of better-quality cloth a day. The workers at home used their hands and feet as a power source, while the new factories used coal to generate steam power to drive the new machines. This industrialisation led to a rapid growth in the size of towns and cities, and, by 1850, the majority of the British population lived in urban areas. The population grew at a rapid rate and became wealthier overall.

Economic change brought social change, as a middle class formed and grew and an industrial workforce emerged in the towns and cities. There was also major political change as the aristocracy was no longer able to dominate parliament and the government.

Whether or not these huge changes amount to a 'revolution' or not has, naturally, been debated. 'Revolutions' are often seen as dramatic political events, such as in Russia in 1917, when the Bolsheviks seized power by force. Anyone standing in Manchester in 1850 and remembering what it looked like in 1780 would see immediately that there had been huge economic, social and political changes which affected every member of society. The process might have taken longer than the Russian Revolution, but it might well have had a greater impact on the lives of the people.

Britain was fortunate in 1750, compared with other nations, in having good foundations on which to develop industrialisation. Its agricultural system was capable of feeding a growing population, including the rapidly increasing section of the population who lived in cities and did not produce their own food. The general good health of this population and its willingness to be mobile were additional benefits. The country's banking system and currency were stable. There was **capital** available and a willingness to invest it in new commercial ventures. Similarly, an increasingly wealthy population were anxious to buy the goods and luxuries being produced and imported. The country's enormous supply of coal was supplemented by the overseas empire, which produced other raw materials such as cotton, and created a further great demand for manufactured goods. These colonies could also provide additional foodstuffs to those grown at home. Some excellent ports, navigable rivers and **canals** helped to transport all these goods. The stable social structure meant that society's leaders, the aristocracy, were happy to invest in commerce and industry, and so make money. The aristocracy dominated parliament and the government, and were supportive of industrialisation. Britain was also politically stable, with an attempted invasion by the Scots in 1745 defeated. However it was involved in several overseas conflicts, but these stimulated manufacturing and gained

KEY TERMS

Capital: Sources of money needed to purchase land and equipment, and to pay wages and other costs until a project can start to make a profit.

Canal: Human-made channels wide and deep enough for boats carrying goods in large quantities to pass through.

49

Britain many colonies. Even the climate was helpful. The mild and damp weather conditions were particularly suitable for the development of textile industries.

Developments in agriculture

Britain, and England in particular, underwent some significant changes to its agricultural system in the century before 1750. Whether these changes amounted to another revolution has been debated by historians, as has the question of how these changes impacted on the rapid industrialisation. However three key factors must be stressed:

- For most of the period, there was sufficient food to feed the population, unlike in France, for example.
- Agricultural output increased substantially and diet improved. This was important in supporting a growing population and in reducing infant mortality.
- Britain was able to feed not only a growing city population, which did not produce its own food, but also a rapidly growing population overall.

Agricultural output in Britain had increased in the century before 1750 and a variety of new techniques for improving output had been developed. The other significant change to occur before 1750 was the move towards larger farm units. These developments led to a gradual change in attitudes towards agriculture. Farming was seen increasingly as a way of making money and not just as a way to feed a family. For a long time, these changes were referred to as the 'Agricultural Revolution', but that term is now rarely used, as the changes happened over such a long period of time. However, it is agreed that, after 1750 there was a rapid spread of new ideas and practices in Britain and a growing entrepreneurial attitude towards agriculture.

The factors which played a major part in increasing both the quality and quantity of agricultural output were:

- the enclosure movement and the growth of larger farming units
- improved soil fertility
- crop rotation
- selective livestock breeding
- better cereal cultivation: wheat/corn, barley, oats and rye
- the spread of scientific knowledge about farming.

ACTIVITY 2.1

Put the factors listed above in order of importance for future industrialisation and give reasons for your prioritisation. What do you think would be the key factor in setting off the whole process of industrialisation?

The enclosure movement and the growth of larger farming units

The enclosure movement broke up the traditional farming units that had belonged to a small community, and merged them into a larger unit owned by a single individual. This process had started decades before 1750, but moved much faster between 1750 and 1800. The traditional agricultural unit in much of southern and central England was known as the 'open field' system. Families cultivated small strips of land in various parts of the village and also had the right to let their animals feed on common land. In order to prevent soil exhaustion, up to 35% of the cultivated land was left **fallow** each year. The aim of this type of cultivation was to produce sufficient food to feed a family, and, if things went well, a surplus which could be sold at market. The 'fallow' system was wasteful, however, with potentially productive land unused each year. Livestock shared the same grazing land, which made it difficult to breed quality animals. Overall, it was not a productive method of farming.

 KEY TERM

Fallow: Of farm land, left unused for a year, in order to avoid soil exhaustion.

Enclosure meant that farming land was joined into larger units of 100 acres or more. The original peasant farmers lost their various rights to use common land for their animals, and the fields were hedged and ditched. Often the process required an Act of Parliament, a complex and expensive legal process. However, as members of parliament were all landowners, they were usually sympathetic to such requests, and pushed them through. Enclosure enabled these larger units to be farmed more efficiently and productively, increasing the amount of food being produced and meaning that better-quality animals could be reared. Between 1750 and 1800, more than 7 million acres of farmland were enclosed, which played a huge part in increasing agricultural output.

Improved soil fertility

Farmers made greater use of fertilisers, such as lime, and crops which increased nitrogen levels in the soil. With more animals being bred and crops developed that enabled them to be fed over the winter rather than being slaughtered, more manure was available to prevent soil exhaustion. Greater profits meant that land previously considered unproductive and unprofitable could be brought into use with just a little investment in fertiliser and drainage improvements. There was also greater awareness that certain types of soil suited specific crops or animals, which allowed for specialisation, with the emphasis on profit and increased productivity.

Crop rotation

One technique spread widely in the period after 1750 – crop rotation. It had been known for decades but was not widely used. Traditionally, on the open-field system, some areas of farmland were left fallow every third or fourth year in order to prevent soil exhaustion. This was replaced by a system whereby land would be planted with wheat, barley, clover and turnips in a four-year cycle. Clover put nutrients back into the soil and turnips provided good animal feed. This meant that significantly more land could be used productively every year.

Selective livestock breeding

Enclosing land and putting up fences and hedges meant farmers could ensure that animals were bred selectively. The breeds of cattle which were best for milk or meat, for example, could be encouraged, and isolating animals in separate fields reduced the risk of spreading animal diseases. There was a growing awareness throughout the agricultural community that demand was growing for food and that prices were rising, and therefore good profits could be made by an efficient food producer.

Better cereal cultivation

Growing the right crops on the right soil, preventing soil exhaustion, using fertilisers and manure effectively, and a greater awareness of the different types of seed all resulted in an increase in output per acre. With more land under cultivation food crops such as wheat increased in output.

Many members of the aristocracy took the lead in agricultural innovation, even the king. George III (1760–1820) had a model farm in which he took great interest. It was quite fashionable for the leaders of British society to be involved in developing their lands efficiently, as well as making money out of them. This was different from countries like France, where the aristocracy did not participate in such matters.

Links between agriculture and industry

So, many factors in the process of industrialisation are interconnected. More food enabled a growing urban population to be fed and producing this food was also more profitable for farmers. These profits created a demand for manufactured goods and produced capital for investment in new forms of transport and manufacturing. More efficient transport enabled fresh food like vegetables to be transported quickly to cities, helping to improve diets, which led to more babies living and, therefore, more demand and greater profits for farmers.

ACTIVITY 2.2

Why do you think agricultural change proved so important to later industrialisation?

Identify at least three important reasons, making full use of the source about enclosures (below) in your answer, and ensuring that your explanation is clear.

To what extent do the changes in agriculture that took place in Britain in this period merit the title of 'revolution'? What do you think are the criteria for calling something a revolution and how did you decide this?

Inclosing has many benefits. The benefits and advantages that would be derived from a general enclosure of common lands, are so numerous as to far exceed my powers of description or computation. The opportunity it would afford, of separating dry ground from wet, or well drain the latter and fertilising the rotten parts, is of infinite consequence. Also it would, with the help of intelligent breeders, be the means of raising a breed of sheep and cattle far superior to the present race of wretched half-starved animals now seen. It may be further observed that the common lands are entirely defective in terms of labour use. No sooner has enclosure taken place than the whole scene is changed from dreary waste to one of great activity. Every man capable of working, is finished with plenty of employment in sinking ditches and drains, making banks and hedges, and in planting. There is also a need for new houses, making roads, bridges. This change will provide food and employment for a very increased population.

Source: Middleton, J. (1798). *View of the Agriculture of Middlesex*. https://archive.org

Development of capitalism: investment, trade and commerce

There was already a healthy economic and commercial structure and a reliable currency when the period of rapid industrial growth started in Britain. In 1720, there had been an outburst of speculation which had damaged the economy, and the government had reacted quickly to ensure that it did not happen again. There was a central bank, the Bank of England, which had been set up in 1694. Governments took care to manage the economy sensibly and, as far as possible, government expenditure matched its income.

Investment

Britain had an established system of country banks and respected local money lenders. They were able to lend money at low interest rates to people who wanted to start a business. Men who had either made large sums of money in overseas trade or who had profits from their land were accustomed to investing it in further enterprises. Many aristocrats developed large coal mines on their own land. The profits from those mines were then invested in improvements in transport, such as roads and canals, which helped to lower prices but increase profits. There was a general belief that it was sensible to invest surplus money in business and social enterprises. With an established insurance market, the risks of investment could be spread. There were already plenty of success stories to show potential investors that their money would be secure and that there was a good chance of a reasonable return on their capital.

Overseas trade

Foreign trade was an important feature of the British economy in the decades before 1750. Those who wished to sell goods abroad found there was a well-established system to assist them. The Royal Navy was the most powerful in the western world at the time and saw as one of its principal functions – after defending the country – protecting and advancing British trading interests overseas. The government and influential parliament at the time were determined to protect and develop British trade. The government raised much of the income it needed to run the country through taxes on imports and exports, but was willing to adjust, or even end, such taxes if they were felt to damage trade in any way.

Alongside the Royal Navy, Britain had developed a large merchant navy in the course of the 18th century, capable of carrying finished goods all over the world. Britain was overtaking the Dutch as the carriers of Europe. Many aristocrats and members of parliament were directors or shareholders in the two great overseas trading companies: the West India Company, which traded in the Caribbean, and the more famous East India Company, which traded with, and eventually owned, large parts of India. They formed extremely powerful pressure groups which ensured that those involved in overseas trade had a real influence on policy making. One of the reasons why a reluctant Prime Minister Walpole went to war with Spain in 1739 was the pressure on his government from trading interests. Britain fought four wars with other European powers between 1739 and 1783, primarily to advance its commercial interests and acquire new colonies. New colonies meant more markets for British goods, which in turn meant increased profits for British companies, their owners and investors.

Some of the country's rivers leading to major ports, such as Bristol and Liverpool, were developed as far as possible to make it easy to import and export goods. (Figure 2.1 highlights this.) There was huge investment in the ports themselves to make them more efficient. As early as 1700, groups of British merchants placed agents, known as 'factors', in major ports throughout the world, from China to South America. These men were responsible for importing goods to Britain but, above all, for developing markets for British goods overseas. While domestic demand for manufactures steadily increased in the early 18th century, foreign demand grew at a faster rate. Not only could the factors sell every item of woollen cloth and cotton that they could import, but demand around the world was rising for British manufactured goods such as those made from pottery, glass and metal. Manufacturers in Britain knew that they could sell abroad almost anything they could make and that the means were there to ensure the goods arrived and their profits returned.

Underpinning much of this overseas trade was slavery. A significant amount of the investment in the great ports of Liverpool and Bristol came from merchants who made huge sums of money in this trade. Ships sailed to Africa with cargoes of metal goods and textiles, which were sold in return for slaves. The slaves were then transported to the

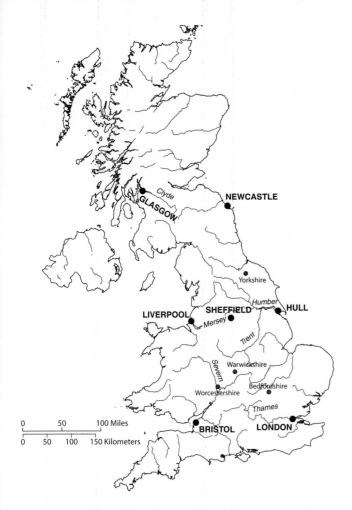

Figure 2.1: A map of the UK showing major ports and rivers during the 18th century

British colonies in the West Indies and North America and sold there. The proceeds were used to buy sugar, cotton and tobacco, which were sold at immense profit back in Britain. Although a risky – and barbaric – business, returns of 200–300% on investments were not unusual. Much of the capital earned this way was used to fund other major entrepreneurial projects, such as canals and railroads.

This thriving overseas trade and developed system of importing raw materials and exporting goods made in Britain were further factors, like the growing population and availability of coal and sufficient food, that enabled British manufacturing to increase in the course of the 18th century.

ACTIVITY 2.3

Why was Britain in such a good position to expand its exports? What were the key factors? On your own, or in a pair, focus on the 'such' part of the question, making sure that it is very clearly explained.

Reflection: Discuss how you reached your conclusions with another student. Did you decide on different key factors and if so, why do you think this was?

Commerce

Britain in the 18th century did not suddenly go from a nation where the vast majority of the population were engaged in subsistence farming to a nation where the majority of the population worked in city factories making manufactured goods. In 1750, it already had a flourishing trade in woollen goods, which were sold all over the world. This trade had been going on for centuries. There were also many other industries, such as nail making, boot and shoe making and cutlery manufacture, that exploited their products and provided for a growing domestic market. Many of these centred on specific areas (often those with low agricultural productivity), like the wool industry in Yorkshire, lace making in Bedfordshire and metal work in Sheffield. Sophisticated systems of bringing in raw materials and distributing the finished products around Britain, as well as exporting them abroad, had existed for a long time. In 1750, for example, over 70% of the woollen goods manufactured in Yorkshire were exported to Europe or America. A highly complex production and distribution network for textiles, as well as other industries, which involved large amounts of capital, already existed when the industrial 'revolution' came to Britain.

The major difference between this type of manufacturing and in the period between 1750 and 1800 was that, in the earlier period, the manufacturing process occurred largely in the home. This was known as 'cottage' or 'domestic' industry. Families – and often the entire family was involved – might primarily work on their land, or the land of others, during the spring and summer months. For the rest of the year, they might spin raw wool into yarn, or weave the yarn into woollen cloth, for example. In parts of Worcestershire and Warwickshire, they might make nails in small furnaces attached to the rear of their cottages, and, in the area around Sheffield, they might make knives and forks. Pins and needles made in homes in Worcestershire were being sold in New York and Hamburg in 1750. So, Britain already had a thriving commercial system by the middle of the 18th century. What happened in the decades after was that mass production built on an already established system of commerce, which was capable of almost indefinite expansion.

53

Early mechanisation: steam engines and spinning machines

Technical innovation played a critical role in the process of industrialisation in Britain. Before the era of rapid growth in manufacturing output after 1780, there had been several vital innovations which enabled the manufacturing industry to expand at an exceptionally high rate later on.

Iron and coke

Essential for making all machines was good-quality iron. There was little available in Britain in 1700, but the demand was there. There were two problems facing those who wished to meet that demand. The first was getting sufficient energy for the furnaces which heated the iron ore to extract the iron. The second was getting the right sort of energy to remove the impurities from the ore, in order to make quality iron that was easy to use in making machines.

The principal source of energy for iron manufacturing was wood, and Britain was running out of it by 1700. The wood had to be made into charcoal, and over five tons of charcoal were needed to make one tonne of even quite low-quality iron.

In 1709, Abraham Darby of Coalbrookdale in Shropshire developed a technique for using **coke**, a by-product of coal, instead of charcoal, for melting the iron ore. There was a vast supply of coal available locally, and the coal was of a type which enabled many of the impurities to be eliminated from the iron ore. Now a better-quality iron could be produced at a lower price. This higher-quality iron was to prove essential in developing the machinery needed for industrialisation. Darby placed his iron works next to the River Severn, which provided water power and was near to both coalfields and iron ore sites, and was also an outlet to the sea through the port of Bristol. Geographical factors were tremendously important to successful industrial development.

KEY TERM

Coke: A hard fuel made from coal, but containing fewer impurities. It burns well and is better for melting down iron ore to make iron.

Steam power

Another major invention which was to prove essential to industrialisation was the steam engine, which generated power using coal and water. There was a great deal of coal in Britain and a huge demand for it. Landowners who had coal under their land wanted to extract it for profit. The main problem they faced was that their mines filled with water and became unusable. The water had to be pumped out and there was simply no known way of draining mines properly.

In 1712, Thomas Newcomen invented an atmospheric steam engine, powered by coal, which could pump large quantities of water out of deep mines at a low cost. (Figure 2.2 shows Newcomen's steam engine.) This not only reduced the price of coal, but also assisted in doubling the quantity produced (from around 2.5 million tons in 1700 to about 5 million in 1750, and about 15 million by 1800). Newcomen's invention was later developed to drive machines in factories and, most significantly, railway engines.

Textiles

Two other inventions in the period before 1780 played a major part in assisting later industrialisation. Britain produced two main types of textile in the 18th century: wool and cotton. Both were in high demand throughout the world. British businessmen realised that increasing both output and quality without raising the price would produce enormous profits.

Woollen and cotton cloth were both made in basically the same way in the early 18th century. The raw material – wool taken from sheep, and raw cotton – had to be spun or made into a thread. The thread was then woven or knitted into a piece of cloth which could be made into clothing or blankets. Spinning and weaving were done by hand by individuals working in their own homes. Middlemen would bring in the raw materials, take the yarn from the spinners to the weavers, and then collect the finished cloth.

The first major invention in this craft was John Kay's 'flying shuttle' (1733). This greatly improved both weaving speeds and the quality of the finished cloth. Figure 2.3 shows an example of the shuttle; it has pointed metal ends and wheels which let the shuttle be used mechanically, rather than by hand. Using the flying shuttle meant fewer people were needed to produce woven cloth. It was not until the late 1760s, however, that use of the shuttle became widespread, partly because of the shortage of yarn, and partly because of opposition by many weavers who thought they might be put out of a job by this new machine.

Figure 2.2: Newcomen's steam engine. Water in the boiler (the large metal container) was heated and the steam forced into the pipe above, which pushed the piston up. The steam then cooled, turning into water and leaving the pipe, which lowered the piston. What information about the steam engine is not shown in this drawing? Does this change your opinion of the drawing's usefulness as a historical source?

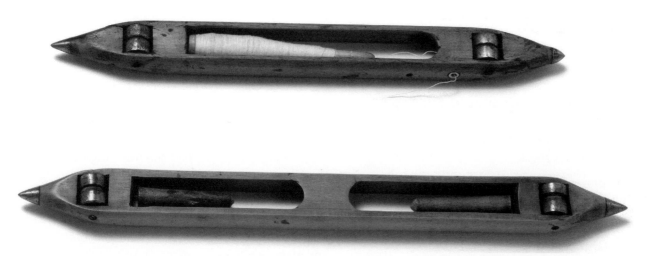

Figure 2.3: John Kay's flying shuttle. How useful is this photograph in showing how and why textile production in Britain increased quickly?

The second breakthrough came in 1765, when James Hargreaves invented the 'spinning jenny'. This speeded up the spinning process, with the 'jenny' initially capable of doing the work of eight spinners, and then 120.

Once steam power and further technical innovations were applied to both processes, then a real revolution could take place. In 1775, Britain's cotton cloth production totalled 57 000 yards. By 1783, it was 3.5 million yards. The quality was better and the price rapidly decreased, creating further demand. Cotton went from being a luxury for the rich to an everyday material for everyone.

ACTIVITY 2.4

Research Newcomen, Kay and Hargreaves. Organise your research by making notes on each of the following areas. What sort of background did they come from? What skills did they have? Why do you think they proved to be such able innovators? How much did they rely on the work of others?

From what you have learned so far, what factors need to be present to encourage technological innovation? Which do you think are the most important and why?

Early developments in transport: canals and roads

As mentioned at the beginning of this chapter, geography had been kind to Britain. The country was in an ideal location to trade by sea with Europe, the Mediterranean and the Americas. It had good sites for ports. It was not too mountainous, and there were plenty of rivers suitable for navigation by cargo-carrying boats. However, roads in the early 18th century were generally in poor condition and unsuitable for carrying heavy goods. There was a limit to the amount of much-needed coal that could be carried to a factory, or iron ore moved to a foundry. High transport costs hit profits. There was real pressure to develop a better transport system. Large-scale industrialisation demanded cheap transport for large cargoes.

Transport improved in three principal ways in the period before 1780, and all three proved to be vitally important to industrialisation. They were:

- making more rivers accessible to large cargoes and improving the ability of ports to handle bulk imports and exports

- improving roads and making local transport more efficient
- building canals.

Rivers and ports

Manufacturing industries needed to bring in energy supplies and raw materials. They also required solid transportation networks to take their goods to market. Britain had natural advantages in this respect, with navigable rivers such as the Severn, Humber, Trent, Mersey, Clyde and Thames. Cargo had been carried up and down these waterways for centuries. In the first part of the 18th century, however, in response to demand, substantial engineering projects were carried out to improve them so that bigger cargoes could be carried further, with expenditure on locks, weirs, dredging and towpaths. Most of these vital developments were made by local groups of manufacturers attaining an Act of Parliament to give them the necessary powers to make the improvements. All the major ports, such as London, Liverpool, Bristol, Newcastle and Glasgow, underwent redevelopment in the first half of the 18th century. This enabled them to deal with the huge increase in both imports and above all, exports, in the second half of the century. As in so many other instances, the existence of useable rivers and good harbours were not the only cause of industrialisation, but they were very important in helping it.

Roads

In 1700, Britain's roads were generally in a poor condition, especially in winter. There had been little improvement since the Romans had departed well over a thousand years before. The inability to move goods quickly and cheaply was a major barrier to industrialisation. Local villages were expected to maintain the roads in their area. They often had limited interest in doing this and did not have the money to do it anyway. The solution, developed in the late 17th century, was a system called 'Turnpike Trusts'. A company could be formed, which, backed by an Act of Parliament, had substantial powers to acquire the land in question. In return for radically improving and then maintaining a stretch of road, the Trust could charge a fee to all those who travelled on it.

Between 1750 and 1770, Parliament passed over 500 acts creating Turnpike Trusts covering over 24 000km of road. This was in response to major demand from both farming and manufacturing businesses. The whole of England and Wales was now connected by a well-maintained road.

Local citizens invested in these companies, which, in the period to 1780, mainly returned good **dividends** which encouraged investment in other major projects and allowed considerable experimentation with different types of foundation and construction of roads. The projects were also a great stimulus to engineering, resulting in the development of new types of bridge, drainage techniques and ways to deal with gradients. The system also helped commercial agriculture and a developing retail trade, as foodstuffs and goods could move around the country more easily.

 KEY TERM

Dividend: When an individual invests in a company, known as buying a share, they expect to get a return on that investment. Companies pay this out every year in what is called an annual dividend. So, if a dividend is 10%, and you have invested $100 in a company, you will get $10.

Canals

In the years immediately before the rapid industrialisation process canals were perhaps the most important improvement in transport. There was great demand for large quantities of coal by the middle of the 18th century. The coal was available, and there were mine owners willing to meet the demand, but it was difficult to move it by cart or on horseback. Transport costs were extremely high.

The breakthrough came in 1761, when the **Duke of Bridgewater** built a canal from his coal mines in Worsley to the centre of the growing industrial city of Manchester. His engineer, James Brindley, used aqueducts, tunnels and locks to overcome a series of major geographical obstacles while building the canal along its 14-km route. The cost of transportation went down significantly. One horse could pull 50 tons of coal on a canal barge while one horse could only carry about a quarter of a tonne on its back on a road. So, the price of coal in Manchester dropped and the enormous demand meant that the duke's profits soared.

Between 1759 and 1774, 52 Acts of Parliament were passed to allow canals to be built, mainly in the Midlands and the north. By 1800, nearly 3000 km of canals had doubled the length of navigable rivers. Cities were linked to factories and to ports. Bricks and slates needed for city houses and factories could be easily moved from the brickworks of Bedfordshire and the slate mines of Wales, along with the coal to warm those houses and provide the energy to drive factory machinery. Many of the early canal companies returned

Seen as the founder of modern British inland navigation, the Duke of Bridgewater owned a great deal of land, and was determined to develop its potential, especially the coal on his estates at Worsley, near Manchester. He instructed his engineer, James Brindley, to construct the canal between Worsley and Manchester to carry coal. In 1762, Bridgewater received permission from parliament to build another important canal; this time an even larger enterprise between Liverpool and Manchester.

huge profits for their **shareholders**, as well as providing substantial employment for the builders and engineers. Skills learned in canal building were to be vital in the later development of the rail network, which played a decisive role in industrialisation. Cheap capital, an absence of obstacles, good support (or at least no opposition) from government all played their part the success of the canals.

 KEY TERM

Shareholders: Those who invest in a company, often before it starts to make a profit from its business (such as building canals).

The growth of population

People are essential to any industrialisation process. The rapid growth of population in this period was an important factor behind industrial growth for two reasons. Firstly, a manufacturer needs people to work in his factories and a railway company needs men to build and run the railway. Secondly, there is no point in producing large amounts of textiles if there are few people to buy them. Domestic demand is important. Figure 2.5 shows

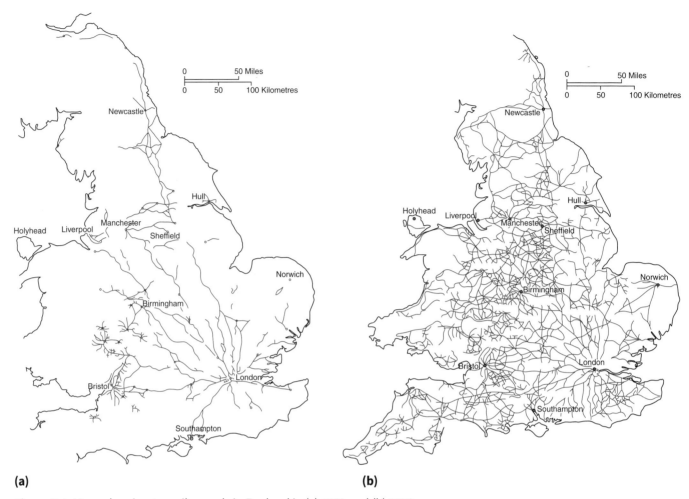

(a)   (b)

Figure 2.4: Maps showing turnpike roads in England in (a) 1759 and (b) 1770

ACTIVITY 2.5

Working in pairs, and using the maps in this section and the extract from Adam Smiths *Wealth of Nations* in the source, identify the specific geographical advantages Britain had which were important to its industrial development. Why were they so important? To what extent do you think geography influenced Britain's economic development in this period?

As by means of water-carriage a more extensive market is opened to every sort of industry than what land carriage alone can afford, so it is upon the sea coast and along the banks of navigable rivers, the industry of every kind naturally begins to sub divide and improve itself. A broad wheeled wagon, attended by two men and drawn by eight horses in about six weeks' time carries and brings back between London and Edinburgh four ton weight of goods. In about the same time a ship navigated by six or eight men, frequently carries and brings back about two hundred ton weight of goods.

Source: Smith, A. (2008). *The Wealth of Nations*. Oxford: Oxford World Classics, p. 93. (Smith was a Scottish economist writing at the end of the 18th century.)

what happened to the population of England (not Britain as a whole) in this period.

There is some debate about whether this population growth was a cause or a consequence of agricultural and industrial change, but the link between the growth and industrialisation can be clearly seen. The population tripled in the 150 years to 1850. It provided labour for the factories, and the essential domestic demand for Britain's manufactured goods.

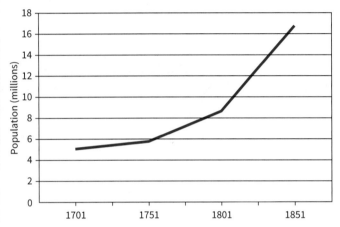

Figure 2.5: Population increase in England 1701–1851

2.2 Why was there a rapid growth of industrialisation after 1780?

The decades after 1780 saw real acceleration in the industrialisation process. It is the truly 'revolutionary' period. Productivity in all areas of manufacturing soared. The conditions were right and there were no major obstacles. A large number of interconnected factors influenced the changes. They included:

- high levels of demand both at home and abroad for British manufactured goods
- the ability to supply that demand and make a substantial profit from it
- innovators capable of developing new techniques for increasing production and quality
- capital available for investment and a social climate which supported **entrepreneurship**
- the ability to transport large quantities of raw materials and manufactured products, not only around Britain but throughout the world
- a system of government which largely supported the process and encouraged **laissez-faire** policies and **free trade**

- prevailing social attitudes, which were largely sympathetic to capitalism and industrialisation
- an absence of international competition
- an unlimited supply of cheap energy
- a growing and mobile population who had a sound supply of basic foodstuffs.

All these factors proved vital in the Industrial Revolution.

KEY TERMS

Entrepreneurship: A willingness to set up and develop a new business and take risks in order to become successful.

Laissez-faire: This translates roughly as 'leave it to happen'; a reluctance to regulate or interfere in business or industry.

Free trade: A commercial situation in which no barriers are placed in the way of businesses buying or selling, such as governments imposing taxes on imports or exports.

Development of the factory system: steam power and machines

The period after 1780 saw important innovations in three connected areas, each of which played a major role in the rapid expansion of industry.

Iron

While Abraham Darby had made a vital innovation in 1709 with the use of coke rather than charcoal in making iron (see 'Early mechanisation: steam engines and spinning machines'), it was still an expensive process and difficult to achieve a high-quality product. It was still cheaper to import iron. In 1783 and 1784, Henry Cort took out two **patents** on '**puddling**' and rolling iron which were to lead to the production of better-quality, cheaper iron in Britain.

KEY TERMS

Patent: The official or legal right to be the sole manufacturer or seller of an invention for a number of years. There were heavy penalties for breaking this law.

Puddling: A vital process in making better-quality iron, in which molten iron was stirred to reduce impurities.

As with many other inventions, Cort's innovations were built on the work of others and needed others to make them fully commercial. Peter Onions, an ironmaster working in Wales, had carried out many experiments in puddling, which Cort both knew of and refined. Then, a series of Welsh ironmasters in the late 1780s and early 1790s took Cort's innovations and developed them commercially. One iron foundry in south Wales produced 500 tons of quality iron in 1785. After adapting the new techniques, it produced 10 000 tons in 1812. Britain now had all the good-quality iron it needed.

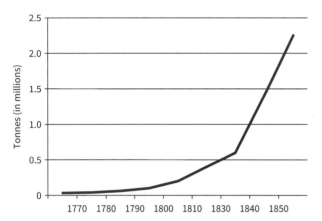

Figure 2.6: Iron production in Britain, 1760–1850

These figures show clearly the statistical evidence of a revolution. It is worth stressing that so many of the key causes of this change are relevant here. There was capital (Cort borrowed £30 000 to fund his experiments), there was cheap coal and the means to transport it, there was iron ore available, there was a huge demand, and there was entrepreneurship and a willingness to take risks.

Steam power

Arguably, the development of Newcomen's steam engine was the vital spark which made Britain's industrial development 'revolutionary'. As with Cort's inventions, the decisive development in steam power was not the invention itself, but how it was adapted to other uses. For example, **James Watt** developed Newcomen's great invention – which was designed for pumping water out of coal mines – into a multipurpose source of power. He made the powered mechanisation of industry possible.

By the early 1760s, Watt was experimenting with Newcomen's engine, with the vital support of John Roebuck, who had not only the money, but also the vision to see where Watt's ideas might lead. In 1769, Watt had patented a new type of steam engine which could be adapted to do more than simply pump water out of mines. When Roebuck could no longer support Watt financially, Watt moved to Birmingham and, with the far-sighted support of Matthew Boulton, started to build a range of steam engines which could be used in many different ways.

Watt came from a skilled working-class background in Scotland, and originally made mathematical instruments. On being given a Newcomen steam engine to repair, he realised the inefficiencies of the machine, and decided to improve it. The key to much of his success lay in the backing given to him by, initially, fellow-inventor and iron works founder John Roebuck, and then by Birmingham entrepreneur and manufacturer Matthew Boulton. The engineering firm of Boulton and Watt became the biggest and most important in Britain by 1800.

Mathew Boulton manufactured a range of metal goods in Birmingham and depended on water power for energy. In the summer, this was insufficient for his needs, and he had the foresight to see the potential of James Watt's designs. There was plenty of coal available locally, and canals had been built which could bring in the iron ore and coal. By 1776, Watt's steam engines were successful in pumping water out of coal mines more efficiently and cheaply than Newcomen's, and were powering blast furnaces, enabling them to achieve higher temperatures and better-quality iron, which also meant a substantial reduction in the amount of coal needed per tonne of iron made. With better-quality iron available, more efficient engines could be made. Industrialisation was developing rapidly.

By 1800, variants of Watt's engines were providing power for hundreds of different enterprises, ranging from cotton and woollen mills to powerful steam hammers at iron foundries and corn grinders at flour mills. They were also being sold abroad at a substantial profit. Made in Birmingham, they were loaded onto canal barges in parts, taken to large ports such as Bristol and London, and then shipped overseas.

Watt showed how to innovate and adapt with steam power, and others followed. One of the most influential in terms of industrialisation was Richard Trevithick. A mining engineer anxious to develop steam power to transport bulk cargoes over distance, he developed a more powerful – mobile – steam engine. By 1804, he had built the first railway steam locomotive.

Demand and vast profit potential had led to remarkable innovations utilising local skills, quality iron, lots of available coal and a good transport system.

ACTIVITY 2.6

Do you think that James Watt should be seen as the 'engineer' of the Industrial Revolution? Working with another student, and using the Source below and your own knowledge, list the criteria for being the 'engineer' of the Revolution. Develop an argument both for and against this view, using evidence to support your points. Which do you think is the stronger argument and why?

What specific factors made this period such a productive one for entrepreneurs like Matthew Boulton? List the main factors you have identified and add your reasons why.

> There are many engines made by Boulton and Watt over 40 years ago which have been in constant use since then with few repairs. What a large number of horses would have been worn out in doing the service of those machines. What a large amount of grain would they have consumed. Without Watt's invention there would have been great barriers to further advancement in inquiry. Steam engines give us the means not only of driving cotton machines but allowed great profits to manufacturers. They create a vast demand for fuel and they lend their powerful arms to draining the mines and raise the coal. They create employment for thousands of miners, engineers, shipbuilders and sailors, and cause the constitution of canals and railways. The leave thousands of fields free for growing food, which before would have been required to feed horses. They make cheap goods and procure in their exchanges a good supply of the necessities and comforts of life, produced in foreign lands.
>
> Source: Ure, A. (1835). *The Philosophy of Manufactures*. London. https: archive.org

Textiles

Textiles, mostly wool and cotton, were central to the industrialisation process in Britain. They were the biggest employers after agriculture, and many agricultural workers also spun or wove in their own homes. Innovations such as those of Kay in weaving and Hargreaves in spinning (see 'Early mechanisation: steam engines and spinning machines') came before the period of rapid growth. It was later developments that led to a massive increase in output.

The first major development came in 1771, when Richard Arkwright patented his water frame. This invention revolutionised the spinning process, which made raw cotton into a useable thread. Now one worker with a machine could produce 128 threads at the same time, instead of one. As well as this significant increase in productivity, the finished thread was stronger and of a consistently high quality. The price of cotton cloth soon dropped substantially, which increased demand. With Eli Whitney's invention of the **cotton gin** in the United States increasing the availability of cheap raw cotton, further growth was possible.

 KEY TERM

Cotton gin: A machine which removed the unwanted seeds from raw cotton quickly and efficiently. Originally it had to be done by hand. As with the spinning 'jenny', 'gin' is an abbreviation of 'engine'.

Further innovation in spinning was a result of the work of Samuel Crompton, who patented his spinning mule – so called because it was a hybrid machine combining the features of the spinning jenny and the water frame. This further revolutionised the spinning process and meant that more high-quality thread could be produced by fewer workers at a lower price. This naturally led to increased demand around the world, which boosted profits for the manufacturers and merchants, and made more money available for investment. By 1820, more than 4 million mules were operating in British factories. Once Watt's steam engines replaced water power or hand-driven power to drive these new machines, output soared still further, as did profits.

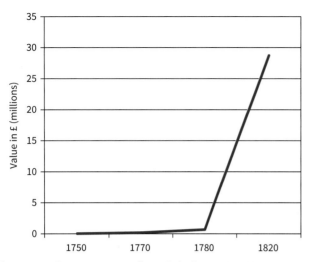

Figure 2.7: Cotton exports from Britain, 1750–1820

1775	1783
57 000 yards	3 500 000 yards

Table 2.1: Cotton output in Britain

Between 1779 and 1830, the price of a yard of finished cotton dropped by 93%. Statistics like this, and those shown in Figure 2.7 and Table 2.1, explain why the events in industry in the late 18th century can be called a 'revolution'. The inventions and advances had solved the problem of demand, improved productivity and employment, and further stimulated demand and developments in a wide range of other industries, ranging from tool making, through engineering to mining.

The factory system

With the new techniques in both spinning and weaving, the growth in demand, the availability of raw materials, the new transportation methods and Watt's developments in steam power, the next step was to combine the production process in a single site. There was plenty of money available for investment and owners saw the large profits that could be made by making quality textiles. With this, factories were built.

The first modern factory was built by **Richard Arkwright** in 1769 in Derbyshire. He chose the site partly because it was easy to access for raw materials, but also because of the availability of good water power. He built the first cotton mill on five floors, each housing the latest machinery. It was capable of operating 24 hours a day and initially employed over 200 people – a mixture of skilled men, women and children. The workforce was effectively trained, regulated and disciplined. With a labour shortage in the area, Arkwright built housing for his workforce to attract more workers, and in so doing, he founded a small town. He paid good and, more importantly, regular wages by the standards of the times. Initially, children as young as seven were employed; later the age was raised to ten. He provided an education for the children, partly because their parents could not read or write so could not keep any records at work. He made a fortune.

Between 1770 and 1835, about 1200 cotton factories and 1300 woollen factories were built in Britain. The age of the factory had arrived, and textile output soared.

ACTIVITY 2.7

On the 16th of December 1775, Mr Arkwright took out a second patent for a series of machines, comprising the carding, drawing and roving machines, all used in preparing silk, cotton, wool and flax for spinning. When this admirable series of machines was made known, and by their means yarns were produced far superior in quality to any spun before, as well as lower in price, a mighty impulse was communicated to cotton manufacture. Cotton fabrics could be sold at a lower price than ever before. The demand for them consequently increased. The shuttle flew with fresh energy and the weavers earned high wages. The fame of Arkwright resounded through the land and capitalists flocked to him. By 1782 he employed upwards of 5,000 persons and a capital of not less than £200,000.

Source: Sir Edward Baines, 'History of the Cottom Manufacture in Great Britain'.

Quoted in Pike, E.R. (2005). *Human Documents of the Industrial Revolution in Britain*. London: Routledge, pp. 32–33

What reasons can you identify from this source to explain why so many entrepreneurs were successful in the period after 1780? Put the reasons in order of importance and think of the reasons for your ranking.

Figure 2.8: Cromford Mill in Derbyshire (UK), where Richard Arkwright built his revolutionary water-powered cotton-spinning frame. Built in 1771–1972, the five-storey mill employed over 200 workers. How useful is the photograph for explaining why Arkwright chose this location for his mill?

RICHARD ARKWRIGHT (1732–92)

Arkwright came from a skilled working-class background. He became both a fine inventor and an entrepreneur, and is seen as the founder of the modern factory system. His great achievement was to combine the latest developments in energy supply and technology (and invent more as needed), and to employ semi-skilled and unskilled labourers to use the increased supply of raw cotton in making good-quality cheap yarn. His factory workers often had to work 13-hour shifts in a disciplined atmosphere.

ACTIVITY 2.8

Look back over the information in this chapter regarding supply of and demand for materials, goods and services. Look especially at the graphs (Figures 2.5, 2.6, 2.7, 2.11, 2.12 and 2.14). One view of Britain's Industrial Revolution is that it was 'demand led'. Work with another student to develop a case supporting this view, and then a case against. Copy and complete the table to help you.

Britain's Industrial Revolution was 'demand led'	
Arguments for	**Arguments against**

On balance, which do you think is the stronger case, and why?

Developments in transport: canals, railways and steamships

Canals

For the period between 1780 and 1830, canals were essential to industrial growth. By the end of this period, there were over 6000 km of navigable rivers and canals in Britain. Large sums of money were invested in canals in what was known as the era of 'canal mania'. While many of the canals paid huge returns to the investors, some did not, as they cost too much to build, duplicated existing ones, or were not completed in time for their full benefits to be enjoyed before the arrival of the railways. They did, however, show clearly the determination to invest in industry and that in many cases great profits could be made by the adventurous.

One writer in 1785, at the height of the canal-building boom, wrote that 'canals converted the inland parts of an island into coast'. Most parts of the country were now accessible for bulk cargoes, especially coal. Major navigable rivers, such as the Mersey and Severn, were linked by canals. In many cases, canals enabled industrial development and new towns to be created where before there had been open fields. In south Wales, the building of the Glamorgan Canal enabled coal to be carried to the newly built iron works inland, and the finished bar iron moved back down to the coast for export or to be taken by canal barge to build steam engines in Birmingham.

The small town of St Helen's in Lancashire developed large-scale industries in copper, glass and iron once the canals could bring in the coal and raw materials and ship out their finished products. Josiah Wedgwood sited his vast new pottery factory at Etruria in Staffordshire next to a new canal so the clay needed could be easily unloaded from barges. Coal could be brought in at low cost and Wedgewood's finished crockery could be shipped out to Bristol and Liverpool for export. The tsars of Russia and the Spanish rulers of South America dined on Wedgwood's products.

Canals also employed thousands of workers in their building, and they developed a new class of engineers. Thousands more were employed in building the barges and making the bricks and lock gates. The wages these employees made created more demand for manufactured goods and also for shops and shopkeepers to sell those goods. A growing population could now find employment. Canals were one of the many essential factors behind the rapid industrialisation of the period between 1780 and 1850.

Railways

Large-scale industrialisation was well under way when the railways arrived. Iron railway tracks had been used in mines to transfer coal to barges for some time, but the power to pull the trucks was provided by a stationary steam engine. Engineers Richard Trevithick and **George Stephenson** and his son Robert, had been experimenting with mobile steam engines since about 1800. Advances in metallurgy and developments on Watt's engines also helped. As with many inventions, a combination of demand, profit potential and willingness by practical men to experiment led to a breakthrough.

Self-educated and from a working-class background, Stephenson developed an interest in steam engines while working in coal mines. He designed and built systems for carrying coal from mines, then in 1821, received parliamentary approval to build a railway from Stockton to Darlington. He surveyed the whole line and had the railway built. He also developed the first fully mobile steam engine capable of pulling both freight and passengers. In 1830, he built the first intercity railway, between Manchester and Liverpool.

GEORGE STEPHENSON (1781–1848)

In 1825, a railway line opened between Stockton and Darlington, with the trucks of coal being pulled by a mobile steam engine. Then in 1829, George and Robert Stephenson's *Rocket*, which could travel at 48 kph and was capable of hauling large amounts of coal and other goods, won a competition as the best steam engine for locomotives. The following year, a line opened between Manchester, one of the great urban manufacturing centres of Britain, and Liverpool, one of Britain's major ports. So, the cost of transport was radically reduced, increasing demand. To the surprise of the Stephensons and their backers, more than 400 000 passengers were carried on the railway in its first year. No one had foreseen this demand for transporting people as well as goods. Equally important, there was a 10% dividend paid out to investors for the first ten years. Rail was a faster, more reliable and cheaper means of transport than canals, and railways did not freeze over in winter or run out of water in a severe drought. By 1844, there were 3000 km of railway in Britain, and 6000 by 1852.

On the whole, the government played a quiet, but important role in this. Parliament provided the necessary acts enabling the railway companies to purchase the land for tracks and stations. The fact that over 100 members of parliament had invested heavily in shares for the railway companies might have helped. Initially there was no regulation, which would have stood against the prevailing laissez-faire ideas of the time. In 1844, however, an Act of Parliament required every railway company to run at least one service a day on every line, each way, for a maximum of 1 pence per mile. They had to provide this public service, but in other ways they were left unregulated in spite of the fact that the first man killed in a railway accident was a government minister. Competition between the large number of railway companies ensured that market forces kept prices down.

Railways enabled people to travel in a way impossible only a decade or two before, and freight transport costs to manufacturers reduced radically, while delivery became more reliable. While canals inevitably went into decline, railways generated significant employment opportunities. Thousands of men worked in building the tracks, railway stations, bridges, tunnels and viaducts. This gave a huge stimulus to engineering of all types, especially civil and mechanical. Railway engines became increasingly sophisticated and powerful. Meanwhile, thousands of engines and carriages, as well as hundreds of thousands of kilometres of track, were exported. Once up and running, rail transport employed thousands of drivers, clerks and porters, meaning more people had a regular income and demand for consumer goods.

Rail transport also meant that labour became more mobile. Men and their families could move more easily in search of work. Urbanisation intensified, as commuting to work became practicable, and railway 'towns' such as Crewe and Swindon emerged and grew into key junctions and repair centres for engines and carriages. Demand for all types of iron and steel soared. Demand for coal also rose, partly to power the engines themselves and partly to us in making the iron for rails and engines. The railway, as with many of the other major innovations, showed that no one single innovation could transform the economy and create a significant amount of growth, but it was one of the many factors which kept the acceleration going and was a vital stimulus.

> **ACTIVITY 2.9**
>
> Using the maps in Figures 2.9 and 2.10, compare and contrast the impact of canals and railways on Britain's industrialisation. In your answer, consider the following questions:
> * Could railways have happened without canals?
> * Did each have a different impact?
> * Which had the greater impact?
> * How great a role did improvements in transportation play between 1750 and 1850? Would there have been a 'revolution' without it?

Steamships

Between 1800 and 1850 there was a lot of experimentation and innovation with steam-driven ships at sea and canal barges. Sail and horsepower were still the main sources of power, but steamships were faster and more reliable than sail, as they were less dependent weather conditions. However, at first a ship's steam engines were only introduced when the wind failed. The first steamship to cross the Atlantic was the *Savannah* in 1819. In 1838 the *Great Western* completed its first transatlantic journey in 14 days. This was the first steamship built especially for the transatlantic crossing. The first regular transatlantic cargo and passenger service began in 1840, and the first wrought-iron ship, the *Great Britain*, was built and launched in 1843. Several different shipping companies formed in the following years, competing in speed and efficiency. This competition and technological innovation laid the foundations for the dominance of steamships in the later 19th century.

Steamships continued to be fitted with sails until late in the 19th century, as the space needed for coal to power engines reduced the cargo the ships could carry. It was not until well into the latter part of the century that steam-driven ships, with no sails, made entirely out of iron and steel, became the means by which Britain's imports and exports were transported to India, North America and the Far East.

Figure 2.9: Britain's canal network, c.1835

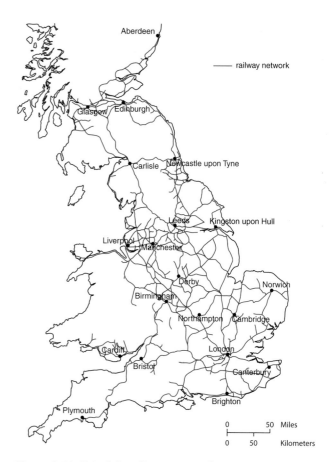

Figure 2.10: Britain's railway network, 1850

Raw materials

The availability of large quantities of the relevant raw materials needed for manufacturing was very important in the rapid industrialisation process which Britain underwent in the period after 1780. There were huge supplies of coal, iron ore, wool and cotton.

Coal

Coal was available in unlimited quantities at a reasonable price once transport costs dropped. Newcomen's steam-engine pump and the development of canals and, later, railways, ensured that as much coal as necessary could be transported efficiently to where it was needed. Britain also had the different types of coal required for different processes, such as making iron, heating houses and driving steam engines. Coal was mined in many parts of Britain, from Kent to central Scotland, which made getting it to where it was needed easier.

The importance of coal to the industrialisation process cannot be underestimated. Figure 2.13 shows the extent of coal deposits in Britain; these were spread over much of the country.

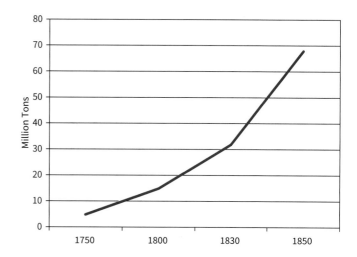

Figure 2.11: Coal production in Britain, 1750–1850

Iron

To produce iron for factory machines, steam engines and railway lines, there has to be iron ore in the ground. Britain was again fortunate in having large supplies of iron ore, and it was quite easy to dig out. Again, the development of canals made transporting the ore to where it was refined straightforward. There were large iron ore deposits in south Wales, central Scotland, and the north-east and north Midlands of England. Many of these deposits were close to major coal mines, which led to the growth of large-scale iron-making industries nearby, including near the ports of Cardiff and Swansea in south Wales.

Good-quality iron ore and vast quantities of coal meant that iron could be made on a large scale and, of course, transported out via the canal system. The interconnection between the various causes of industrialisation is evident here.

Textiles

Cotton was not grown in Britain; it had to be imported. Britain had an advantage again, however, in having (before 1783) colonies which could produce large amounts of raw cotton and a large merchant navy to transport it from America to Britain under protection by the highly effective Royal Navy. After the War of Independence between Britain and the new United States of America, political relations between the two countries were not good, but cotton growers in the American South and British cotton manufacturers took great care to ensure that this vital trade was not affected.

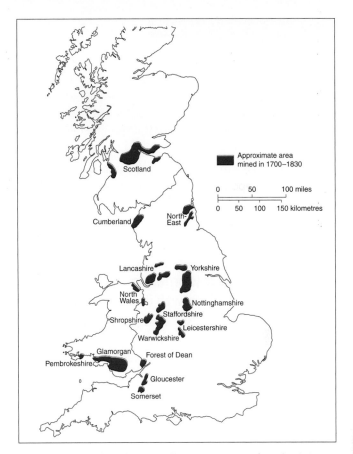

Figure 2.13: A map showing the main areas of coal mining and iron ore deposits, 1700–1830

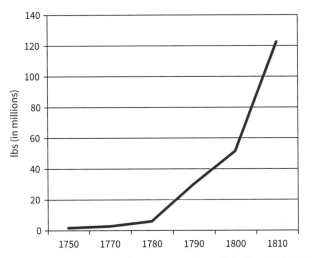

Figure 2.12: Imports of raw cotton into Britain, 1750–1810

For quite a large part of the period, Britain was engaged in major wars, including the global Seven Years War (1756–63), the American War of Independence (1775–83) and war with France for many years between 1792 and 1815. The importance of the Royal Navy in protecting these cotton imports was critical.

The other vital raw material behind industrialisation was wool. The wool trade had existed in Britain for centuries before cotton began to arrive on a large scale, and there was more than enough raw wool to meet the demand before mechanisation of the industry. Mechanisation, however, increased the quality and supply, and price reductions along with this improvement in quality also increased demand. While the wool industry did not enjoy the huge increases in output that cotton did, there was steady growth throughout period. Until about 1815, Britain could produce sufficient raw wool, with specialist breeding and greater use of marginal land ensuring greater output. When British farmers could not produce enough raw wool to meet demand, as in the early 19th century, sheep farming was developed in British colonies such as Australia and New Zealand. These colonies were themselves growing rapidly, which further increased the demand for British manufactured goods – and so industrialisation continued.

ACTIVITY 2.10

From what you have learned so far, do you think that without a good supply of raw materials and the means to transport them easily, there would have been no Industrial Revolution in Britain? Was the availability of raw materials or the ability to transport them more important to industrialisation?

Make a list of the reasons why each factor could be considered important. How important were other factors? Use your notes to help you to answer these questions.

Growth of markets (domestic and international) and growth of free trade

Overseas demand for British goods did not cause industrialisation, but it contributed to its 'revolutionary' nature. Growing domestic demand was essential to the process, and rapid population growth, coupled with rising real wages, ensured this. Britain had real advantages in having overseas markets in which to sell the goods it made. Because Britain was the first country to rapidly industrialise, it had no serious competition when it came to producing textiles and many other manufactured goods. As was the case with so many other aspects of the Industrial Revolution, statistics show remarkable increases.

The importance of British exports

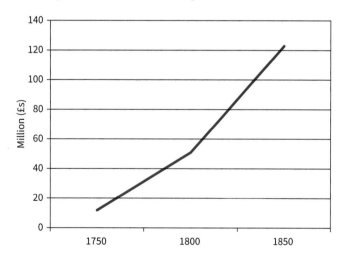

Figure 2.14: The value of British exports, 1750–1850

About 30% of exports from Britain went to its colonies or former colonies in North America and the West Indies, about 30% to Europe, about 20% to Asia and the rest to South America, Australia and New Zealand. The markets

in these last three places grew rapidly after 1820. Exports proved to be great generators of rapid growth and overseas markets were great incentives, as there were vast profits to be made. By 1850, exports generated over 10% of Britain's **national income**.

KEY TERM

National income: The total value of the output of all a country's goods and services in a year.

The infrastructure needed to serve a growing overseas market was already in place at the start of this period. There were well-established ports and a large merchant marine service. In 1760, Britain had about 600 000 tons of merchant shipping. This was 1.5 million tons by 1792. The canals and railways delivered goods to the dockside to load directly onto ships. A sophisticated banking and insurance system supported manufacturers and merchants. A manufacturer of cotton goods in Lancashire, for example, knew that he would get paid for the cloth he had made which was sold in Moscow, Calcutta or New York. Specialised commercial and financial institutions, alongside the development in commercial practice and law, assisted this rapid growth. There was an entrepreneurial revolution here to accompany the industrial revolution.

The government played an important and active role here too. One of the dominant political figures of this period, William Pitt, Earl of Chatham, was the son of a merchant who had made huge sums of money trading in India. In 1763, at the end of a war with France fought largely over colonies, he ensured that Canada became British and that British commercial interests in India and the West Indies predominated. His son, also called William, became prime minister in 1783. In 1786, he established a commercial treaty with Britain's traditional enemy, France, which enabled British goods to sell more freely in France. In return, the French could export products, such as wine, to Britain. The 1783 peace treaty with the new United States took great care to ensure that trade flowed freely between both countries. By 1800, the United States was taking 25% of all British exports. Another peace treaty in 1815, at the end of the long war with France, ensured that British commercial interests in Africa, as well as the West Indies, India and Australasia, were fully protected.

One of the main reasons why Britain was the first to recognise the independence of the breakaway Spanish colonies in South America in the 1820s was to ensure that British merchants could sell there. The British foreign secretary responsible for this, George Canning, was MP for the great port of Liverpool. It was the merchants and ship owners of Liverpool who had chosen him as their representative.

The British government believed that its main role was not only to maintain law and order and defend the country, but also to defend and advance Britain's commercial and industrial interests. While the principal source of income for government throughout this period (except during wartime emergencies) was a tax on imports and exports, the government took great care not to use this power in any way which might damage trade or industry. Instead, and increasingly throughout the period, it encouraged free trade without **tariffs**.

KEY TERM

Tariffs: Taxes imposed on goods when they are being either imported into or exported from a country.

●●● THINK LIKE A HISTORIAN

Consider the role of government. It has been suggested that one of the reasons why Britain had such great economic growth during this time was because the government did so little and just let people 'get on with it'. Identify examples where government inaction was beneficial, and where government action did more harm than good.

When the East India Company – which not only administered the trade between Britain, India and the Far East, but also owned large parts of India – fell into difficulties, the British government intervened to ensure it was regulated and, above all, that trade could continue. It was very aware that there were millions of people in India who could buy British goods.

By the end of the period, Britain exported a higher proportion of industrial output, and had more exports overall, than any country in the world.

ACTIVITY 2.11

Work in a group to identify the factors which played a part in the rapid acceleration of industrialisation after 1780. Which was the most important, and why? Allocate a specific factor – such as the availability of capital or the degree of government support – to a member of the group. Each member should argue why their factor was the most important and why. After the discussion, each member of the group should say which factors were more decisive.

Reflection: Discuss how you reached your conclusion with the rest of the group. How did you decide on the relative importance of the different factors? Would you change how you decide on the relative importance of different factors after listening to other members of your group?

2.3 Why, and with what consequences, did urbanisation result from industrialisation?

The growth of towns and the impact on living conditions

Although Britain was the most developed and urbanised nation in the world in 1750, only 15% of the population lived in towns. In 1775, just seven towns had a population of over 30 000 and five of them were ports. However, the national growth of commerce, finance and, above all, manufacturing industry, led to a steady growth of urban areas. By 1800, 25% of the population lived in towns. By the end of the period, it was over 50%. This move from country to town, from agriculture to industry, finance and commerce, was a key part of the industrialisation process.

Urban growth overall was about 25% each decade between 1800 and 1850, but some towns experienced more spectacular growth in certain periods. For example, Glasgow's population increased by 46% between 1810 and 1820, and Manchester's by 46% between 1820 and 1830. Bradford, a town at the centre of the textile industry, had a population of approximately 4500 in 1780, which rose to 103 000 in 1850.

The causes of the rapid growth of towns

One of the most important factors in the growth of towns was the rise in Britain's overall population. It more than doubled between 1750 and 1800, and the national **census**, carried out every ten years, shows that it went from about 15.7 million in 1801 to 27.3 million in 1851. This stemmed from a combination of 'push' and 'pull' factors.

A push came from agriculture. As agriculture became more efficient and productive, there was no longer the need for a large workforce in the countryside. Rural living tended to be healthier than in the towns, so more babies survived, but rural areas could no longer usefully employ all the people born there. So, the pull came from the towns which provided jobs for the rural unemployed. The towns that grew most rapidly were those at the centre of industrialisation. The establishment of textile

69

factories (woollen goods in Leeds and cotton ones in Manchester, for example) drew people from rural areas as well as providing employment for those born in the towns themselves. The population of Leeds grew from 53 000 in 1801 to 172 000 in 1851, and Manchester's rose from 75 000 in 1801 to 303 000 in 1851.

> **KEY TERM**
>
> **Census:** A count of every person and household in the country. The first national census in Britain was in 1801. Population figures before 1801 are less accurate.

Moreover, the changes in agriculture led to more, and better-quality, food being produced to provide for this growing population. With an expanding empire overseas and a superb merchant navy, Britain was secure in the knowledge that it could import food if needed.

In addition, there was no restriction on the movement of people. Those who worked on the land were no longer tied to it in any way. Those living in a town with limited employment opportunities could move easily to one which needed workers.

In many cases, these towns had enjoyed long traditions of relevant crafts skills. Other towns became centres of different types of manufacturing, such as Birmingham with its metal industries and Merthyr Tydfil in south Wales with its iron works. Birmingham's population grew from 71 000 in 1801 to 233 000 in 1851 and Merthyr Tydfil's from 8000 to 46 000 in the same period. The great ports of Bristol (61 000 to 137 000) and Liverpool (82 000 to 376 000) also experienced rapid population growth in these years. In every case, it was the promise of employment and a steady wage for all the family that attracted people to urban areas.

The industrial towns provided employment for those who worked in the new factories, and for a growing middle class whose employment was linked to industrialisation. Factory managers were needed, as were bankers and lawyers. Men were required to promote and organise the distribution of manufactured goods. Engineers were needed to innovate, design and build.

At the same time, people needed to buy goods for themselves and their families, which led to the growth of large stores which needed managers and employees. With improving literacy and a cheap press, there was also a demand for quality newspapers and this meant a need for journalists. Towns needed men to be in charge

of civic affairs, to deal with problems of welfare and the provision of services. This growing middle class wanted to educate their children, and so schools grew. Middle-class wives, with their large houses and large families, needed servants, and domestic service came to be the biggest employer of young working-class women in this period.

The changes in transport were also important reasons for the growth of towns. Without the ability to bring in large supplies of coal and raw materials, and move out the finished products, there could have been no factories to provide employment. Improved transport also meant that food could be brought in to feed the workforce, along with the bricks and slate to house them. Railways also played a significant role in the expansion of towns. In some cases, as we have seen in examples such as Crewe and Swindon, the railways really created the towns themselves, as they became not only vital rail junctions, but also the centres for manufacturing and servicing locomotives and carriages. By 1840, cheap transport was available for moving people, too. Suburbs sprang up on the outskirts of towns, and commuting became possible.

This combination of 'push' and 'pull' factors was important. A growing population needed work and food. Industrialisation, and what went with it, provided much of the work; the changes in agriculture provided the food.

> **ACTIVITY 2.12**
>
> In a small group, discuss whether population growth was the principal factor behind the growth of towns in this period. Each member of the group should take on a specific cause – such as agriculture change or population growth – and present a case arguing that it was the key factor.
>
> What benefits and disadvantages did urbanisation bring? Make a two-column list and compare the two sides. Which list is longer? Which contains more important items? List the main factors you think are the most important, giving reasons why you think they are the most important.

Urban conditions, housing and health

The combination of a rapid growth in population together with a significant move of people from the countryside to the towns meant that there was a large demand for houses for this new population to live in. While some employers took care to provide decent housing for their workforce, in the vast majority of towns, the solution to the housing problem was appalling.

Building entrepreneurs, aiming for a quick profit, brought land near factories and placed as many houses as possible on that land, often multi-storeyed and extremely close together. There was no civic planning and no control by any authority. The simple aim was to get as many families as possible into as little space as possible. Virtually no attention was paid to the need for adequate clean water supplies or sewage disposal. Factors such as heating and ventilation were ignored. Whole families would live in a single room. In winter, diseases like tuberculosis and infections like pneumonia were common. In summer, cholera, linked to contaminated water supplies, became a major killer. In the 1830s, around half of all children in towns died before their fifth birthday. The rise of these working-class tenement areas, known as slums, is one of the biggest criticisms that can be made of the impact of industrialisation.

Part of the problem was that local government was simply not suited to the needs of rapidly growing industrial cities. The system had been created centuries before and was designed to manage small market towns and rural areas. Controls were, therefore, insufficient, and managed by unpaid local volunteers, usually local landlords in the countryside and wealthier merchants in the towns. In 1835, however, the government passed the Municipal Corporations Act, which meant that:

- a new system of local government was set up for towns
- local property owners could elect local officials to manage a town
- local taxes could be raised and that money used to improve the towns, if so desired; local police forces could also be established.

The biggest drawback to the act was that it was permissive. Local governments did not have to improve living conditions unless they wanted to. Few did. Many people were reluctant to pay the increased taxes needed to improve the living conditions of others. The rich could simply move out of the squalid towns and build in the suburbs. These were often to the west of a town, as the prevailing winds in most areas came from the west, so the smell and smoke of the new towns would not affect them.

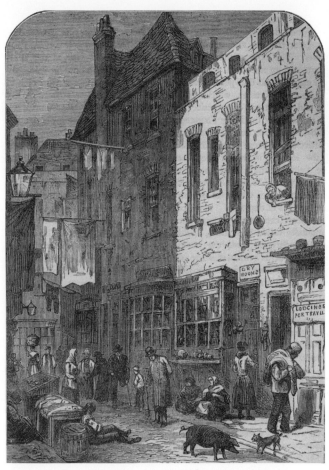

Figure 2.15: The Rookery of St Giles in London was a notorious slum, housing the poorest and including immigrants. In what ways are contemporary drawings and paintings useful as historical sources?

There was concern among the ruling classes about working-class dissatisfaction in the late 1830s and early 1840s but it took some time before anything happened. **Edwin Chadwick**, who also played an important role in reforming working conditions in factories, was asked to investigate. He was responsible for a **Royal Commission** report which was published in 1842. This report, with a great deal of impressive statistical evidence, made clear the damage done to the health of very many people by dreadful environmental and living conditions. Action to try and remedy the worst problems caused by bad housing was taken in the first Public Health Act of 1848. This was prompted by further outbreaks of cholera across the nation, which affected all classes. The act was a compromise between two groups. There were those who wanted the state to take firm action and to compel local authorities to improve amenities like water supply

Trained originally as a lawyer, Chadwick was deeply concerned by the impact of industrialisation on the way many people lived and worked. He became a committed reformer. His detailed, highly scientific, investigations into both individual welfare and public health led to both the New Poor Law of 1834 and the Public Health Act of 1848.

and sewage disposal. They anticipated further laws by parliament and controls from central government. This would naturally mean more taxation, more bureaucracy and more inspectors. On the other side were those who still supported laissez-faire ideas and objected to government interference in local matters. In particular, they wanted to avoid the increased taxation needed to fund improvement.

KEY TERM

Royal Commission: An enquiry into an issue set up by the government. It has the power to summon witnesses to give evidence and is expected to write a detailed report making recommendations for changes. It was customary for those recommendations to become law.

The act did create a central Board of Health in London, which reported to parliament and encouraged the creation of local health boards that had the power to make improvements. The only firm powers that the act gave central government, however, was the right to impose local health boards on areas where the death rate rose above the national average. Otherwise, there was no national pressure to improve the quality of housing – that was left to the local authorities, and few exercised the powers they had to do so.

ACTIVITY 2.13

From the report of the Royal Commission of 1842

First, as to the extent and operation of the evils which are the subject of this inquiry: –

That the various forms of epidemic, endemic, and other disease caused, or aggravated, or propagated chiefly amongst the labouring classes by atmospheric impurities produced by decomposing animal and vegetable substances, by damp and filth, and close and overcrowded dwellings prevail amongst the population in every part of the kingdom, whether dwelling in separate houses, in rural villages, in small towns, in the larger towns – as they have been found to prevail in the lowest districts of the metropolis.

That such disease, wherever its attacks are frequent, is always found in connexion with the physical circumstances above specified, and that where those circumstances are removed by drainage, proper cleansing, better ventilation, and other means of diminishing atmospheric impurity, the frequency and intensity of such disease is abated; and where the removal of the noxious agencies appears to be complete, such disease almost entirely disappears.

That the formation of all habits of cleanliness is obstructed by defective supplies of water.

That the annual loss of life from filth and bad ventilation are greater than the loss from death or wounds in any wars in which the country has been engaged in modern times.

Source: www.bl.uk/collections-item/1842

What causes of poor health are described in this source? Why do you think this report proved to be so influential, and persuaded parliament to act? Why do you think these conditions were tolerated by those who lived in them and those who created them?

KEY CONCEPT

Cause and consequence

Look back at the information in this chapter on living conditions in towns during this period. Were poor living conditions solely the consequence of large and rapid population growth in towns, or did other causes contribute? Make a list of as many such causes as you can that explain why urban living conditions for the working class were poor. In what ways can you link these reasons together?

Working conditions: child labour, hours, pay and safety

By 21st-century standards in developed economies, those who worked in the factories had to put up with appalling working conditions and, for most, exceptionally low pay. The average working day ranged from 12 to 14 hours for six days a week, often in a dirty and dangerous environment. The work was tedious and the atmosphere noisy and polluted. Many of the workforce learned to lip-read, as communication was otherwise impossible with the noise of machinery. There were few breaks, and many factories had terrible sanitation.

Over 65% of the workforce in the textile mills were women and children. They performed the menial and unskilled roles. In the past, women had often performed more skilled roles in the making of textiles when working at home, but now their role was reversed. Men had the skilled roles: designing, installing and maintaining the machinery, and earning between £2 and £2.25 a week – more than enough to maintain a family. Unskilled men, however, could earn as little as 70p a week, which was not enough, and they would be dependent on their wives and children making up the difference needed to survive. Women usually earned between 35p and 60p a week, and children even less. These were near starvation wages. Unmarried women lived with their families, and married women used their pay as a vital supplement to their families' income. For many families, the income earned by children, who often started working from age six or seven, was essential. In many factories, children made up about 30% of the total workforce.

Some employers took real care of their workers. One example is the socialist writer and thinker Robert Owen, who developed a huge factory complex in New Lanark in Scotland, employing nearly 2000 workers, the majority of whom were women and children. He introduced an eight-hour day and provided education for his child employees. He took care to create safe working conditions for all his workers, as well as providing them with decent housing. However, few employers followed his example of making a substantial profit as well as providing good working and living conditions and reasonable hours.

Other factory owners treated their workforce badly, especially the women and children. Children had to clean moving machinery (stopping the looms lowered production and so cost money) and many serious injuries

happened. It was easy for a child who had been working for ten hours straight to make a mistake. There were no health and safety regulations and machinery was not guarded. There was no compensation for those injured or killed at work. Certain poor children, known as 'paupers', who were either orphans or had been abandoned by families unable to care for them were exploited. This became a national scandal. They were used as cheap and expendable labour by some factory owners, and deprived of adequate food, play, education and housing. Many suffered lifelong disabilities, becoming known as the 'factory cripples', and it took several decades of pressure and agitation to remedy these abuses.

Impacts on different social classes

Britain had always been a socially diverse country. Society was not formed into rigidly defined social groups in the 18th century. While there was an aristocracy – a small landowning elite that dominated politics and much of the economy – outsiders could join this class. It was possible for other successful men to buy great landed estates and gradually gain aristocratic status and a title, or for women to marry into the aristocracy. The prime minister in 1763 was William Pitt, grandson of a successful trader in India, and he became the Earl of Chatham in 1763. One of his sons, William Pitt the Younger, became prime minister in 1783. Meanwhile, men from working-class backgrounds could and did rise into the middle class through hard work and good fortune, purchasing their own houses and businesses.

The aristocracy

Throughout this period, the aristocracy remained the dominant political, economic and social influence in British society. Its members remained firmly in control of a large proportion of the land and wealth of Britain. They controlled the **House of Lords** and had a lot of influence over the **House of Commons**, which, although elected, contained many men related to the lords or who gained their election through support from members of the House of Lords. In many cases, aristocrats made large amounts of money out of both agricultural improvements and industrial investment. They also invested in overseas trade. Making money was not seen as damaging to their social status, as was the case in France. The Duke of Bridgewater, for example, made a great deal of money by building the first large canal to transport coal from his mines to sell in Manchester.

KEY TERMS

House of Lords: One of two parts to the British parliament. The House of Lords was made up entirely of lords; the majority of them men who had either been made lords by the king, or who had inherited the title from their father or other male relative. It was an unelected House. Its other members were serving bishops of the Church of England.

House of Commons: Unlike the House of Lords, all the members of the House of Commons were elected. This was where key issues like the government's budget were decided and the most important laws initiated. The House of Lords, however, could veto any measure which the Commons decided on.

Many of the great landowners were keen to develop new agricultural techniques and publicise them, and to exploit any mineral resources they might have had to the full. The lists of investors of many of the early railway companies, for example, contained members of the House of Lords. Many of them educated their sons in **public schools** alongside the sons of many of the new entrepreneurs. In some cases they were more than happy for their sons to marry the daughters (and receive the dowry) of men from the ranks of the growing middle class. One of the reasons why parliament was so supportive of change, or at least put up few barriers to industrialisation, was that many of its largely aristocratic membership stood to make money from it. They still managed to pass laws which protected their interests, such as keeping the price of corn artificially high and preventing cheap foreign imports in the Corn Laws of 1815.

Britain benefited from having a **constitutional monarchy**. George III (1760–1820) and his successors throughout the period were usually prepared to accept the decisions of their parliaments and prime ministers. While British monarchs still retained influence over appointments and some policy, ultimately, if the prime minister and parliament wanted something, they got it. Compromise and adapting to changed circumstances helped the aristocracy to retain its power and influence.

The aristocracy was also willing to accept political change. This helped it to keep its largely dominant position and to avoid what happened in France. In 1832, there was a demand for radical change in who was allowed to vote, which would lead to a weakening of the aristocracy's control of parliament. Faced with serious rioting and demonstrations across the nation – and another revolution in France in 1830 – the British aristocracy wisely compromised.

Overall, the rich got richer. The aristocracy did retain much of its power and influence, but it took enough care to adapt to a rapidly evolving economy and accepted that the interests of other social groups had to be considered.

KEY TERMS

Public schools: Privately run boarding schools, which, by this stage were not 'public' at all and charged high fees for attendance. It was customary for boys to be sent to them from the age of 11.

Constitutional monarchy: A political system in which the ruling king's or queen's power is set by constitutional limits. They are not above the law and cannot make laws on their own. Government ministers accountable to an elected national assembly carry out the day-to-day work of running the country.

ACTIVITY 2.14

From what you have learned so far, why was the British aristocracy able to retain so much of its wealth, power and influence in this period?

Make a list of the reasons for this, placing them in what you think is the order of importance. Include evidence to support your case. Explain why you have placed these reasons in this particular order next to the list.

The growth of a middle class

Perhaps the greatest social change which resulted from industrialisation was the growth of a middle class. While there had always been professional men such as lawyers and bankers, as well as wealthy merchants, they were few in number before 1750. Industrialisation led to the rapid expansion of this group, which gradually became known as the 'middle class' during the 19th century. Entrepreneurs and innovators, factory owners and architects, station managers and slum builders and landlords emerged in large numbers. Great engineers like Isambard Kingdom Brunel, responsible for much of the innovative railway building of the 1830s and 1840s, gained wealth and status. Robert Peel, prime minister from 1841 to 1846, who pushed through many major reforms, was the son of a successful textile manufacturer. He was educated at a public school and Oxford University, alongside the sons of many of the aristocracy. He married the daughter of a minor aristocrat and his eldest daughter married the son of an earl.

There was a growing need for civil servants and local government officials as bureaucracy grew. The railways needed architects for their great new stations and surveyors for their new lines, and accountants to manage the large amounts of money involved in building and running the railways. The new middle class, with its surplus income, demanded servants and luxury goods, and simulated the growth of an enormous retail system. Industrialisation fuelled great social, as well as economic, change.

Segregation by housing emerged and increased throughout the period, particularly after the railways made cheap commuting possible. While factories remained surrounded by often appalling working-class housing, the middle class, able to afford a horse and carriage, or regular rail fares, migrated to the suburbs. The suburbs, away from the pollution and filth of the industrial towns, required major investment in building and many domestic servants were employed to work there.

Progress into the upper reaches of society was possible for the most successful. A banker named Robert Smith was made a member of the House of Lords in 1797, partly because of his loyal support for the prime minister (who usually decided on such social promotions), but also because he agreed to write off a personal loan to him. The British aristocracy did not close its ranks to such people during the Industrial Revolution. Naturally, Smith ensured that the interests of progressive bankers such as himself were well represented in parliament. Overall, this group was a substantial beneficiary from the industrialisation process.

ACTIVITY 2.15

Working with another student, identify the specific factors which enabled the middle class to grow in both size and influence in this period. Make sure you clearly separate the 'size' and the 'influence' factors.

Do you think economic change always leads to social change? Make a table listing the reasons why you would agree or disagree with this question.

The working class

The rest of the population enjoyed no real benefits from industrialisation. In fact, the condition of some groups actually got worse. The most desperate poverty was felt by agricultural workers in the south and east of England, and by those who had been involved in making textiles by hand in their own homes. These people often faced both starvation and homelessness.

Just as there were distinctions between the rich and successful members of the aristocracy and those

whose fortunes declined, and between the successful and prosperous members of the middle class and the bankrupt, there were considerable variations in how industrialisation treated what were known as the 'lower orders'. (The term 'working class' emerged during the course of the 19th century.)

Those who worked in the new industrial towns and coal mines experienced mixed fortunes. In terms of income, real wages actually rose for this group, so, matters might have been better for the industrial worker. This does not, however, reveal the whole picture.

The majority of semi-skilled and unskilled men depended on the additional incomes of their wives and children for survival. They had no educational opportunities, so rising out of the working class was unlikely. Work was not guaranteed and, in recession, thousands could be thrown out of work. If there was illness or industrial injury (and both were highly likely), there was no assistance.

By the late 1830s, cheap rail transport meant that, it was possible to move in search of work, and for most of the period there was work available. Conditions in the increasing number of coal mines, however, were invariably terrible. While some improvements had been made in safety, working conditions overall were among the worst in the country. Serious injury and death were common. Wages were low and often men were not paid in normal currency, but in their employers' private currency, which could only be used in shops owned by these employers. Prices there, unsurprisingly, were often higher than elsewhere.

From a report on working conditions in Yorkshire, 1842

Young girls, often under the age of 10, regularly perform all types of works in the coal mines, although they do not often cut the coal at the face. One of the most disgusting sights I have ever seen was that of young females, dressed like boys, crawling on all fours, with belts around their waists and chains passing between their legs, pulling small trucks of coal underground along small tunnels, about 2 ft. high and running with water. They may do this for up to 13 hours a day.

Source: Adapted from Pike, E.R. (2005). *Human Documents of the Industrial Revolution in Britain.* **London: Routledge, p. 254**

The only real beneficiaries in the working class were the skilled workers: the men who made the machine tools, built the new looms and helped to develop the concepts of men like Newcomen and Cort into actual machines. There was a shortage of such men and they were paid accordingly. The skilled engineer or factory worker could earn over £4 a week, more than double what a semi-skilled weaver could earn, and nearly three times that of the unskilled and casual labourers who made up the majority of the working class. These skilled workmen would move in search of work if necessary. They also took great care to restrict entry to their ranks, in order to preserve the difference in wages. The other real advantage they had was that they were always guaranteed work. This wasn't the case for the rest of the new working class.

ACTIVITY 2.16

Did the Industrial Revolution lead to major social change? Work with another student to identify how much influence the Industrial Revolution had on social change, making sure you provide evidence to back up these points. Think carefully about the word 'major': is this question encouraging you to accept an idea you do not agree with?

Government responses to the consequences of industrialisation: early moves towards regulation and control of working and living conditions

Before 1750 working-class men, women and children often had poor working and living conditions but rapid industrialisation brought in real change. Poverty itself was not new. However, the visibility and extent of the poor working and living conditions was new. This was particularly true for the women and children, who were seen as unable to protect themselves from exploitation. Traditional thinking was that it was not the role of the state to interfere in the relationship between an employer and their employees. A ten-year-old child was believed to be perfectly capable of making decisions about whether or not to work, and whether or not to put up with the conditions in which they worked. Employers argued that better pay and working conditions would drive them to bankruptcy. They believed that market forces should apply and capitalism should not be regulated in any way.

Some attempts were made to control child labour before 1830, with parliament passing acts in 1802 and 1819 to restrict the hours that children could work and to stop those under the age of nine from being employed. However, no effective system of inspectors was created to ensure the rules were obeyed, and attempts to prosecute law-breakers proved difficult and expensive.

There were some real improvements in the early 1830s. The working class relied on others to make their case for them as they weren't represented in Parliament. Gradually, a factory reform movement was organised, focusing primarily on child labour. Some of the reformers were genuinely humanitarian; others were strongly opposed to capitalism and the spread of industry. One important factor in driving forward this reform movement was religion. While some of the clergy and members of the Church of England were content with society as it stood, others, motived by a strong Christian belief, were determined to see society change for the better. Neither of the two main political parties at the time, the Whigs and the **Tories** were particularly interested in social and economic reform. The Tories tended to be conservative and the Whigs, while prepared to favour political reform, preferred a laissez-faire approach in other areas. Nonetheless, two prominent leaders of this new reform movement, Tory MPs Richard Oastler and Michael Sadler, began to gain support from many workers hoping to see a reduction in working hours for all.

KEY TERM

The Tories: The political party that dominated British politics throughout this period. In the course of the 1830s, it changed its name to the Conservative Party.

It was a letter in a Leeds newspaper in 1830 that gave the idea of regulation for children some momentum. At the time, Leeds was the centre of the woollen industry. Written by Richard Oastler, the letter called for an end to what he called the 'Yorkshire Slavery'.

Thousands of our fellow creatures are at this very moment existing in a state of slavery more horrid than the victims of that hellish system – colonial slavery. The streets which are now receiving the petitions of the Anti-Slavery Society are every morning wet with the tears of innocent victims at the terrible shrine of greed, who are compelled, not by the whip of the negro slave driver, but by the equally dreadful whip of the factory overlooker to hasten these half-dressed and half-fed children to those evil centres of British child slavery, the mills in this town and neighbourhood.

Source: Richard Oastley's letter to a Leeds newspaper, 1830. From: the University of Huddersfield Repository

The letter was published in a local newspaper, but it gained national attention, and national debate followed. The largely uncensored press played an important role in making the wider public aware of what was happening in factories and in the countryside. However, with an even greater debate raging in Britain over whether parliament should be reformed and whether the vote should be extended to more men, the matter was not dealt with until 1833. Oastler's fellow MP Michael Sadler did manage to get a bill introduced into parliament giving a maximum ten-hour day for all workers under 18 years old. The bill did not pass, but did achieve extensive publicity during its passage through parliament. Sadler was able to set up a committee of MPs to examine the bill in detail and ensure that its supporters dominated it. He also managed to persuade a large number of witnesses to give evidence of the many abuses and bad practices that went on in the textile factories.

Evidence of Samuel Coulson, given to the committee of MPs on factory conditions

Qu. At what time in the morning, in the brisk time, did those girls go to the mills?

Ans. In the brisk time, for about six weeks, they have gone at 3 o'clock in the morning, and ended at 10, or nearly half past at night …

Qu. Had any of them any accident in consequence of this labour?

Ans. Yes, my eldest daughter when she went first there; she had been about five weeks, and used to fettle the frames when they were running, and my eldest girl agreed with one of the others to fettle hers that time, that she would do her work; while she was learning more about the work, the overlooker came by and said, "Ann, what are you doing there?" she said, "I am doing it for my companion, in order that I may know more about it," he said, "Let go, drop it this minute," and the cog caught her forefinger nail, and screwed it off below the knuckle, and she was five weeks in Leeds Infirmary.

Qu. Has she lost that finger?

Ans. It is cut off at the second joint.

Qu. Were her wages paid during that time?

Ans. As soon as the accident happened the wages were totally stopped; indeed, I did not know which way to get her cured, and I do not know how it would have been cured but for the Infirmary.

Source: Pike, E.R. (2005). *Human Documents of the Industrial Revolution in Britain*. London: Routledge, p. 126

77

Sadler lost his seat in parliament in the general election of 1832, being strongly opposed by many factory owners and those who believed strongly in laissez-faire policies. However, another MP, Lord Ashley, took on his mission. Although Ashley's ten-hour bill failed to pass (by just a single vote), the government of the day, acknowledging the degree of public concern, agreed to set up a Royal Commission to examine the subject.

Unlike Sadler's committee, which tended to present and publish evidence which only supported its case for reform, the Royal Commission under the leadership of Edwin Chadwick gave plenty of scope for manufacturers to present their views. The recommendations of the commission were accepted by the government and made into law in 1833. This Factory Act was an exceptionally significant piece of legislation. The most important terms were as follows:

- It applied to most textile mills.
- No child under the age of nine could be employed.
- Restrictions were placed on the number of hours people under the age of 18 could work.
- Children over nine and under 13 had to receive two hours of education a day.

- Inspectors were appointed by the government to check that the law was being obeyed and had some powers to enforce the law.

●●● THINK LIKE A HISTORIAN

Some MPs, although elected by men of property to represent the interests of men of property, voted against the wishes of their constituents because they felt it was in the interests of the country and those who could not vote to regulate factories. What should dictate how an elected representative votes? Their conscience? What their voters tell them to do? What their party tells them? What they think is in the best interests of the country? What might win them the next election?

Many people hopeful of reform were disappointed by the act. It only covered some factories and not, for example, coal mines, where many children also worked in dangerous and unhealthy conditions. It did not include women. Men who were looking for a shorter working day were also disappointed. In addition, the act proved difficult to enforce, and many factory owners simply ignored the requirement to educate children. Parents, desperate for money, often colluded with the factory owners to ignore the rules. If rule-breaking was discovered, the financial penalties imposed were small and hardly a disincentive to employers.

This 1833 act was, however, a critical first step. While the Royal Commission and this law revealed the reluctance by government to interfere with the way industry managed its employees, it did accept that children needed protection from exploitation by unscrupulous employers (and their parents). By appointing inspectors with powers to investigate and prosecute, there was the crucial acceptance that the state had a responsibility to protect the interests of vulnerable people. This was a vital new principle and it led to many significant changes of legislation in the future. Men whose instincts were laissez-faire and non-interference had been persuaded to take action. This was because of humanitarian instincts and public opinion, a free press and evidence that was often very upsetting. However it is worth stressing, that many factory owners were already operating within the guidelines of the act.

Lord Ashley continued to focus on the employment conditions of women and children. He had the 1833 act reviewed by a **select committee** of parliament. Again, he used this committee to publicise the failings of the 1833

act and those in areas such as coal mines, not covered by the act. This was to lead to the Mines Act of 1842, which stopped all children under ten and women from underground work and established inspectors with the power to investigate and prosecute. It also informed the 1844 and 1847 Factory Acts, which reduced the maximum working hours for 8- to 13-year-olds to 6½ a day, increased the amount of education required each day to 3 hours, stopped women from working night shifts, and laid down a maximum 12-hour day for women. This was later reduced to 10 hours a day with a maximum of 58 hours a week.

KEY TERM

Select committee: A group of members of parliament which examines a specific problem and makes recommendations for addressing it.

ACTIVITY 2.17

Prepare two presentations. In the first, make a case on behalf of factory owners, arguing against any government regulation of hours and working conditions. You need to bear in mind the sort of evidence that your opponents will offer and the best way to counteract this. You might also consider the likely sympathies of MPs in the 1830s.

In the second, put forward an argument for the need for government regulation of working hours and conditions. You need to bear in mind that all MPs were property owners and taxpayers, and many might have investments in factories.

Reflection: Discuss your presentations with another student. Which did they find more persuasive, and why? How far might they have been influenced by hindsight in making their decision – in other words, by the knowledge that the Factory Acts were eventually passed?

These two Acts of Parliament represent a significant step forward in terms of state intervention as they provided more inspectors who had more powers, and greater protection from exploitation for women and children. However, while some of the worst results of the impact of industrialisation on the majority of the population were eased, both working and living conditions for the working classes of Britain remained poor.

2.4 Why, and with what consequences, did industrialisation result in popular protest and political change?

Reactions to mechanisation and economic change

Radical economic change came to Britain after 1750. While some people benefitted, there were others who suffered because of this change. In rural areas, before the full impact of agricultural changes was felt, there was rarely unrest. The population remained reasonably static. Most of the rural working class had small plots of their own land which allowed them to survive. In many cases, they also had other occupations, such as weaving or spinning in the home, to provide additional income. There would also be a degree of support from their communities in times of financial hardship. Poor harvests could lead to food riots, but these were comparatively rare in the first part of the 18th century.

Towards the end of the century, however, protest grew in many rural areas. The causes of these protests were similar to the reasons why many left the countryside for the towns:

- There was rapid population growth in rural areas. There was no longer work for so many on the land at the same time as factories were reducing the demand for products which had been made in homes.
- Food prices rose, especially for the rural workers' staple diet, bread.
- Enclosure farming began to impact more and more parts of rural Britain, leading to the loss of common land for grazing and the small plots for agricultural workers.
- Landowners needed fewer full-time workers, just those on a temporary basis at harvest time, so regular paid work was less available.
- Parliament passed laws with heavy penalties against poaching (catching animals for food on someone else's land).
- The limited welfare system could not cope with the number of people needing help and landowners were not willing to pay additional taxes to fund it.

There were scattered food riots between 1790 and 1810, usually in years when the price of bread was exceptionally high. The participants were mainly agricultural labourers or miners, but the incidents rarely involved more than a few hundred people. They tended to attack and loot the property of the 'middlemen', those involved in transporting wheat and flour, who were suspected of hoarding and profiteering. The riots were invariably suppressed and those involved severely punished. They were never well organised as there was limited scope for communication outside the immediate area, as almost all rioters were illiterate.

There were also some riots directed against enclosure, but, like the food riots, they were scattered and poorly organised. Enclosure was a significant change to rural life. However, there were few protests because the actual enclosure processes needed a large amount of additional labour, initially. This meant that the negative impact was not felt immediately. The growing demand for labour in the towns also reduced some of the distress felt in the countryside. Also, the fact that Britain was at war for much of the period between 1792 and 1815 meant that there was a great demand for men for the army and the navy.

It was in the years after 1815 that most protest was seen in rural areas. Peace with France left thousands of former soldiers and sailors looking for employment. Agriculture prices collapsed, which, although it meant slightly cheaper food, meant that farmers cut wages and reduced employment. The limited amount of welfare available was not enough to cope with mass unemployment and poverty, and landowners who paid for this welfare refused to contribute more into a system which they did not feel benefited them. The burning of haystacks, local food riots and attacks on livestock spread throughout the 1820s as poverty grew among the rural poor.

Another factor which led to unrest was the increase in the number of radical newspapers. Some were aimed at a middle-class readership and focused largely on issues like the taxes imposed on imported corn to benefit farmers and the harsh methods that the government used to keep order. Others were aimed more at the rural working class (where they were read out in inns, for example) and attacked the taxes that had to be paid to support the rich who ran the country in their own interests. The messages of the vast majority of these publications were highly critical of the government and were important in fuelling unrest.

The Captain Swing riots

The 'Captain Swing' riots of 1830–31 brought these protests to a conclusion. Captain Swing was a mythical figure allegedly organising the movement, whose name appeared on various threatening letters to landowners. They were called 'riots' by the government and local landowners, suggesting that the protests were illegal, violent and destructive. The protesters might have seen them in a different light! The protests highlighted several related issues:

- lack of regular employment
- low wages and bad housing and working conditions
- lack of welfare support
- having to pay taxes to support the Church of England (even people who were not members had to do this; members of other churches thus paid twice)
- the arrival of threshing machines, which helped harvesting, but reduced the demand for labour
- hunger.

The main areas of protest were in southern England and in East Anglia, where there was little alternative employment. The majority of the new factories were in the Midlands and the north of England. The railway had not yet arrived to provide cheap transport to areas where work was available.

The government reacted quickly and decisively. Troops were sent into the area to keep order. Normal judicial processes were suspended. Some rioters were executed, some transported to Australia and many others imprisoned.

Ultimately, the protests achieved little, and conditions for the agricultural labourer remained poor throughout the period. The protests did delay the use of threshing machines for some years, so wages increased slightly, but attempts by agricultural workers to organise themselves into a trade union in the 1830s were stamped out and its leaders transported to Australia. The unrest in the countryside in 1830–31 formed part of a wider protest throughout Britain, demanding political reform. However, the reforms of 1832 (see 'The Great Reform Act', later) did nothing to improve conditions for the agricultural worker in Britain.

The Luddite riots

Despite the huge impact that industrialisation had on the working classes, there was surprisingly little protest against the changes that the factory system imposed. There were occasional attacks on the new machines

before 1830, but few later. There were, however, two more significant attempts to prevent the establishment of the new machines. Both mostly involved skilled men in the textile industries whose roles were now performed more cheaply and efficiently by machines. The first was in Lancashire in the 1770s, caused by the arrival of machinery which improved both the output and quality of finished woollen cloth. The men and women who had made textiles by hand found themselves without their well-paid work. There was some smashing of the new machines, but it was confined to a small area and attracted no support from other members of the working class. The workers had failed to stop the arrival of the machine.

The other main outburst gained more publicity and historians have paid greater attention to it. This was known as the 'Luddite' movement, between 1811 and 1816, with the main incidents of machine-breaking between 1811 and 1812. In several parts of the north of England and the Midlands, mobs broke into factories and smashed the new machinery, spinning jennies and water frames in particular. A great deal of damage was done to property and, in one case, a mill owner was killed. Most of the men involved had been skilled workers employed in making textiles by hand in their homes, and their income and independent status was threatened by the new machines.

There were other factors which might have played a part in this protest. Britain was at the time involved in a major war, and both its European and American markets were disrupted while there was also a shortage of vital raw materials. Although this was a temporary problem, it led to high unemployment in the textile industry. This, added to wage cuts and exceptionally high bread prices, fuelled further protests. The fact that miners, whose livelihoods were not affected by these new factory machines, were also involved indicates that wider issues were at stake.

As with other protests, the Luddite uprising was firmly repressed by troops and offenders were imprisoned. There is some evidence that the local magistrates responsible for law and order were sympathetic towards the machine breakers, as they disliked the arrival of the factory owners and their rise in the social hierarchy. There was not always a great effort made to investigate and prosecute offenders.

By the end of 1814, machine breaking had died out. Trade had improved and the price of bread had dropped by half from its all-time high of 1811. Some historians have seen the Luddite movement as the start of a class struggle by the 'lower orders' against the excesses of capitalism; others suggest that it was a more straightforward case of hungry men faced with the loss of their jobs, homes and status in their communities.

The political and constitutional consequences of industrialisation

For the first 50 years of this period, industrialisation had a limited impact on the political process. George III, who ruled between 1760 and 1820, was broadly sympathetic

to economic progress, but while he had influence, he had limited power. Parliament was also sympathetic to both economic and social change, and so by extension was the government, since the custom was that all government ministers were also members of parliament.

There were few obstacles to industrialisation. Enclosure acts were passed easily. Inventors had their innovations protected by patents. Canal and railway developers had permission to build. Overseas trade was protected by the Royal Navy. Tariffs were modified to assist exports.

ACTIVITY 2.18

How useful is the cartoon in Figure 2.16 in explaining the causes of the Captain Swing riots? Consider the different elements in the source, including which figures seem ugly and which attractive, and what that tells us. Don't forget to consider the text in the drawing.

Given your analysis of these details, does the cartoon as a whole seem hostile to the Captain Swing rioters or to the authorities, or both?

Figure 2.16: In this political cartoon from the 1820s called 'State of the country', published at the time of the Captain Swing riots, rioters carry banners declaring 'Swing for ever!' and 'No Machines'. Others are saying, 'Well I don't think Mr Swing can come here', 'Oh L[or]d Master!!', 'fire fire fire!!!', 'I Recommend to this meeting the formation of a yeomanry Regiment of which I am willing to take the command, then if the base peasantry wont stare quietly we can cut them down like chaff', 'I think that would only make worse, what we want is Reform in Parliament, with Lower Rents Taxes & tithes, you that think with me hold up your hands' and 'all all all'.

Foreign policy was geared to the needs of British commerce as well as national security. Taxation was low and laissez-faire was the attitude of the government. The ruling classes – the aristocracy and the richer members of the middle class – were all involved in making money and naturally took great care to protect their interests. Any serious threat to their incomes received immediate attention from the government. There was a threat by France to the profitable sugar-producing islands in the Caribbean in the wars of the 1790s. Immediately, troops and ships were quickly diverted there. Only the lower classes would have wanted political change, but they were unrepresented in Parliament and generally focused on their own economic survival.

The first real demands for political change came in the 1790s. There is limited evidence to link it with industrial change, however. Three factors appear to have encouraged this process. The first is a movement started by a group of liberal MPs in the early 1780s which aimed to reduce the amount of control that the king and aristocracy had over parliament, and to ensure instead that there was fairer representation of all classes in parliament. The second factor is that, people were taking notice of the example of a revolution breaking out in France, with its radical political ideas. The third was the writing of Thomas Paine in his famous book *The Rights of Man* (published in 1791), which demanded votes for all men, a democratic society, equality for all and a welfare state.

Because of these factors, groups of men started to organise themselves in 'Corresponding Societies'. These societies were almost entirely made up of skilled and literate workers in trades such as weaving, shoemaking and metalwork. They were sympathetic to Paine's ideas, but showed little interest in the many problems which faced those who suffered most from industrialisation: the agricultural poor and those working and living in dreadful conditions in the factories and the slums.

The Corresponding Societies had limited impact. Most aristocratic and middle-class opinion was largely hostile to the societies. They felt that their ideas might lead to the anarchy and chaos that seemed to be taking place in France in the 1790s. Britain was at war with revolutionary France, and revolutionary ideas were seen as disloyal at the very least. Some of the homes of these radicals were destroyed by what were known as 'Church and King' mobs, made up largely of working-class people. The only time that there was the chance of a link between these radicals and the working class was in times of hunger and

unemployment, and fortunately, from the government's point of view, there were few of those before 1815.

The long war with France came to an end in 1815. This had an immediate economic effect, in that over 300 000 soldiers and sailors were no longer needed and came onto the job market. There was also an inevitable economic dislocation as the £40 million that the government had been spending annually on the war suddenly became available for other uses. This had a major impact on industry. In addition, there was an exceptionally bad harvest in 1815 which led to distress in 1816. The government also passed the Corn Laws of 1815, which prevented the import of cheap corn and was designed to help landowners maintain their profits. Hunger and unemployment among the working classes grew. The radical ideas of the 1790s Corresponding Societies reappeared and this led to some strong, and occasionally violent, demands for both political and economic change.

However, these protests achieved little, as the government took care to repress them as far as was possible without, generally, overreacting. In the early 1820s, bread prices fell again. Meanwhile, the alliance between the aristocracy and the richer middle classes held firm, while those seeking change were badly divided. Some advocated peaceful protest while others felt that violence was the only way to achieve change. Some wished for moderate political reform, others demanded revolution. Some worked for political changes, others focused on economic issues such as wages and the price of bread. Some supported industrialisation, others opposed it. There was little unity betwen these groups with their various aims.

Peaceful protest was sometimes dealt with brutally. In 1819, over 60 000 people, including many women and children, attended a public meeting at St Peter's Fields, a large open space near Manchester. They went to listen to a speech by radical political speaker Henry Hunt, advocating the reform of parliament. The local magistrates (judges) aided by the local **yeomanry** were determined to stop this assembly. An armed cavalry charged the crowd and killed 11 people. This became known as 'Peterloo' – a sarcastic reference to the battle of Waterloo, in which the British army had played a key role in the defeat of France. While many people agreed that this was a serious overreaction by the local forces of law and order, it did demonstrate that many of the middle-class factory owners and shopkeepers, who made up the yeomanry and magistrates, were less than enthusiastic about radical reform, and the agitation died down.

Figure 2.17: A cartoon showing Britannia defying the 'monster' republicanism attempting to cross from Europe. The author uses satire and ridicule, giving republicanism a thick French accent in which to threaten England: 'All de Nations in Europe has <u>accepted</u> de Liberty la Francois. – Now Me be delegated to you from de <u>Great Nation</u> to offer you de same Liberty. Which if you refuse to accept, you call de Vengeance of de Great Nation upon you. We <u>will</u> come and plant the Tree of Liberty in your Hearts & make your Nation <u>free</u>'. How do humour and imagery combine to reveal how the cartoonist truly feels about republicanism?

KEY TERM

Yeomanry: A force made up of local volunteers, usually of middle-class background. It had been created to support the regular army in case of invasion by France during the Napoleonic Wars, but was now used to prevent domestic disorder.

When major political and constitutional reform did happen in Britain, the influence of industrialisation was indirect rather than direct. Between 1829 and 1830, a series of events happened to raise the issue of political reform.

A bad harvest in 1829 led to bread prices rising rapidly and real difficulties in rural areas, while a trade downturn led to high unemployment in urban areas. This caused serious distress for thousands. Meanwhile, among many middle-class men, there was growing dissatisfaction that the Conservative government, which had been in power since 1812, was no longer governing in their interests but was more concerned with farming and preserving aristocratic status and power. In fact, the party was badly divided between those resistant to any change and those who felt change was needed to survive.

There was growing dissatisfaction too with the system of representation in parliament. It was felt to be corrupt and out of date, having changed little since the 16th century. Many felt it was dominated by the aristocracy and agricultural interests, and that industry was being ignored. Many of the new industrial towns did not send MPs to parliament, while towns which had been important in the 16th century, but had declined in population, still did. Some small towns, known as 'rotten boroughs', made possible to buy the right to represent them in parliament. The king died in 1830, precipitating a general election that the ruling Conservatives lost. It was extremely rare for a sitting government to lose an election, as they had the means to manage them to their advantage. However, the 1830 election brought in a new, more liberal, government under Earl Grey – a long-time advocate of reform.

The years between 1830 and 1832 were dominated by campaigning for parliamentary reform. An unusual and critical factor in the final result, was the alliance between a middle class determined to reform a political system which they felt was no longer acting in their interest, and a working class with its own set of grievances. A series of organisations demanding political change developed. In 1831, the National Union of the Working Classes was set up in London, demanding the vote for all adult males. There were other organisations with a purely middle-class membership. For some who joined these groups, political reform was the main objective. However, others believed that these organisations were the only way out of poverty and hunger. Some were skilled workers in employment; others were unemployed unskilled factory workers; still others were handloom weavers opposed to industrialisation.

This mass of protest, with the middle class clearly joining with the working class, was critical in forcing king, parliament and government into major constitutional and political reform.

ACTIVITY 2.19

How far do you think the demand for political change caused by earlier economic change? What other causes could be considered? Which was the most important and why?

Make a list of all possible causes of political change and place them in order of importance according to your view. Explain which you think are the most important and why.

The Great Reform Act, 1832

In 1832, parliament was finally reformed. Aristocratic control over the political process was reduced. The new industrial towns were able to send MPs to parliament. The proportion of middle-class men from a background in manufacturing, commence, banking and industry did increase (but not substantially). Government and parliament would become more responsive to the wishes of the middle class. The middle class gained the most from the extension of the franchise (the right to vote). This proved to be an important step on the path towards full democracy in Britain.

It could be claimed that the working class gained nothing from the 1832 act. The few men from the working class who had the vote before 1832 lost it, as now only men of property could vote. It was not until 1867 that the better-paid working man had the right to vote. The new parliament elected in 1832 looked like the old one in its membership. The laws that it passed in the next decade did little to help the working class. Disappointment with the 1832 reforms led to further demands for change, notably the Chartist movement.

The part that the working class had played in these reforms was, however, important. The mass protests of the skilled and unskilled, in both rural and urban areas, as well as serious rioting, played a critical role in persuading the government – terrified of a middle-class/working class alliance along the lines of what had happened in France in the 1790s – to make concessions.

ACTIVITY 2.20

Why did political reform come to Britain in 1832? Identify and make notes on the key reasons and make sure you explain which was the most important and why. What did the 1832 Reform Act reveal about the British class system?

The reforms of 1832 rewarded and empowered the middle classes, but many-working class men, both skilled and unskilled, educated and illiterate, felt they had done much of the work and taken most of the risks in getting parliament reformed, and instead of gaining from it, they actually suffered as a result.

Figure 2.18: This cartoon from December 1836 comments on conditions before and after the New Poor Law. The text on the left of the image reads 'Wot only one Pound o Roast Beef and half Pound o Pudding for a Man's <u>Christmas Dinner?</u> & no Horse Raddish!! I'm bless'd if they'll get any body to stop in the <u>Work House</u> if they goes on <u>Starving</u> em in this ere Way.' and the text on the right reads: 'Wot that ain't good enough for yer eh? Just think on the many poor creaters as ain't got no <u>Christmas Dinner</u> at all. I spose you'll be wanting a <u>Fire</u> next.'

ACTIVITY 2.21

How does the cartoon in Figure 2.18 add to your understanding of contemporary debate concerning the New Poor Law? What contrasts do you notice between the two panels in this cartoon, and what do you think they signify? Who do you think the intended audience was for this source?

The New Poor Law, 1834

One of the first actions taken by the first government formed in the newly reformed House of Commons was to deal with the problem of poverty in Britain. The government was well aware of the part played by an angry working class in bringing Britain close to revolution in 1829–32. A repeat of such disorder was to be avoided at all costs. Parliament was made up of wealthy men who had no wish to pay increasingly heavy taxes to support the poor. For a variety of reasons, there was a strong demand to change the old Poor Law which dated back to the 16th century. It was modified in the 1790s by what became known as the 'Speenhamland System', named after the village where the local magistrates first developed the reform. This system was mostly used in the south of England.

- It continued to be paid for by local landowners and led to their contributions increasing. (This was known as the Poor Rate.)
- It depended on the size of the recipient's family; the larger the family the more help it received.
- It varied with the price of bread, so, if prices rose, the recipients were paid more.

The system was widely disliked, as it was expensive and many felt it didn't encourage the unemployed to find work. Landowners, who paid good wages and increased them in times of high food prices, resented having to subsidise others who paid lower wages and had their employees' wages made up out of the Poor Rate.

In fact, the system was simply was unable to cope with the sort of mass unemployment that could happen in industrial towns with a trade downturn, and the riots of 1829–32 demonstrated that it was not working.

As was increasingly becoming the custom, the government set up a Royal Commission in 1832 to investigate and recommend action about poverty in Britain. The commission, dominated by middle-class men, took care to ensure that the evidence taken supported their ideas and exaggerated the failings of the old system. They produced a long report, which few really understood, in 1834.

This resulted in parliament passing the Poor Law Amendment Act the same year, with the intention of creating a welfare system designed to deal with the new industrial society. Under the act, which aimed to give as little welfare as possible and cut the costs to landowners, the Speenhamland System was abolished. All those needing help would only get it in a workhouse. There would be separate types of workhouse; some for destitute women and children, the old and the sick; others for unemployed men able to work. So, men and women would be separated. This was intended to prevent the poor having too many children. Those capable of work would be made to do tedious, monotonous jobs and wear distinctive prison-type clothing. The inmates' standard of living was deliberately made less comfortable than that of the lowest paid labourer outside the workhouse.

The Poor Law was centrally monitored by the government in London, but was managed by locally elected, middle-class officials: men who actually had to pay support for the poor. Naturally, they had a vested interest in paying as little as possible.

For many in the working class, this act was very disappointing. Not only had no working-class men been given the vote in the 1832 Reform Act, but the men of property who made up the new parliament had also passed an act purely in their own financial interests. The poor felt the law was a direct attack on them. While there might have been some who took advantage of old Poor Law, the New Poor Law seemed to view poverty as a crime, punishable by a sentence in the workhouse.

These were called **Bastilles** and were bitterly resented. Often the intended segregation between the old, women and children and those men capable of work did not happen, and all were treated equally badly. Riots often occurred when the workhouses were being built. Opposition in the textile areas in the north was strong, as the new system could not cope with mass unemployment when a whole town would be out of work during a trade downturn. In some northern industrial towns, the old Poor Law had been sensibly adapted to deal with this event and had no need of what proved to be an unworkable system. Nonetheless, the New Poor Law remained for the rest of the 19th century. It was hated and often brutally administered.

KEY TERM

Bastilles: A sarcastic reference to the old French prison famous for having been stormed during the French Revolution (see Chapter 1).

Demands for political reform, including the Chartists

The Reform Act failed to provide the vote, or hope of any improvement to the working class, a new movement emerged in the 1830s called Chartism. Many working-class families felt it might bring real improvement to lives so affected by industrial and agricultural change. A series of factors gave rise to this working-class movement, which lasted from the late 1830s until 1848. Bad harvests in 1837–38 led to high food prices. There was severe unemployment in 1842 and further bad harvests in 1847–48 led inevitably to food price rises again. The main incidents of Chartist activity and protest happened during these years.

In the 1830s, the trade-union movement had failed to improve wages or working conditions. At the same time, reforms and Acts of Parliament had done little for the working classes. They had not enfranchised them, but had produced the despised New Poor Law. Parliament had concerned itself with issues that were of no interest to a Lancashire mill worker. The slave trade was abolished in 1833 and millions of pounds were given in compensation to the slave owners – though nothing to the slaves – while nothing was done to deal with poverty in rural Britain or the situation of the handloom weavers.

There was, however, growing literacy among the working classes and a cheap radical press encouraging action. There were also enough educated and able men who could provide organisation and leadership to the angry working classes.

Chartists

In 1838, a small group of skilled working-class men, led by Francis Place and William Lovett, met in London and drew up a programme which they hoped would unite the working classes across Britain. They hoped that the purely political objectives of their programme would enable all the many different aims and complaints of the British working class to be dealt with.

This 'People's Charter' had six seemingly simple points:

- Universal manhood suffrage – all men would have the vote in national and local elections.
- There would be no property qualification required before someone could stand for election to parliament. In the 1830s, only men who owned property could become MPs, which excluded almost all working-class men.
- Annual parliaments would be held. There had to be an election for a parliament every year.

- Equal representation – each area that sent an MP to parliament had to contain the same number of voters. There were wide variations in this in the 1830s.
- Payment for MPs – in the 1830s, MPs were unpaid. This meant that only wealthy men could afford to become MPs.
- The ballot, or voting in secret – in the 1830s, voting was done in public. This often meant that landowners and rich factory owners could dismiss or otherwise punish those that voted against their interests. It also led to substantial corruption.

There were three main periods of Chartist activity, in 1838–39, 1842 and 1848–89. All were linked to periods of high food prices or high unemployment. **Petitions** were sent to parliament each time, containing millions of signatures requesting the implementation of the charter. Parliament met none of the demands. There were huge rallies throughout the country, often with over 50 000 attending to listen to the Chartist speakers.

KEY TERM

Petition: A written request delivered to parliament, signed by citizens, asking it to take steps specified in the petition, such as pass a particular new law.

Figure 2.19: An illustration from 1848, showing the Chartist rally on Kennington Common in London. How useful is this image in understanding the growth of Chartism?

In some cases, there was violence. For example, in South Wales in 1839 a group of miners and iron workers marched on the town of Newport, in what became known as the Newport Rising. Some of them had weapons with them. Some of the marchers just wanted to demand the Charter and protest at the arrest of a prominent Chartist speaker, but others had more revolutionary intentions. Fearing the worst, the local authorities brought in soldiers (police forces were still in their infancy) and they shot 12 of the demonstrators. The Chartist organiser, who had tried hard to make the protest peaceful, was arrested and transported to Australia. Over 500 Chartists were arrested nationally and many were imprisoned.

There was further trouble in 1842, especially in the north of England and the Midlands, which led to some damage to factory machinery, but, again, once employment rose with a period of rapid railway building, unrest died out.

The free press played an important part in Chartism. One of the many publications that supported it, the *Northern Star*, which had been strongly opposed to the Poor Law, came out as the major Chartist newspaper in the 1840s, selling more than any of the other provincial newspapers read by the middle class.

The final activity of the movement came in 1848. A huge demonstration was planned in London to try to really put pressure on Parliament to adopt the Charter. However, the meeting was banned and far fewer protesters turned up than anticipated anyway. The presence of 10 000 specially recruited policemen would have frightened many people and may have stopped them from attending. The Chartist leader at the time, a charismatic and radical Irish speaker called Feargus O'Connor, went to parliament on his own to present the final Chartist petition. The large numbers of signatures on this final petition, like the large numbers attending what were called 'monster meetings', were intended to put pressure on the government and parliament, but the petition was unsuccessful. That was the end of Chartism. The 1850s were to be a period of rising employment and real wages, while food prices dropped and there was less to protest about.

Why did Chartism fail to achieve its objectives?

Like many working-class movements, Chartism was badly divided and largely fuelled by hunger and unemployment. When conditions improved, the movement declined. The government usually didn't react with unnecessary violence or harshness. The officer in charge of the troops keeping order, General Napier, was generally sympathetic to many of the Chartists aspirations and did not want to fight the movement. The movement itself faced divisions over many issues, for example:

- the use of force or peaceful protest
- a revolution or moderate change
- support for industrialisation or opposition to it (such as the handloom weavers)
- collaboration with the middle class or staying separate
- whether Chartists were religious or not
- wanting the focus to be on education and banning alcohol, or not wanting to ban alcohol
- a focus on self-improvement within the working class or more action by the government to improve living and working conditions
- hate for O'Connor (a brilliant speaker but no organiser) or support for him
- whether Chartists were socialists or not.

Given the many different objectives and dependence on prevailing economic conditions, it was perhaps not surprising that the movement seemed to achieve little.

So, a combination of rising prosperity, firm government action, evidence of the strong alliance between the aristocracy and middle class, and its own many internal divisions, led to Chartist failure in the short term. Ultimately, however, all its demands were met, except annual parliaments. From that point on, governments learned to consider more carefully working-class interests, and the working class itself might have learned lessons about how to gain improvements in the future.

ACTIVITY 2.22

One early 19th-century writer wrote, 'I defy you to agitate a man on a full stomach'. In your opinion, how much influence did hunger have on all protest in this period? What other factors could be considered? Make a list of other causative factors of protest and explain why they should be considered.

KEY CONCEPT

Significance

Historians are likely to regard something as 'significant' if it had important consequences or if it tells us a lot about what was happening in a particular place, at a particular time.

The Chartist movement failed to achieve its aims by 1850, but that doesn't mean it was historically unimportant. Discuss with a partner reasons why the Chartist movement could be described as significant. Which reasons do you think are the most important? What connections can you see between these reasons?

Origins of organised labour

Trade unions

Trade unions were to have limited impact on the lives of the working classes in this period. This is perhaps surprising given that more and more people were working closely together in factories, often with valid grievances such as low wages and poor working conditions.

KEY TERM

Trade union: A group of workers who join together to defend their work-related interests and put concerns to their managers. They usually aim to improve pay and working conditions.

Although technically illegal throughout the 18th century, trade unions did exist. The ruling class did not like the idea of the working people coming together to attempt to improve wages, working hours or working conditions. Called 'combinations', groups of men did organise together, usually in towns. Invariably they were skilled workers in specific trades, such as tailors or watchmakers. The reasons for setting up their organisations tended to be:

- to provide insurance benefits for their members, in case of illness, or benefits to their widows and children if the working man died
- to give themselves more bargaining power against employers
- to restrict entry to their professions, insisting on long periods of training, to protect their status and income.

The groups tended to be conservative and defensive, and were anxious to exclude unskilled workers. Their main reason for existing was to preserve the interests of their members, and they were not interested in wider social, economic or political issues. There is little evidence of any 'combinations' among the unskilled, either in agriculture or industry during the course of the 18th century.

During the period of fear caused by the French Revolution and the wars against France in the late 1790s, the illegality of these early unions was reinforced in 1799 and 1800 by new Combination Laws. Frightened of any revolutionary activity or restriction of trade, the government made membership of a union punishable by imprisonment. There was an intense fear of conspiracy at the time, and the combinations were seen as potentially dangerous conspiracies because they tried to keep their work secret.

Despite this 'paranoia', there is little evidence of much prosecution of the combinations. Generally, they were tolerated by authority, particularly locally.

Membership of unions of skilled men began to grow in the boom years of the wars, and there were successful strikes for higher pay and better conditions by shipbuilders and cotton spinners. Economic depression and government repression after 1815 reduced union activity, and an attempt to coordinate it on a national level in 1818 failed totally.

In 1824, however, the Combination Laws were repealed as part of a relaxation by parliament of a range of repressive laws which had been passed to deal with the perceived crisis after Peterloo. Trade unions were now legal, and from this came a sudden outbreak of strikes, which led to the new law being modified in 1825. This stated that unions were still legal, but could only negotiate on hours and wages. There was no right to strike, for example.

It was still possible to prosecute union leaders who tried to improve conditions for their members. Striking miners, for example, were prosecuted under an old 'Master and Servant' law, which had been designed for a totally different purpose. The most famous anti-union action occurred in the village of Tolpuddle in Dorset in 1834. A local Methodist preacher, George Loveless, tried to form a union to improve conditions for agricultural workers. Well aware that local farmers would be hostile, members swore an oath of secrecy. When discovered, Loveless was prosecuted under an old Act of Parliament against secret oaths, and was transported to Australia as one of the Tolpuddle 'martyrs'. This stopped any further activity among agricultural labourers.

Those who wished specifically to improve wages and working conditions were distracted by the campaigns for the 1832 Reform Bill and later the Chartist movement. Attempts to form national unions by trades such as carpenters failed in 1827. There was an attempt to form a 'Grand National Consolidated Trade Union' to gain an eight-hour day. This was inspired by the socialist Robert Owen in 1834 but it also failed.

Overall, trade unions achieved little in this period. The defensive and conservative aims of the skilled men contrasted with the perhaps more radical ambitions of the unskilled. There was also the division between those who had political objectives such as parliamentary reform, and those who simply wanted more pay, shorter hours and better working conditions. The vast majority of working-class men did not join a union in this period. What unions did exist tended to be small, local and confined to skilled men whose work was in high demand. The radical press that developed to support the skilled unions tended to put forward socialist and anti-capitalist ideas. These ensured little middle-class support and felt alien to most of the working class. The development of mass trade-union membership and its real impact on economic and political life would come later in the 19th century.

Cooperative societies

Some members of the working classes attempted to improve conditions for themselves. This was because of the failure of Chartism, the fact that trade unions did not achieve much for the working classes, and the reluctance of the government and Parliament to act positively to improve the lives of working-class people. An example of this was the foundation of what became known as the Cooperative Movement.

In 1844, 28 working-class people set up a shop in Rochdale, Lancashire. They were mainly skilled workmen in regular employment and idealists possibly influenced by some of the socialist ideas of Robert Owen; several had a background in the Chartist movement.

The shop, initially selling food, but soon also clothes and other necessities, was owned and run by its members. The prices were reasonable, as the shop was not designed to be profitable, but rather any surplus income was paid back to those members who shopped there – and anyone could become a member. It was run, democratically, by its members. Unusually, women could also be members and vote at meetings. It was completely neutral towards any religion or political party and it had a further motive to encourage education for all. This was to be the start of a vast retail operation that would cover the whole country. Local cooperative societies sprang up everywhere, giving many people their first opportunity to participate in democratic management. These societies later played a significant role in the formation of the Labour Party, which was set up specifically to get working-class men into the House of Commons, giving that class a political voice for the first time.

ACTIVITY 2.23

Work in a group to discuss why the working class was unable to improve its living and working conditions in this period. Then consider to what extent repression by the state was the main reason for the lack of improvement in working-class conditions in this period.

Government reaction to demands for change

The reactions by government to protest and demands for political reforms varied. Sometimes the government simply ignored them, sometimes they opposed them and sometimes they agreed to them. The government rarely took positive initiatives to help the working classes with the difficult impact of industrialisation. Its approach tended to reflect the social and economic interests of the upper and middle classes who had the vote and were overwhelmingly represented in parliament. The reaction to Luddism and Chartism was always to maintain law and order and the property rights of landowners and manufacturers. This was sometimes backed by force and the law. The government was consistently opposed to the ideas behind trade unionism.

When faced with real pressure and the threat of possible revolution, however – as in 1832 – it made concessions. Those concessions were limited, though, and designed to win back the middle-class support which had briefly deserted it. Although the government was well aware that the Corn Laws had a negative impact on food prices, it maintained them until 1846. When famine struck in Ireland, then part of the United Kingdom, in the 1840s, it declined to take any action to prevent or mitigate it. Over a million people died of hunger in Ireland even though Britain was the richest country in the world at the time, and had the ships, means and money to bring aid. Meanwhile, the government passed Factory Acts and the New Poor Law, but, in both cases, took care to protect the interests of the classes it represented, and rarely the interests of those it did not.

ACTIVITY 2.24

In the period covered here, France had three political revolutions: in 1789, 1830 and 1848. In 1848, Britain was one of only two countries in Europe that did not have a 'political' revolution. Why do you think this was the case?

Reflection: How did you decide on the most important reasons? Join another student and explain to each other how you made your choices. Did you make different choices, and if so, why do you think this was? Following your discussion, do you think your approach was effective in answering the question?

Exam-style questions

Source analysis questions

Read the four sources, then answer both parts of question 1.

SOURCE A

Robert Owen, factory owner and socialist writer, 1831

The practice of employing children in mills of 6–7–8 years old was discontinued in my factories and parents advised to acquire health and education for their children until at least the age of 10. The children were taught reading, writing and arithmetic from age 5 to 10 in the village school without any expense to their parents. Their homes were made more comfortable, their streets were improved, the best foodstuffs were sold to them at low rates and fuel and clothes were obtained in the same manner. Those employed became more industrious, sober and healthy, faithful to their employers and kind to each other.

Robert Owen, Selected Works *(Farnham, Ashgate, 1993) [author doesn't have page ref]*

SOURCE B

From a Factory Inspectors Report, 1843

Twelve hours daily work is more than enough for anyone. However desirable it might be to prevent excessive working, there are great difficulties in interfering with the labour of adult men. The case is very different for women. Not only are they much less free agents, but are physically incapable of bearing work for the same length of time as men and the deterioration of their health has far worse consequences for society. The substitution of female for male labour, recently greatly increased, has worse consequences for the social condition of the working classes because women are withdrawn from domestic duties.

Source: E Royston Pike, Human Documents of the Industrial Revolution, London: George Allen and Unwin 1966, pp.98-99

SOURCE C

J.R. McCulloch, Scottish economist, 1835

We do not say that the statements made in the Poor Law Commissioners Report are completely without foundation, but we believe that they may have been extremely exaggerated. That some abuses exist in some factories is certain, but these are rare and generally factory workers, including children, are healthy and contented as any class of people. Were children forbidden to work in factories four fifths of them would be thrown out of work and onto the streets and acquire a taste for idleness and the many other bad practices present amongst the worst inhabitations of our cities. Conditions for the poor would be ten times worse but for the factories. They have been the best schools for the children. Besides taking the children out of harm's way, they have got them in to regular, orderly and good working habits.

https://archive.org/details/edinburghreviewo35/

SOURCE D

After conversations with old farm labourers recalling their lives in the 1820s and 1830s

These poor labourers, spiritless slaves, moulded by long years of extreme poverty and constant oppression, finally rose against their hard masters and smashed the agricultural machines, burnt haystacks and broke into the houses of the rich. The introduction of the threshing machines was a terrible blow to them. Wages were only 35p a week, not really sufficient to keep a family from starvation and clothed only in rags. Unless they broke the law and poached animals for their cooking pots they would not have lived. It was customary to get rid of the men after the harvest and leave them to exist on the old Poor Law in the bitter winter months. Alongside these there were the aged and the sick, and the young men who had not yet got a job.

Source: Adapted from W.H. Hudson, A Shepherd's Life*, published in 1910*

1 **a** Compare and contrast the attitudes towards factory reform in sources A and B.

b 'All workers were treated harshly in this period.' How far do sources A to D support this view?

Essay based questions

Answer both parts of the questions below.

2 **a** Explain why British towns grew so rapidly in the period 1780–1850.

b 'The rich got richer and the poor got poorer.' To what extent is this an accurate picture of Britain in the period 1780–1850?

3 **a** Explain why there was so much popular unrest in Britain after 1815.

b Evaluate the reasons why there was limited improvement in the living and working conditions of the British working class in this period.

Sample answer

Explain why there was so much popular unrest in Britain after 1815.

There were three main, interconnected, reasons for the growth of unpopular unrest in Britain after 1815. One was the growth in the numbers of middle-class men, increasingly educated and wealthy, who did not have the right to vote and lived in towns which did not have representation in parliament. They disliked the control that the aristocracy had over the government and parliament. Another reason was hunger. The wars with France ended in 1815 and thousands of soldiers and sailors were now unemployed. There was no welfare system to support them. With a growing population and fewer workers needed in the countryside, thousands also headed for the towns in search of work. In many of the new factories there were harsh working conditions and the factory workers often had to live in bad housing. There was a great deal of poverty in rural areas as agricultural changes meant that fewer workers were needed, and often only for a few months a year. Trade unions were banned until the 1820s, so many workers were not able to have their grievances seen to. It was the mixture of the middle classes wanting political change, and the working classes, in both towns and in rural areas, wanting an end to their hunger and improved living and working conditions that explains why there was so much unrest. The government, largely controlled by the aristocracy, did little to help and

was more concerned with stamping out trouble than curing problems.

> This is a competent response. There is good focus on the question. There is nothing irrelevant there. There is a good range of valid points and they are sensibly developed. It gives reasons why both the middle and working classes had grievances, and each point is backed up with relevant detail – for example, the middle class because they did not have political representation and the working class because of unemployment and the lack of any welfare system. The answer centres on explaining *why* there was the unrest, and not just describing it or listing the grievances. The response also deals clearly on the 'so much' part of the question. The level of knowledge and understanding is also sound.

Summary

After working through this chapter, make sure you understand the following key points:

- how the geography, natural resources and social, political and economic conditions in Britain in the middle of the 18th century provided the vital basis for future industrialisation

- identification of the principal factors that enabled rapid and large-scale industrialisation to take place and how change stimulated even more change

- the social and economic implications of rapid industrialisation, particularly on the growth of urban areas, and the impact it had directly on the lives of so many citizens

- how industrialisation also led to political and constitutional change.

Further reading

Daunton, M.J. (1995). *Progress and Poverty: An Economic and Social History of Britain 1700–1850*. Oxford: Oxford University Press. (This covers in depth every aspect of society and the economy in the period studied.)

Evans, E. (2001). *The Forging of the Modern State: Early Industrial Britain 1783–1870*. London: Routledge. (This is particularly good on the politics of the period, especially on the 1832 Reform Act. Part Three covers topics including the Poor Law, factory reform and Chartism well.)

Morgan, K. (2004). *The Birth of Industrial Britain: Social Change, 1750–1850*. Harlow: Longman. (This is a good introduction to the topic, with useful chapters on population change and its impact and also on the changes in transport and their impact.)

Griffin, E. (2010). *A Short History of the Industrial Revolution.* **New York: Palgrave.** (While perhaps a little more 'technical' than some books, it is useful in the opening two chapters on the various debates that have arisen over the causes and results of the revolution.)

The UK's Historical Association has a wide range of resources specifically designed for AS and A Level students, and all those resources are available online for students in schools around the world, or for download. There are articles on, for example:

- the causes of the Industrial Revolution
- the transport revolution
- the commercial revolution
- Oastler's campaign against 'slavery' in Yorkshire
- Chartism
- child labour in Britain.

There are also podcasts to download on:

- the Industrial Revolution and the cities
- child labour in Britain.

Chapter 3
Liberalism and nationalism in Germany, 1815–71

Learning objectives

In this chapter you will:

- understand why it took so long to achieve German unification
- analyse the part played by the forces of liberalism and nationalism in 19th-century Germany
- learn why the 1848–49 revolutions occurred in Germany, and assess their significance
- understand the role of a key individual, Otto von Bismarck, in bringing about historical change.

Timeline

Jun 1815 German Confederation is established

Jun 1840 Friedrich Wilhelm (Frederick William) IV becomes king of Prussia

Jan 1834 *Zollverein* is founded

Mar 1848 Revolution begins in Austria and Germany

Jun 1849 Collapse of Frankfurt Parliament

Mar 1850 Erfurt Union of German states formed

Nov 1850 Humiliation of Olmütz: Prussia abandons Erfurt Union plan

Jan 1861 Wilhelm (William) I becomes king of Prussia

Sep 1862 Bismarck becomes minister-president (prime minister) of Prussia

Jan 1864 Austro-Prussian War against Denmark begins

Jun 1866 Austro-Prussian War

Aug 1866 Treaty of Prague

Jun 1867 North German Confederation set up under Prussian leadership

Jul 1870 Franco-Prussian War begins

Jan 1871 German Empire established

Before you start

Look at the map in Figure 3.1, which shows central Europe in 1815, at the end of the **Napoleonic Wars**. List the main states which then lay within the area that was to become Germany.

Figure 3.1: The German Confederation in 1815 (map by Sperber, J. (2004). *Germany, 1800–1870*. Oxford: Oxford University Press.

95

🔑 KEY TERMS

The Napoleonic Wars: A conflict between Napoleon Bonaparte's France and alliances of various European states, which began in 1803 and ended with Napoleon's defeat in 1815. (See Chapter 1.)

Confederation: A loose association of states which retain some control over their own policies.

3.1 What were the causes of the revolutions in 1848–49?

You will have noted that Germany did not exist in 1815 as a single unified country. Instead it consisted of a series of different states. Much of the territory lay within the boundaries of an organisation known as the German **Confederation**. This chapter explains how these states came to be united in the mid-19th century.

Figure 3.2: Delegates at the Congress of Vienna in 1814. What information would you use to asses this image's usefulness as a historical source?

The impact of Metternich's System on the states of Germany

Before the Napoleonic Wars, most of the area that we know today as Germany had been part of the medieval Holy Roman Empire, a collection of semi-independent states under the Austrian emperor. This had collapsed in 1806, as a result of Napoleon's invasion. He reorganised the west German states into a single organisation, the Confederation of the Rhine.

The French armies brought with them the ideas of the 18th-century Enlightenment, an intellectual movement which stressed the power of reason and sought to sweep away outdated political and social structures. For example, they replaced the diverse laws and judicial processes of the various German states with their own legal system. In reaction, many German thinkers began to emphasise the distinctiveness of their own culture. Romantic writers stressed the importance of emotion and imagination, in response to the rational ideas of the French invaders, and they encouraged interest in the historical past of the German people. Particularly

influential was the writer J.G. Herder, who popularised the concept of *Volksgeist* ('spirit of the people'), the idea that each nation had its own individual identity, based around a shared heritage and language. These were the first stirrings of a sense of German nationhood.

German people began to understand the importance of uniting against the French occupation. After its defeat by Napoleon, Prussia, one of the most important states, reorganised its government and army. This enabled it to join with Austria and Russia to expel the French forces. The decisive Battle of Leipzig (1813), a major defeat for Napoleon, helped to develop a sense of national pride. It was later commemorated as a symbol of emerging German identity, with a 91-metre high monument constructed on the site to mark its centenary, even though German-speaking troops had fought on both sides.

The post-war settlement

In September 1814, a congress of European nations met in Vienna to discuss the problems caused by the wars, and to establish new boundaries on the continent. The most important states represented at this series of meetings were Austria, Prussia, Britain and Russia. France, whose monarchy had been restored after the defeat of Napoleon (see Chapter 1), attended the congress but had no decision-making powers. The decisions made at this meeting changed the face of Europe.

The European leaders faced a challenge from the related ideas of **liberalism** and **nationalism**, which were products of the French revolutionary era. The representatives of the countries who met at Vienna regarded these ideas with anxiety.

 KEY TERMS

Liberalism: A belief that government should be reformed to allow as much personal and economic freedom as possible. Nineteenth-century liberals also favoured the concept of representative assemblies, although these would not necessarily be elected by all adults.

Nationalism: A belief that people with a common language, culture or history should have the right to govern themselves, and that the boundaries between states should be based on this idea.

These leaders were political and social conservatives. They were determined to restore stability after the years of upheaval caused by the revolution in France and the movements of French armies across the continent. They wanted to recreate the rule of the old royal families who had lost power during the previous 20 years.

The most significant individual at the Congress was the Austrian foreign minister, **Prince Klemens von Metternich**. The Austrian Empire had a population of 25 million and extended over 647 000 square kilometres. It comprised present-day Austria and Hungary, together with a range of other territories in central and eastern Europe. In addition to Austrians (who spoke German) and Hungarians, among the many different ethnic groups under its rule were Czechs, Slovaks, Croats, Poles and even some northern Italians. The majority of the empire's subjects were Roman Catholics, loyal to the Pope.

The 'Metternich System' was designed to maintain the rule of absolute monarchy in the Austrian Empire, and the continuation of similar political systems in other European states. Metternich was deeply suspicious of change, once describing the words 'liberty' and 'equality' as the source of evil because they were liable to mislead the masses of the people. He was aware that the empire was a fragile

PRINCE KLEMENS VON METTERNICH (1773–1859)

Metternich was Austria's foreign minister from 1809 to 1848 and its chancellor (chief minister) as well from 1821 to 1848. He played a key role in creating the alliance of Austria, Prussia and Russia which defeated Napoleonic France in 1813–14. Metternich was a conservative whose main aim was to uphold international order to protect Austria's interests. He was determined to suppress liberalism and nationalism. Metternich fell from power when the 1848 revolutions broke out, and went into exile. He returned to Austria in 1851, after the power of the monarchy had been re-established, but he never again played an important role in politics. Always sure of his own abilities, Metternich famously said of himself that 'error has never approached my spirit'.

97

structure and that nationalism threatened the rule of its royal family, the Habsburgs. He feared that if Germans, or members of other nationalities, were allowed their independence, the empire might collapse. He avoided stationing troops in the parts of the empire from which they came, as he believed this would reduce the chances of organised nationalist opposition developing. His was a negative policy, which relied on repressive methods such as press censorship. He created a network of secret agents who spied on political radicals and intercepted their correspondence. The Metternich System kept the peace in Europe, but at a cost of stoking up resentment from the peoples under its rule.

The German Confederation

The Metternich System's solution for Germany was to reorganise it into a confederation (*Bund*) of 39 states under the control of Austria. These varied considerably in size, from kingdoms like Bavaria and Saxony to self-governing city states like Hamburg. It was not a united Germany and in fact the intention was to avoid such a development.

The Confederation was based on the boundaries of the old Holy Roman Empire. It contained some non-Germans, for example Czechs in Bohemia (a region in present-day Czech Republic) and French-speaking people in Luxembourg. At the same time, it excluded some areas with German-speaking populations, including parts of Prussia. Presiding over this structure was a conference of ambassadors from the member states, known as the Diet, which met in Frankfurt. The Diet controlled the foreign policies of the member states, but the individual rulers continued to manage their own internal affairs and the Confederation never developed a strong identity of its own. It did not have its own civil service and there was no attempt to develop it as an economic area. In 1821, an attempt to create a federal defence force failed as a result of conflict over who should command such an organisation and how it should be funded.

The structure of the Confederation was designed to maintain Austria's power over the German states. The Diet was always chaired by the Austrian representative. Austria also had a veto over any attempt to change the constitution, and it could usually count on the support of the main southern states – Bavaria, Württemberg, Baden and Hesse-Darmstadt – in a vote. These states were near each other and, with their predominantly Catholic populations, were culturally more sympathetic to Austria than to northern, Protestant, Prussia. The rulers of these southern states granted their subjects constitutions, with certain civil rights in law, but they retained the real power over the government. Most of the German princes followed Metternich's lead in governing in an authoritarian fashion.

The largest German state was Prussia, a mainly rural state in the north-east, with Berlin as its capital. It was ruled by an authoritarian monarch, King Friedrich Wilhelm III, who governed with the support of a conservative landowning class, the *Junkers*. The *Junkers* also provided the core of the Prussian army's officer class. In the 1815 peace settlement, Prussia gained a great deal of territory, including the Rhineland in the west, an industrialised area separated from the main part of Prussia. This doubled the population of Prussia to more than 10 million. It was the only possible future rival to Austria for the domination of Germany, but at this stage it did not offer a challenge to its more assertive southern neighbour. With their conservative, monarchical forms of government, both Prussia and Austria had an interest in preventing political change in Germany.

The influence of liberal ideas and the emergence of a middle class

Liberalism, which the Metternich System sought to suppress, was primarily an ideology of educated middle-class people. These consisted of two main groups: business people and professionals, such as lawyers, officials, doctors and university teachers. The growing business class was mainly concentrated in the cities of the Rhineland, and in ports such as Hamburg. They were not, for the most part, owners of large factories. Most were merchants who controlled small workshops or employed large numbers of domestic workers who produced goods in their own homes. In Prussia, they had benefited from the removal of privileges that had been enjoyed up to the early 19th century by the traditional **guilds**, allowing anyone to become an employer without first joining one of these organisations.

KEY TERMS

Guilds: Associations of merchants or craftspeople, often dating back to medieval times, set up to protect the interests of their members. By the 19th century, they were widely seen as outdated and restricting free competition.

The most successful merchants often had a well-developed sense of civic responsibility, which led them to become leaders in their communities. Many middle-class men acquired a university education, which was the gateway to the professions. Germany's university population doubled between 1817 and 1831. The emergence of the middle class was also instrumental in the growth of a thriving newspaper press, as levels of literacy and awareness of public affairs increased, as did the establishment of societies to promote cultural activities. The middle classes experienced a sense of exclusion from the upper levels of the social order, which were still dominated by a privileged landowning aristocracy. In Prussia, for example, the aristocratic *Junker* class, which owned large agricultural estates in the eastern part of the country, controlled most of the higher positions in the army and civil service. The desire of many members of the middle classes to gain access to the opportunities offered by these public service careers made liberal ideas attractive to them.

Middle-class liberals wanted the people to have some say in government, but they did not want to see the establishment of fully democratic, **republican** systems of government. Liberals wanted countries to have representative assemblies or parliaments, elected by property-owning people like themselves, with **constitutional monarchy** as their preferred form of government. They also wanted certain guarantees of freedom, such as the rights to free speech and fair trials. This was a middle way between the authoritarian rule of an old-style monarchy, and democracy, which was seen as a dangerous system leading to mob rule and the seizure of power by masses of poor, uneducated people. Memories were still fresh of the French Revolution, which had been marked by violence against people and property.

Many political liberals also believed in the idea of laissez-faire economics (meaning 'leave it alone'), in which trade and business functioned without government interference. They wanted to remove **tariffs**, which restricted trade between countries. Economic liberals wanted to promote competition between businesses, which they argued would reduce prices and improve the quality of goods for consumers.

Underlying these ideas was an optimistic belief in humans' capacity for self-improvement. Liberals believed that, if given freedom, people would work to improve their circumstances, and this would help society as a whole to make progress.

It is difficult to gauge the influence of liberal ideas among the wider population. There was a great deal of intellectual excitement in the period 1815–48, with the publication of books and pamphlets and the staging of public lectures. It seems unlikely, however, that this activity reached more than a limited circle of

like-minded, well-off, educated people. Some liberals took their ideas to working-class areas, for example in Hamburg. In so far as workers were interested in political ideas, however, they tended to be **radicals** who favoured the creation of a democratic republic. Many of them expected to achieve this through popular uprising rather than rational debate.

 KEY TERMS

Republican: A form of government in which the head of state is not a hereditary ruler, such as a king, but a leader chosen directly or indirectly by those people in the state who have the right to vote.

Constitutional monarchy: A system of government in which a monarch's powers are limited by laws and rules.

Tariffs: Taxes or duties imposed by a government on goods imported into a country.

Radicals: People who want far-reaching changes to a political or social system.

Growth of nationalist ideas

How strong was nationalism in Germany?

In the first half of the 19th century, liberalism was often associated with nationalism. Nationalists believed that people of the same race, language, culture or history should be united in an independent nation of their own. They should govern themselves without interference from any other country. Support for national unity in Germany at this time was limited mainly to small sections of society – literate,

99

ACTIVITY 3.1

Draw a table like the example below to show the differences in mid-19th-century Europe between the three terms: liberalism, conservatism, radicalism. What types of people in society were most likely to support each idea?

	Liberalism	Conservatism	Radicalism
Definition of the term			
Examples of how each philosophy viewed human nature, society and politics			
Groups in society who supported the idea			

professional people and members of student associations known as the **Burschenschaften**. They were not typical of German society at the time. The majority of people were peasants who worked in agriculture. They faced a daily struggle for existence and were likely to have had little interest in abstract ideas of this kind.

Rather than a strong sense of national identity, most ordinary Germans felt greater loyalty to the region where they lived. Communications were poor and people were usually born, lived, married, worked and died in the same villages or neighbouring towns. Each region had its own traditions and customs. There was little desire to see the creation of a strong central government, which might impose additional taxes on the population, interfere with civil liberties and draft people into the armed forces.

In Germany, there was a common language and culture, but there was no religious unity. The southern states, such as Bavaria and Baden, were mainly Catholic. So, too, were the western provinces of the Rhineland and Westphalia, and West Prussia and Posen in the east, which Prussia had recently acquired. By contrast, Prussia proper, like most of northern Germany, was largely Protestant. In addition, the industrialised Rhineland was economically very different from the agricultural regions to the south and east. Germans enjoyed relatively high levels of literacy, but most early-19th-century newspapers concerned themselves with local rather than all-German issues.

As we have seen, a sense of German cultural nationalism first emerged in the late 18th and early 19th centuries, in reaction to the invasions by France. Between 1815 and 1848, these ideas filtered through to the educated middle classes. In the cities, some workers were influenced by more radical democratic ideas, based on the **sovereignty** of the people, but they remained a minority of the population.

> ## KEY TERMS
>
> **Burschenschaften:** Student organisations which developed after 1815 to promote ideas of German nationality, freedom and civil rights. (The singular is *Burschenschaft*.)
>
> **Sovereignty:** Ultimate political authority within a state.

The conservative reaction to nationalism

Metternich was successful in containing liberal and nationalist movements in the decade and a half after the Congress of Vienna. After a member of a liberal student association murdered a conservative writer and Russian spy,

August von Kotzebue, Metternich secured the agreement of the main German states in August 1819 for the repressive Carlsbad decrees. These had three key features:

- Universities: Each university was to have an 'extraordinary commissioner' assigned to it, to supervise the teaching programme. Liberal professors who undermined the established order were to be removed from their posts. Unauthorised student organisations were to be dissolved.
- The press: The member states of the Confederation, and the Diet, were to censor the newspaper press.
- A central investigating commission was to be set up in Mainz to root out organisations promoting liberal and nationalist ideas.

In time, however, liberalism took a stronger hold across Germany, especially in the south. This was partly in response to a revolution which occurred in Paris in July 1830. Charles X, last ruler of the old Bourbon dynasty, was replaced by King Louis Philippe, a representative of another branch of the French royal family. Charles had never been reconciled to the ending of old-style absolute monarchy, and had tried to govern like his predecessors had before 1789. By contrast, Louis Philippe established a parliamentary monarchy, based on the consent of the educated, property-owning middle class.

In four small German states – Saxony, Hanover, Hesse-Cassel and Brunswick – rulers were obliged to grant constitutions. Increased press freedom allowed more criticism of governments. In May 1832, nationalists organised the Hambach Festival in Bavaria, where liberal and nationalist ideas were openly discussed. A group called Young Germany was established, which called for a united Germany based on liberal principles.

Metternich reacted to these developments with predictable harshness. Although the organisers of the Hambach Festival were acquitted of wrongdoing by an ordinary court, they were then tried and imprisoned by a special police court. As in 1819, Metternich persuaded the princes to accept a new round of repressive measures. The Six Articles of June 1832 limited the rights of elected assemblies in states which had constitutions, and also declared the supremacy of federal law over the laws of the individual states. The Ten Articles, passed the following month, banned political meetings and festivals. It was even illegal to wear the colours of the student associations in scarves and ties.

In fact, there was never a real danger of revolution in Germany in this period. The liberals and nationalists were too few, and Austria could always count on its control of the Confederation, and the support of Prussia in suppressing opposition. In 1837, the new king of Hanover, Ernest Augustus, abolished the constitution that had been granted by his predecessor, and seven professors who objected lost their posts at the University of Göttingen. The 'Göttingen Seven' included Jacob and Wilhelm Grimm, two famous brothers whose collection of traditional folk tales helped to promote a sense of German culture.

This was typical of most German states at the time, where demands for political change failed to achieve anything substantial. Most of the princes ensured that they kept the levers of power in their hands when they granted constitutions. They retained the right to veto unwelcome proposals and could usually rely on the support of the upper houses of parliament, dominated by the aristocracy. The princes used a variety of means to limit the power of elected assemblies: restricting the vote to wealthy property owners, using **indirect voting** or having different classes vote in separate estates, with greater weighting attached to those in which the upper classes were represented. These devices had the effect of restricting the free expression of public opinion.

KEY TERM

Indirect voting: A system in which voters choose delegates who then elect the representatives to sit in a central assembly or parliament.

In Prussia a new king, **Friedrich Wilhelm IV**, succeeded to the throne in 1840. He was a complex and unstable character, who believed that God expected him to rule his subjects firmly but kindly. Friedrich Wilhelm combined this conviction with some more modern reforming instincts. He relaxed censorship and gave greater powers to the provincial Diets or assemblies, but he rejected demands for a single parliament for all Prussian territories.

FRIEDRICH WILHELM IV (1795–1861)

Friedrich Wilhelm IV became king of Prussia in 1840. He was a romantic and often unpredictable figure, who unintentionally caused liberals to believe that he sympathised with their ideas. He was really a conservative, whose handling of the revolution of 1848–49 left reformers disappointed. He was unable to rule for the last three years of his reign as a result of a stroke, and the country was governed by his younger brother, Wilhelm I, as regent.

ACTIVITY 3.2

An extract from the invitation to the Hambach Festival, a political demonstration held in Germany, 27 May 1832

> For the German, the seed of great events has not yet germinated. What he desires is a festival of hope; a festival not to celebrate what has been achieved, but what is still to be achieved, in constitutional freedom and German national dignity, not a glorious triumph, but a manful struggle to shake off oppression from within and without.
>
> Source: Kertesz, G.A. (ed.). (1970). *Documents in the Political History of the European Continent 1815–1939.* Oxford: Oxford University Press, p. 70

In what ways does the language of this source extract illustrate the ideas of liberalism and nationalism? Note down the phrases which reflect these ideas.

101

Figure 3.3: *The Procession to Hambach Castle* by Erhard Joseph Brenzinger, 1832. The artist took part in the Festival with three of his friends who later became members of the Frankfurt Parliament. Do you think that this image is expressing a point of view or recording an event? What evidence can you find for your opinion in the image?

> ●●● **THINK LIKE A HISTORIAN**
>
> Based on what you have learned so far, how far do you think that people's actions are influenced by abstract ideas such as liberalism or nationalism? Does their interest in such ideas depend on their social class, their level of education or other circumstances?

The impact of the *Zollverein*

Opportunities and obstacles to German economic growth

One of the most important factors in the long-term development of a united Germany was the economic progress made in the first half of the 19th century. Germany's geographical situation at the heart of Europe was an advantage, because it meant Germany could trade easily with both east and west. We should not, however, exaggerate the extent of industrialisation in this period. Something like 70% of the population still made their living from agriculture. Manufacturing was the main economic activity only in certain areas, notably the Rhineland and Saxony. The main

growth areas were in the production of consumer goods such as textiles. Heavy manufacturing began to take off from the 1840s, with the rapid development of railways, especially in Prussia. Railway building attracted capital investment and stimulated the coal and iron industries. This tended to encourage the emergence of larger industrial firms and the rise of new urban centres.

In the years after the end of the Napoleonic Wars, economic growth was held back by the existence of customs barriers between the members of the German Confederation. This slowed down trade across Germany because every time a product crossed a border it was likely to be taxed by the territory it was entering. On a long journey across Germany, this could happen numerous times. In addition, larger states such as Prussia often had their own internal boundaries and imposed tolls on goods as they moved within their own territory. All this entailed the time-consuming completion of bureaucratic paperwork at borders, increasing the costs of transport. At the same time, German industries had to contend with competition from foreign products, which did not face duties at the external borders of the Confederation. This meant that German firms within the Confederation had no competitive advantage over non-German ones outside.

Prussia led the way in promoting change. In 1818, it abolished its 67 internal customs barriers because they hindered trade, and it encouraged other German states to do the same. It protected its own industries from foreign competition by charging a tariff on imports at its own frontier. This was initially set at a low level in order to discourage smuggling and so that foreign countries were less likely to retaliate with high tariffs of their own. The Prussians worked to remove barriers to trade within the German Confederation, in order to create a larger market and reduce the price of goods. Alongside the appearance of new roads and railways, steamboat services on the Rhine and Elbe rivers also helped the growth of the Prussian economy.

The *Zollverein* and the rise of Prussia

By 1834, Prussia had formed the *Zollverein*, a **customs union** of 18 German states. This was the largest free-trade area in Europe, soon comprising 25 states, with a combined population of 26 million. Income from tariffs was divided between the member states in proportion to their population size. Soon they were linked by a rapidly growing rail network, centred on Berlin, and in time they adopted a common currency and system of weights and measures. The *Zollverein* promoted economic expansion for all its members.

KEY TERM

Customs union: An association of states who agree to abolish tariffs between themselves, and to operate a common set of tariffs on imports from other countries.

ACTIVITY 3.3

How does the map in Figure 3.4 help to explain the growing importance of Prussia in the development of a more unified German economic system?

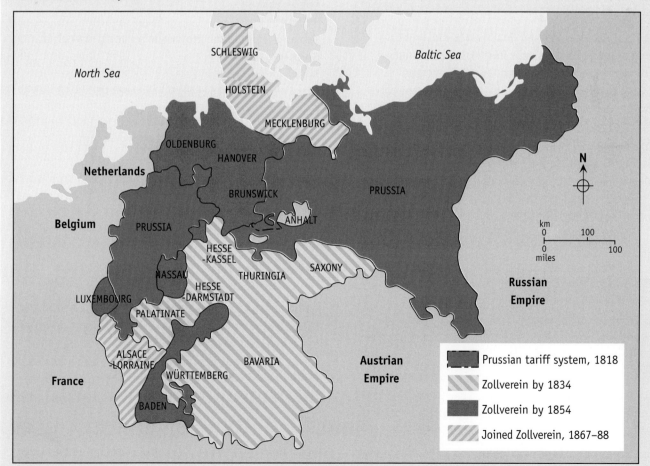

Figure 3.4: A map showing membership of the *Zollverein,* 1818–88

Austria did not join, failing to perceive the importance of economic change and preferring to maintain high import duties to protect its domestic producers from the perceived threat of foreign competitors. Austria preferred to rely on trade within its empire and did not want to lower its tariffs to the level of those within the *Zollverein*. In the long run, this was to be an important reason why Austria lost control of Germany to Prussia. In turn, Prussia became determined not to allow Austria to join the *Zollverein* later, in order to maintain its own advantageous position. It also meant that German economic growth was centred on the ports of the North Sea rather than directed southwards to the valley of the River Danube.

The *Zollverein* helped Prussia assume a predominant economic position within Germany, but it did not follow that it would also take on its political leadership. The states that joined the customs union insisted that decisions in its governing body, the *Zollverein* Congress, had to be unanimous, and the states were determined to retain their independence. Nationalists who hoped that the *Zollverein* might provide a basis for a political union were disappointed.

One of the nationalists' key weaknesses was that they could not agree on where the frontiers of a German state should be. Some favoured a 'large Germany' (*Grossdeutschland*) which would include German-speaking regions of Austria, and which would be dominated by Austria. Others preferred a small Germany (*Kleindeutschland*) without those regions, which would therefore be dominated by Prussia. These preferences to some extent reflected the continuing cultural differences between Protestant northern Germany and the Catholic southern states. The industrialised Rhineland remained more economically developed than the still largely agricultural east.

ACTIVITY 3.4

From what you have learned so far, what do you think were the main obstacles to German unification? List the three most important factors.

Social and economic problems in the 1840s

The year 1848 is known as the 'year of revolutions', when a number of European countries were affected by popular uprisings. The disturbances began in February with the toppling of the monarchy of King Louis Philippe in France. In March, Metternich was forced into exile by disturbances in Vienna. It seemed that the power of the Austrian Empire, and of traditional authorities throughout Europe, was crumbling. Revolutionary hopes proved short-lived, however, and authoritarian regimes soon re-established control.

The revolutions were not just caused by liberalism and nationalism. The events of 1848–49 had a variety of causes – economic, social and political.

Social and economic causes of revolution

Continuing poor living standards for the peasants in the countryside were made worse by high rents and two years of bad harvests in 1846 and 1847. Increasing population size exacerbated the situation. Table 3.1 gives some indication of the rate of growth across the period, with figures for the German states as a whole shown alongside those for Prussia.

	1820	1840	1870
Prussia	10.3	14.9	19.4
Germany	26.1	32.6	40.8

Table 3.1: Population growth (in millions) in Prussia and Germany, 1820–70
Source: Adapted from Breuilly, J. (1996). *The Formation of the First German Nation-State, 1800–1871*. Basingstoke: Palgrave, p. 131

ACTIVITY 3.5

What does Table 3.1 suggest about the growth of Prussia in comparison with the rest of Germany? What other types of data would help you to assess how important it was becoming in this period?

Rising food prices worsened the position of urban workers, especially as they coincided with a recession in the textile industry in 1847. The economic downturn led employers to cut wages. This occurred against a background of poor working conditions in factories, typified by long hours in an unhealthy environment. The poorest workers' protests in early 1848 were mainly about their daily lives and were not explicitly political in character. Skilled workers, however, went beyond these basic demands to call for trade union rights and free education.

The outbreak of revolution in Germany

Educated middle-class people were motivated by a desire to improve their own position as well as being influenced by ideas of liberalism and nationalism. They resented the hold on power of the privileged nobility, who dominated the army and civil service, regardless of their qualifications to fill these posts. These middle-class liberals did not want to overthrow the monarchical regimes in power in the German states, but they did want to put pressure on their rulers to introduce political reforms. They first expressed themselves in the south German state of Baden, where Grand Duke Leopold granted a free press, trial by jury and other reforms. In October 1847, liberal politicians demanded further political changes, including the summoning of a German national parliament. They wanted to replace the German Confederation with a genuinely united Germany.

News of the revolution in France provided a further stimulus to liberal demands for change. The uprisings in the German states were uncoordinated but shared certain characteristics. In Württemberg, the ruler, Wilhelm I, was pressured into appointing liberal ministers and granting a new constitution. King Friedrich Augustus II of Saxony agreed to similar demands. Demands for a bill of rights were accepted by the princes of Hesse-Darmstadt, Nassau and other states. The only German ruler who gave up his throne was Ludwig I of Bavaria. The circumstances here differed from the rest of Germany in that the first disturbances were caused by conservative opposition to the king's mistress, the exotic Irish-born dancer, Lola Montez. Liberal students then took advantage of the situation to demand constitutional reforms. Ludwig made some concessions, but when these proved inadequate, he abdicated in March 1848 in favour of his son, Maximilian.

A meeting at Heidelberg in March 1848, attended by representatives from six states (Prussia, Bavaria, Württemberg, Baden, Nassau and Frankfurt) led to the summoning of a *Vorparlament* or 'pre-parliament'. It met in Frankfurt and resolved to create a national constituent assembly or parliament, whose role would be to draw up a constitution for a united Germany. Each state in the German Confederation would be asked to hold elections to this parliament, using its own voting system.

ACTIVITY 3.6

An extract from the Resolution of 5 March 1848 at the Heidelberg meeting of liberals

> The calling of a national representative assembly, elected in all German states according to population, must not be postponed; [it is needed] in order to avert internal and external danger, and to develop the power and prosperity of German national life.
>
> In order to assist in bringing about an early and complete representation of the nation, those present have resolved:
>
> To approach urgently their respective governments to provide the whole German fatherland and the thrones [of the German states' rulers] as early and as completely as possible with this powerful bulwark [support].
>
> G A Kertesz (ed) Documents in the Political History of the European Continent 1815-1939 (Oxford University Press, 1970)
>
> **Source: Kertesz, G.A. (ed.). (1970). *Documents in the Political History of the European Continent 1815–1939*. Oxford: Oxford University Press, p. 104**

How does this source show the commitment of the Heidelberg liberals to nationalist ideas? What evidence is there in the source to show that they were not seeking the overthrow of the existing political order in the German states?

Reflection: Discuss your reading of the source with another student. Did you reach similar conclusions about its content?

Revolution in Prussia

The combination of economic distress and desire for political change can be seen clearly in the case of Prussia. The Prussian government had decided to build a railway linking the agricultural lands of the east to markets further afield, but it needed to raise money to do this. The people who stood to gain most from this were the *Junkers*. King Friedrich Wilhelm IV called a national assembly known as the United Diet in April 1847 to win support for the project. The Diet assembled against a background of crop failure and rising food prices. There was unrest among skilled workers, who faced competition from factory production. When the Diet met, its members demanded a constitution before they would consider the king's appeal to support funding of the railway. Friedrich Wilhelm turned them down, declaring, in the old-fashioned language which came naturally to him, that he would never consent 'that a written paper should intrude … between our Lord God in Heaven and this country, to govern us through its paragraphs'. He then dissolved the Diet. This failed, however, to quieten growing demands for political change.

Disturbances broke out in Prussia's capital city, Berlin, in March 1848, encouraged by news of the fall of Metternich in Vienna. The first demonstrations involved craftsmen and workers, who were protesting about their pay and conditions. This was followed by demands from middle-class citizens for the protection of their rights. Following a period of street fighting, the army lost control of the situation, leaving the king to attempt to calm the demonstrators. This was the start of the revolution in Prussia.

As we have seen, most of the German revolutions were not violent. The fighting which erupted briefly in Prussia in March 1848 was not typical of events across the Confederation. In some ways, the restraint of the revolutionaries across Germany was surprising. These events were the culmination of a decade of popular discontent, later known as 'the hungry forties'. Economic depression, combined with food shortages which affected working-class people across northern Europe, were the underlying causes of the uprisings. In the months after March 1848, however, the political demands of the liberals came to the fore. The lack of common ground between working-class and middle-class revolutionaries was a fundamental weakness of the movement. The differences between the two were later exploited by the German states' traditional rulers, as they sought to recover the power which had temporarily been taken from them.

The period 1815–48 also saw the emergence of Prussia as a major state within the German Confederation. Its role in the development of the *Zollverein* was a source of future development, which might enable it to compete with its only rival, Austria, for the leadership of a united Germany. It was not clear in 1848, however, that a united Germany would definitely come about. Prussia's king, Friedrich Wilhelm IV, was ambivalent about the new forces of liberalism and nationalism. Moreover,

Austria still remained the senior partner within the Confederation in terms of its political and diplomatic standing.

3.2 What were the consequences of the 1848–49 revolutions?

Initial responses of the German states to the 1848–49 revolutions

The princely rulers, alarmed by the strength of popular feeling in the spring of 1848, made concessions in the short term. They were worried that if they tried to stand against the revolutionary mood, they would be swept away, so most of them granted constitutions. They were careful to retain control of their armed forces, however. They waited until the right moment to reassert their authority. Baden was briefly in the hands of revolutionaries, supported by mutinous troops, but in June 1849, the Grand Duke asked Prussia to restore order in the country. Prussia also offered military assistance to end the revolts in other states, including Saxony and Württemberg.

Weaknesses of the revolutions

In most cases, the recovery of royal power was made possible by divisions within the revolutionary movements. Liberals, who wanted moderate constitutional reform, differed from radicals, who sought more far-reaching political changes. Working-class revolutionaries wanted improvements to their living and working conditions and had little in common with middle-class liberals interested in political ideas. In the Rhineland, for example, better-off activists abandoned the revolutionary movement when they saw armed working-class crowds taking to the streets, fearing a threat to their property rights. Liberals were unwilling to continue their support for protests which might develop into a radical social revolution.

Another important reason for the ultimate failure of the revolutions was the recovery of the Austrian monarchy. Although initially caught off guard in March 1848, it soon recovered and, with the support of Prussia, set about restoring monarchical power in the German lands.

Friedrich Wilhelm IV and Prussia

Friedrich Wilhelm behaved inconsistently during the revolutionary year. After the rioting in Berlin in March 1848, he appeared in public cloaked in the black, red and gold German colours adopted by the nationalist movement, and declared emotionally that 'henceforward Prussia will be merged in Germany'. There has been debate about his motives for this gesture. He was an erratic figure whose actions are hard to judge. Perhaps he was carried away by the emotion of the moment and genuinely, if briefly, imagined himself at the head of a popular movement. Alternatively, he might have been trying to save his own position by taking charge of the revolution rather than submitting to it. Either could be a plausible explanation for his actions.

In the immediate aftermath of the revolution, Friedrich Wilhelm allowed the election of an assembly, whose purpose was to draw up a constitution for Prussia. He then changed his mind and dissolved the assembly. In December 1848, he announced a more restrictive political settlement of his own. The new constitution, which came into effect in February 1850, established a two-chamber parliament but enabled the king to retain the essentials of power in his own hands. In an emergency, for example, he could collect taxes without parliamentary approval. Ministers would be responsible to him, not to parliament, and he reserved the right to change the constitution. The voting system for the Prussian lower house of parliament, the *Landtag*, was designed to favour conservative interests. It was to be elected by a complex 'three-tier **suffrage**', based on the taxes paid by different classes. This ensured that the wealthy had an inbuilt advantage; roughly one-third of the voters chose 85% of the members of the *Landtag*. The upper house, *Herrenhaus*, was appointed by the king. This guaranteed the continuing political dominance of the *Junkers*.

KEY TERM

Suffrage (or franchise): The right to vote.

The Frankfurt Parliament

The most dramatic consequence of the revolutions was the election of a national parliament, which met in Frankfurt from May 1848 to June 1849. Each state was allowed to choose its own voting system to select its representatives. The exclusion of most of the poor

from voting meant that the parliament was not truly representative of the German people, though in this respect it was not dissimilar to national assemblies in other European states. It was all-male and most of the members were well-off professionals. It was often mockingly described as 'the professors' parliament'. Jacob Grimm and three others of the 'Göttingen Seven' were among those elected. Its first president was Heinrich von Gagern, a lawyer who had been a member of the *Burschenschaften* at university. Table 3.2 shows the composition of the parliament.

Occupation	Number of members
Lawyers	200
Nobles	90
University professors	49
Principals and teachers	40
Writers and journalists	35
Merchants and industrialists	30
Clergy	26
Doctors	12
Handicraft workers	4
Peasants	1

Table 3.2: Occupations of members of the Frankfurt Parliament, 1848–49
Source: Adapted from Shreeves, W.G. (1984). *Nationmaking in Nineteenth Century Europe*. Cheltenham: Nelson Thornes, p. 141

ACTIVITY 3.7

Convert the numbers for each occupational group in the Frankfurt Parliament into percentages. How far does it deserve the description 'a parliament of middle-class intellectuals'?

The parliament's members were mostly liberal in politics, although there were also small numbers of radicals who wanted a republic. The parliament wanted a strong central government, with more authority over the German states than the Diet of the old Confederation. However, it was slow to decide what form this would take or exactly what powers such a government would possess. In June 1848, the parliament set up a 'Provisional Central Power' under a liberal Austrian prince, the Archduke Johann, which was to govern until a permanent constitution had been agreed. In December, the parliament approved 50 fundamental citizens' rights, including equality before the law, freedom of the press and freedom from arrest without a warrant. It had still not agreed on a constitution to replace the interim government headed by the archduke.

ACTIVITY 3.8

What symbols of German nationality do you observe in this painting? Find out what the significance of these symbols was in German tradition and write a brief report on their importance.

Figure 3.5: The first session of the Frankfurt Parliament. In this contemporary illustration, the Frankfurt Parliament, elected during the revolutionary period of May 1848, is shown meeting in a church.

The collapse of the Frankfurt Parliament

A divided and ineffective parliament

The Frankfurt Parliament had several key weaknesses. Its members could not agree on the territorial extent of a new Germany. As we have noted, the old German Confederation included some non-Germans and excluded some German-speaking areas, including parts of Prussia and Austria. There was debate in the parliament about conflicting proposals for a *Kleindeutschland*, dominated by Prussia, and a *Grossdeutschland*, which would mean the continued leadership of Austria.

The parliament eventually agreed on a German constitution in March 1849, which was to involve an emperor governing with the support of two houses of parliament, one elected and the other consisting of the princes of the Confederation. The crown of this empire was offered to Friedrich Wilhelm IV. Supporters of the *Kleindeutschland* option believed that he was prepared to place himself at the head of a German national revolution. Prussia was also the only state with the military strength to resist Austria, if it opposed their plans. But Friedrich Wilhelm was a proud man who would not accept a gift from the Frankfurt Parliament, whose legal authority he refused to recognise. He rejected the offer in April, declining to 'pick up a crown of mud and wood from the gutter'. He would only accept an imperial throne offered by his fellow princes.

Why did the Frankfurt Parliament fail?

The parliament's members lacked political experience and they took some time to organise themselves and decide how to proceed. They struggled to resolve differences between moderate liberals, radicals and conservatives.

The parliament lacked the means of enforcing any decisions it made. In particular, it lacked an army of its own. A Prussian general, Eduard von Peucker, acted as war minister, but the Prussian army remained under the authority of the king. The weakness of the army was illustrated by a crisis over the disputed provinces of **Schleswig-Holstein** on the Jutland peninsula, linking Prussia and Denmark. In March 1848, the German-speaking population of these territories rebelled against an attempt to integrate them fully into Denmark. They demanded admission to the German Confederation as a single state. The Frankfurt Parliament authorised the Prussian army to fight Denmark over the issue. The Prussian army advanced, but soon halted and signed a truce at Malmo in August 1848, in response to international pressure. The key point was that Prussia had withdrawn its forces without consulting parliament. This demonstrated the dependence of the parliament on the cooperation of the traditional rulers. It possessed moral authority, but no actual independent power to impose its will.

The German princes did not initially oppose the parliament because their own authority had been weakened by the revolutionary events of spring 1848. By the autumn, however, they were recovering their confidence. The delay in working out a constitution was fatal to the parliament's chances of success.

By the time it was ready to present its proposals, its opponents had regained their strength. The princes mostly withdrew their constitutions after Friedrich Wilhelm's refusal of the crown. Most of the members of the parliament went home. Those who remained moved to Stuttgart, capital of Württemberg, only to be dispersed by troops in June 1849. This marked the failure of middle-class liberalism to establish a united Germany.

KEY TERM

Schleswig-Holstein: Two adjacent territories between the Baltic and North seas. Although not part of Denmark, they were under the personal authority of the Danish king as their duke. Holstein was German-speaking and was also part of the German Confederation. Schleswig had a mixed Danish- and German-speaking population. As a result, their status was disputed, and German nationalists claimed that they should be treated as one, and be part of the Confederation.

ACTIVITY 3.9

From Friedrich Wilhelm IV's message to the Frankfurt Parliament, rejecting the offer of the imperial crown, 3 April 1849

> The German National Assembly has counted on me in all things which were calculated to establish the unity of Germany and the power of Prussia. I honour its confidence; please express my thanks for it ... But I should not justify that confidence – I should not answer to the expectations of the German people – I should not strengthen the unity of Germany – if I, violating sacred rights and breaking my former explicit and solemn promises, were, without the voluntary assent of the crowned Princes and free States of our Fatherland, to take a resolution which must be of decisive importance to them and to the States which they rule.
>
> Source: Kertesz, G.A. (ed.). (1970). *Documents in the Political History of the European Continent 1815–1939*. Oxford: Oxford University Press, p. 118

What reason does Friedrich Wilhelm give for turning down the offer of the imperial German crown? Do you believe that he is sincere in expressing his support for the idea of German unity?

Reassertion of Austrian power: the 'humiliation of Olmütz'

Prussia and Austria after the 1848 revolutions

The Prussian monarchy survived the crisis of 1848–49 intact. Friedrich Wilhelm IV had briefly appeared as a potential leader of liberal nationalism, but this had proved a short-lived phase.

Friedrich Wilhelm might have rejected the Frankfurt Parliament's offer of a German crown, but he was interested in promoting unity in northern and central Germany under Prussian control. In 1849–50, he put forward a plan for a union of German states based on a strong central government, an assembly elected on a limited franchise, and Prussian control of the army. Austria was to be excluded but would be in a special relationship with this new **Reich**. Saxony and Hanover agreed to support the plan, concluding the Three Kings' Alliance with Prussia. Some smaller states agreed to join when the scheme was launched at Erfurt in Saxony in March 1850. Most of the German princes, however, suspected that this 'Erfurt Union' was a vehicle for Prussian domination. Now that Austria was once again able to assert itself, they also feared the consequences of its disapproval. The Revolution of 1848–49 had been only a temporary interruption to Austria's status at the head of the Confederation.

KEY TERM

Reich: A German term for a realm or empire. In modern history, it has been applied to the unified German state of 1871–1918 (the Second Reich) and to Hitler's Germany (the Third Reich, 1933–45).

The collapse of the Erfurt Union

As Austria recovered from the revolution in Vienna, it reacted to the Prussian-led Erfurt Union project by reviving the Diet of the Confederation. By now, Austria had a new and able chief minister, Prince Felix Schwarzenberg, who was determined to uphold the authority of the Habsburg monarchy. He put forward a rival scheme to the Erfurt Union, a *Grossdeutschland* solution in which Austria, Prussia and the larger states would govern together. In response to this proposal,

Hanover, Baden and Saxony abandoned the Erfurt Union, leaving Prussia isolated.

The conflict came to a head when **Elector** Friedrich of Hesse-Cassel (an area between the main part of Prussia and the Rhineland) asked for help in a dispute with his parliament. The Elector appealed to Austria and his parliament asked for Prussian support. Schwarzenberg insisted that only the Confederation could respond to this appeal. Prussia was simply not strong enough to resist when Austrian troops entered Hesse to restore the ruler's authority. Its army was still weak. In addition, Austria acted with the support of Europe's other leading conservative power, Russia. It was not in Friedrich Wilhelm's nature to try to lead a nationalist movement of German states against Austria.

KEY TERM

Elector: A title used by some German princes, derived from the fact that they elected the Holy Roman Emperor until the dissolution of the empire by Napoleon I in 1806.

In the so-called 'humiliation of Olmütz' in November 1850, Prussia agreed to abandon the Erfurt Union. At this meeting, held in present-day Czech Republic, it effectively gave up its claim to the leadership of the German states. It seemed that Austria had triumphed and that the old, unequal partnership with a 'humiliated' Prussia had been restored. On the other hand, the smaller states rejected the Schwarzenberg plan, as it favoured their larger neighbours. The result, in May 1851, was an agreement to return to the old framework of the German Confederation.

Overall, the experience of 1848–49 had demonstrated the weakness of liberal nationalism. The reassertion of princely power showed the resilience of long-established institutions, which had been caught off guard initially, but had proved determined in recovering their status. The revolutions had been unplanned and their leaders lacked the necessary organisation and resources to achieve their goals. Moreover, the division over aims and methods between liberals and radicals was fatal to their chances of success. The working classes, by and large, were not enthused by the political visions of the middle-class revolutionaries. Those who had such high hopes in the spring of 1848 were left overwhelmingly disappointed.

Prussia's prospects

Why then did Prussia emerge as the state that would eventually lead German unification? The reality was that, although Austria formally appeared the victor in the dispute over the Erfurt Union, it had some important disadvantages.

Prussia's position in north-central Germany gave it an opportunity to dominate its neighbours, whereas Austria, despite its status as a great power, had a sprawling southern European empire to govern. Much of its army was tied down by the need to control nationalist movements in Hungary and northern Italy.

Events in Germany were indirectly affected by the outbreak of the Crimean War of 1854–56. Britain and France went to war with Russia, fearing that it was planning to extend its influence in south-east Europe at the expense of the Ottoman (Turkish) Empire. The main area of fighting was on the Crimean peninsula bordering the Black Sea, to which Britain and France sent troops. Austria made a major diplomatic mistake by not backing Russia, the other leading power with an interest in maintaining the 1815 European settlement. Russia had supported Austria over the Erfurt Union and was angered by its apparent ingratitude. This had the effect of weakening the alliance between Europe's two most conservative states. If further change occurred in Germany, it was now much less likely that Russia would intervene on Austria's side. On the other hand, the war had no real effect on Prussia, whose interests were not directly involved. It was wise not to play any part in the conflict, managing instead to remain on good terms with both sides.

Economic developments after 1849: the growth of industrialisation and the *Zollverein*

Prussia's economic growth

Prussia was the most economically advanced of the German states, with its growth outpacing that of its rival, Austria. Between 1850 and 1860, Prussia's rail network increased by 46%. This stimulated other sectors of the economy, such as iron and steel. The output of coal, a vital resource in the age of steam power, grew from 1 961 000 tonnes in 1850 to 8 526 000 tonnes by 1865. Railway expansion was achieved through a partnership between the state and the private sector. In return for supplying

some of the funding for railway building, the government was able to collect interest payments. Combined with import and export dues from the *Zollverein*, the sale of timber from the Crown lands and royalties from mining rights, this boosted the government's income and made it less necessary to raise taxes.

Prussia was in a strong position to lead German unification by the end of the 1850s. The rapid growth of its population, coupled with its successful banking system and coinage, meant that it was well placed economically to dominate its neighbours. Its iron and steel industries provided the materials for its weapons and its expanding rail network could be used to mobilise its troops. In 1862, a Franco-Prussian trade treaty helped Prussia's development by further integrating it into the economy of Western Europe.

Economic growth boosted the material prosperity and self-confidence of the middle classes. Growing numbers of them began to look to the Prussian state to guarantee continued future growth and as a possible agent of unification. They had learned an important lesson from the experience of 1848–49: that idealism without the backing of a powerful state structure was doomed to failure. They therefore took a more pragmatic approach; being more prepared to compromise with the established authorities, so that the latter were not driven into opposing all future reform. In 1859, many business and professional people came together to found the National Society, or *Nationalverein*, an organisation which placed its hopes in Prussia. The society's founding document called for nationwide elections and the creation of a strong national authority, replacing the Confederation. It was prepared to support the transfer of the Confederation's powers to the Prussian government. However, the society was never likely to become the centre of a mass movement. It had only 25 000 members, mostly from the middle classes, so its actual influence was relatively limited.

Prussia's economic lead over Austria made it a plausible focus for such aspirations. Austria was hit hard by the onset of an economic downturn in the late 1850s, and the costs of maintaining military garrisons throughout its empire added to its problems. It lacked direct access to the most rapidly growing trade routes in Germany, the ones that led northwards to the Baltic and the North Sea. Austria relied for its domination of Germany on its prestige and its ability to use diplomatic means to control the other states. Increasingly, it lacked the economic and military might to compel other states to do its will. In the era of Metternich, it had succeeded in keeping Prussia on its side by appealing to its fear of revolution. Since the humiliation of Olmütz, however, this uneasy partnership had been replaced by outright resentment. As Prussia grew in strength during the 1850s, it became possible for it to challenge Austria's supremacy – if it could also find the necessary political leadership to do so.

The *Zollverein* in the 1850s

One of the most important features of the 1850s was the continued growth of the *Zollverein*. Hanover became a member in 1851, which enabled Prussia to control the flow of trade to the North Sea ports. The *Zollverein* was by now Europe's fourth largest economy, after Britain, France and Belgium. Austria wanted the whole of the Habsburg Empire to join, but this was unacceptable to most of the existing members. It would have entailed the introduction of high tariff barriers to protect Austria's less-efficient industries. In 1853, Austria concluded a trade treaty with the *Zollverein*, leaving the question of its eventual admission to the bloc for review by 1860. It never joined. In effect, Prussia had won the battle for economic domination of Germany.

Despite this, we should not exaggerate the importance of the *Zollverein* to the process of political unification. By joining it, German states were seeking material advantages as members of the strongest economic unit in central Europe. This did not mean, however, that they welcomed the possibility of Prussia becoming the dominant political force in Germany. Indeed, some historians have suggested that the *Zollverein* might have held back unification by helping the finances of smaller states which were keen to retain their independence. Christopher Clark, author of a history of Prussia, *Iron Kingdom* (Penguin, 2006), has argued that the main importance of the *Zollverein* was that it encouraged Prussian leaders to think in a wider 'German' way, while also pursuing the interests of their own state. It also demonstrated to liberal opinion in smaller states that, in spite of its conservative reputation, Prussia could represent a more forward-looking, rational approach in some respects.

Otto von Manteuffel's reforms

Otto von Manteuffel was Minister-President (prime minister) of Prussia from 1850 to 1858. He was a conservative who wanted to strengthen the bonds between the monarchy and the people. His aim was to promote economic and social development, without making concessions to radicals who wanted a more democratic political system. He also blocked traditionalists who wanted to restrict the foundation of new banks, which they regarded as encouraging risky financial speculation. He helped to foster a culture of private enterprise by reducing state control of the coal and iron industries.

Manteuffel sought to discourage the poorer members of society from supporting liberal ideas by undertaking social reforms. His government provided low-interest loans to help peasants buy their landholdings from the landowning aristocracy. In areas where there was excessive population pressure on the land, financial assistance was provided to peasants who were willing to move to less densely populated parts of the country. He also introduced measures to improve the working conditions and pay of factory workers. All this was achieved without the involvement of parliament and without harming the interests of the industrial middle classes.

As the 1850s drew to a close, the 'German problem' remained unresolved. Prussia had made great strides in terms of its economic development, and it possessed a strong state structure, which gave it the potential to challenge Austria for the leadership of Germany. Friedrich Wilhelm IV and his successor, Wilhelm I, presided over an exclusively German kingdom, whereas Austria had a sprawling empire to manage and many problems outside Germany which might distract it. Prussia still had significant limitations, however. Its army was in need of modernisation and it could not count on the support of many of the smaller German states. Moreover, any move to dislodge Austria from its position would depend on the attitude of the other great powers. It was by no means a foregone conclusion at this stage that Prussia would emerge a decade later as the centre of a united Germany.

ACTIVITY 3.10

	Percentage of labour force in manufacturing		Per capita Gross National Product (in 1960 US $)		Railways (km in operation)	
	1850	1870	1850	1870	1850	1870
Prussia	20	28 (1882)	308	426	5586	18 876
Austria	14.8 (1857)	13.1 (1869)	283	305	1579	9589

Table 3.3: Some economic indicators in Prussia and Austria

Source: Adapted from Breuilly, J. (1996). *The Formation of the First German Nation-State 1800–1871*. Basingstoke, Palgrave, pp. 131–32

Use the data in Table 3.3 to explain why Prussia was better placed than Austria to become the dominant German state in the mid-19th century. How useful is the information presented here?

Reflection: With a partner, discuss if and how the introduction of economic data in this part of the chapter has changed your view of the relative strengths of Austria and Prussia? Are there differences between your view and your partner's view? Discuss why this may have happened.

KEY CONCEPT

Change and continuity

How much change have you noted in each of the following areas between 1815 and 1860?

- German economic development
- the strength of the German nationalist movement
- the relative power of Prussia and Austria.

What changed very little in Germany in this period?

3.3 What were Bismarck's intentions for Prussia and Germany from 1862 to 1866?

Reasons for Bismarck's appointment as Minister-President; his attitudes towards liberalism and nationalism

Wilhelm I became regent of Prussia in 1858, when his brother, Friedrich Wilhelm IV, fell ill. He ascended the throne in his own right in 1861. Wilhelm was not a liberal, but he accepted the constitution. He was primarily a military man whose main concern was to strengthen the army. His fears for Prussian security were aroused by a crisis in 1859, when the Franco-Austrian War broke out. In

this conflict, which formed part of the process of Italian unification, France supported the Kingdom of Piedmont in driving Austrian forces out of northern Italy. The Prussian army was partly mobilised in order to deter possible French moves in the Rhineland. In the event, it was not called upon to fight, but the experience revealed serious organisational weaknesses. Prussia's professional army at the time numbered some 150 000 soldiers. Approximately 40 000 young men underwent two years of military training followed by two years in the reserve. They then transferred to the *Landwehr*, a semi-civilian militia force separate from the army. Members of this organisation received limited training, and the officers were not professionals.

Wilhelm wanted to reform the army to make it more effective, which meant increasing the military budget. He wanted to double the size of the regular army by increasing the annual number called up for military service to 63 000 and extending their term from two to three years, followed by five years in the reserve. Wilhelm also viewed the *Landwehr* as both militarily ineffective and unreliable in its loyalty to the state. He wanted to reduce its importance by merging it with the army. This ambitious plan would require a 25% tax increase to fund it.

These plans alarmed the liberals, who were the majority group in the *Landtag*, because they feared that a stronger army could be used to suppress them and raise taxes without their consent. They were also concerned at the proposed downgrading of the *Landwehr*, which was dominated by middle-class men like themselves. By contrast, the regular army was largely officered by conservative members of the aristocratic *Junker* class. The liberals, now organised as the German Progressive Party, therefore agreed in 1861 to vote funds for only one year. The king faced a constitutional

113

crisis when the liberals increased their parliamentary representation in new elections, winning nearly 40% of the seats. In September 1862, the Progressives clashed once again with the king over the budget. Wilhelm faced a dilemma: he believed that funds were needed urgently for the army, but the constitution required that taxes be agreed by the *Landtag*. He even considered abdication, rather than give up any of his royal powers. This was where **Otto von Bismarck**, one of the most influential figures in Prussian and German history, became involved in events.

OTTO VON BISMARCK (1815–98)

Bismarck was the son of a *Junker* landowner and a mother who came from a middle-class family of officials and lawyers. He was a boisterous law student at Göttingen and then Berlin University, known for fighting duels.

Although well-educated, as a young man he could not settle to a career in the civil service because he could not put up with authority. After a period spent managing his estates, he was elected to the Prussian United Diet in 1847. He represented Prussia as a diplomat for a decade until his appointment as Minister-President in 1862. When the German states were united in 1871, Bismarck was the first chancellor of Germany. He helped expand the German Empire and had great power until forced from office following a dispute with Kaiser (Emperor) Wilhelm II in 1890.

Otto von Bismarck in power

Bismarck was a politician and former diplomat, who came from a *Junker* landowning family. He had made his name as a conservative member of the Prussian United Diet, where he defended the monarchy against the liberals in the 1848 revolution. He was fond of presenting himself as a typical country squire: unintellectual, with strong prejudices and an ingrained sense of loyalty to Prussian institutions. The truth was more complex, however. Bismarck's mother came from a middle-class professional background, and from her he inherited his quick intelligence. He was cunning,

unprincipled and strong-willed but also emotional and short-tempered. His preferred form of government was a monarchy with few constitutional restrictions, and he had little patience with parliament. Bismarck served as a diplomat, representing Prussia in the Diet of the Confederation in 1851, where he was noted for his rudeness and defiance of the Austrian chairman. He established his standing with other delegates by means of a simple gesture at his first appearance at the Diet: he openly smoked – a privilege which had previously been exercised only by the Austrian representative. In 1859, he was appointed Prussian ambassador to Russia. In the summer of 1862, just as the conflict between the king and the liberals was reaching its climax, he was transferred to Paris.

It was now that Bismarck was recalled to Berlin to serve as Minister-President. The invitation was extended on the initiative of Albrecht von Roon, the minister of war, who believed that Bismarck had the strength of personality and intelligence to overcome the budgetary crisis. Although Bismarck's commitment to the Prussian state was not in doubt, it was still a controversial and risky choice. He was regarded in government circles as extreme and even reckless, and Wilhelm had serious reservations about asking for his assistance. 'He smells of blood,' Friedrich Wilhelm IV had once said, 'and can only be employed when the bayonet rules.' In the tense situation which had developed by September 1862, however, it was hoped that Bismarck could find a way of financing the army reforms while averting the loss of any royal powers.

Bismarck's attitude towards German unification

Bismarck's appointment opened the way to a period in which, after years of frustration, the cause of German unification made rapid strides. This came as the result of a series of short wars in which Bismarck was the key player: Prussia fought against Denmark in 1864, Austria in 1866 and France in 1870–71. It then became the leading state in a new German empire. It is therefore important to understand Bismarck's attitude towards liberalism and nationalism.

Bismarck's role in the achievement of unification has been debated at length by historians. They disagree about the extent to which he set out from the first to unify Germany. Some have judged that this was always his intention; others claim that he was an opportunist who took advantage of successive crises that he did not plan, but which ended in German unification.

The first view sees Bismarck as both a visionary and a ruthless planner. Support for this interpretation comes from his remarks in 1862 to Benjamin Disraeli, the British politician and future prime minister. Bismarck said that his first task was to reorganise the army and after that he would 'take the first opportunity to declare war with Austria, break the German Confederation, bring the middle and smaller German states under control, and give Germany a national union under Prussia's leadership.' These comments suggest that Bismarck did indeed plan events over the long term. In a later conversation with Disraeli, he claimed that he had always planned the stages by which Germany was unified. These conversations should nonetheless be treated with caution as evidence of Bismarck's political vision. It is unlikely that he would reveal accurately his long-term plans to a British politician whom he knew only slightly. Bismarck might simply have been trying to impress Disraeli in the course of a casual conversation.

The alternative interpretation is that Bismarck was primarily concerned with the interests of Prussia. As a *Junker* landowner, he aimed to maintain Prussia's monarchy and its conservative social structure. He did not believe in German nationalism for its own sake but only as a way of advancing Prussia's power. On one occasion he said of nationalism that 'this kind of emotional sentimental policy is totally alien to me; I have no time at all for German nationality; I would as soon make war against the kings of Bavaria and Hanover [as] against France.' Bismarck was determined that if German unification took take place, then it should work to Prussia's advantage. This meant a *Kleindeutschland* solution: one in which Austria was excluded from any new German state. He knew it was unlikely that Austria and Prussia would ever agree to divide Germany between them, and that a conflict between the two was almost unavoidable.

Although sometimes Bismarck liked to suggest that he had a carefully worked-out master plan, at other times he emphasised his pragmatism. For example, he said that one should not play chess on the assumption that one's opponent was bound to make a certain move: 'for it may be that this won't happen and then the game is lost … one must always have two irons in the fire.' This suggests that he was good at making use of opportunities as they arose.

●●● THINK LIKE A HISTORIAN

Do you think that successful political leaders work out detailed plans in advance, or do they tend to have a general objective but are willing to adapt their methods in response to circumstances? What examples can you find of such an ability to improvise successfully, from other countries and periods?

Bismarck's impact on Prussian politics: relations with Wilhelm I and the *Landtag*

Bismarck, the king and the liberals

It was Bismarck's reputation for unswerving loyalty to the monarchy which had persuaded Wilhelm I to take the risk involved in appointing him as his chief minister, but relations between king and minister were often stormy. Although he served the monarchy faithfully, Bismarck was often prepared to push policies through against the king's wishes, resorting to tearful, angry outbursts and threats of resignation when he met opposition. He adopted the persona of an ultra-conservative servant of the Crown, while in reality he was skilled at manipulating Wilhelm. Bismarck was an intensely arrogant, self-confident individual. He once said that he would make his own music or none at all, meaning that he would not take orders from others.

Bismarck promptly resolved the army reform crisis by collecting taxes without parliamentary agreement to a budget. He delivered a speech to parliament on becoming Minister-President which was to become famous. (The key passage is included in the following activity.) Bismarck intended to show the liberals that they had some common ground with him. They wanted to see German unity come about at the expense of Austria, and Bismarck wanted to show them that their aims could only be achieved with a strong army. His words reinforced his image as a ruthless politician who was prepared to govern by force if necessary. He also undertook repressive measures, including censorship of the press, showing contempt for the liberal belief in the rule of law.

Bismarck and the Progressives in the *Landtag* were in conflict over army reform and, in truth, they had little in common with each other. The Progressives resented Bismarck's willingness to disregard parliamentary convention, his use of the press to manipulate public opinion, and his evident contempt for their political values. His insistence that the king's government must be carried on, and that he would still do so in the absence of an agreement with parliament, was a complete rejection of what they stood for. In further elections in 1863, the Progressives won 40% of the seats in parliament, but they could not prevent Bismarck from governing without their consent. The only possible basis for a compromise lay in the fact that, for very different reasons, both Bismarck and the Progressives supported the idea of German unification. If Bismarck was successful in achieving this, it was likely that they would place their nationalist beliefs before their liberal principles and give him their support.

ACTIVITY 3.11

From Bismarck's speech to the Prussian parliament, 30 September 1862

> Germany is not looking to Prussia's liberalism, but to its power; Bavaria, Württemberg, Baden may indulge liberalism, and yet no one will assign them Prussia's role; Prussia has to coalesce and concentrate its power for the opportune moment, which has already been missed several times; Prussia's borders according to the Vienna Treaties [of 1814–15] are not favourable for a healthy, vital state; it is not by speeches and majority resolutions that the great questions of the time are decided – that was the big mistake of 1848 and 1849 – but by iron and blood.
>
> Source: *German History in Documents and Images*, germanhistorydocs.ghi-dc.org

What do you think Bismarck meant by his reference to the 'big mistake' of 1848 and 1849, and by 'iron and blood'? What does this extract say about the way in which he expected Prussia's position in Germany to change?

Bismarck and the Prussian army

The Prussian army was a vital asset for Bismarck. The military was well-respected and was considered an honourable occupation for men of noble families. The training of army officers was well organised, requiring their attendance at a military academy for three years. Elsewhere in Europe, wealthy young men could buy their commissions to become officers and received little further training as they were promoted.

Bismarck was assisted in his battle for unification by two outstanding army leaders – Field Marshal **Helmuth von Moltke**, chief of the **general staff**, and Albrecht von Roon, the minister of war. These two men made a formidable team, and it is unlikely that Bismarck would have achieved his aims without their significant contributions.

Moltke made his name as a skilful battlefield commander and cemented his reputation with his reorganisation of the Prussian army in the 1860s. He modernised methods of training and understood how important railways could be to transport soldiers and supplies. He was chief of the Prussian general staff from 1857 to 1871 and then of the German general staff until his retirement in 1888.

 KEY TERM

General staff: A group of army officers who assist a senior commander in planning and carrying out military operations.

ACTIVITY 3.12

How well equipped was Prussia under Bismarck to lead the process of German unification? What would you need to know about Prussia's potential opponents to assess its chances of success in a war with them?

Relations with, and policies towards Austria: war with Denmark and Austria

Bismarck's main aim in 1862–66 was to make Prussia the dominant power in northern Germany by excluding Austria from the region. He preferred to achieve this peacefully, but was prepared to use force if necessary. He was determined, however, that any fighting would take place at a time of his own choosing, when he had ensured Austria's isolation and was confident of success.

War with Denmark, 1864

The cause of the war with Denmark was a dispute over the duchies of Schleswig-Holstein. This had already inflamed German national opinion during the 1848 revolution (see 'The collapse of the Frankfurt

116

Parliament'). In 1863, a new Danish king, Christian IX, proposed the incorporation of Schleswig into Denmark. This angered the German Confederation. Nationalists put forward a German prince, Duke Frederick of Augustenburg, as a rival candidate for the position of Duke of Schleswig-Holstein. Bismarck, on the other hand, wanted to secure the two duchies for Prussia. He did not want to provoke Austria by acting independently, however, nor did he wish to see Schleswig-Holstein occupied by an army of the German Confederation. He was acting throughout in the interests of Prussia, not of a wider German identity.

Denmark's big mistake was to believe that Austria and Prussia would not cooperate with each other, even in the face of a common enemy. Austria had no direct interest in the region, which was geographically much closer to

Prussia, but, when Bismarck proposed joint action against Denmark, it had no option but to take part. For the sake of Austrian prestige, it could not allow such an important issue to be settled without its own involvement. Bismarck was also confident that other European powers would not intervene in the crisis. They did not sympathise with the claims of either Danish or German national groups, and preferred some kind of compromise settlement. France would almost certainly remain neutral. Britain did not possess a large enough army and did not regard the outcome of the crisis as a vital national interest. Nor was Russia likely to help Denmark. In 1863, Bismarck gave diplomatic support to Tsar Alexander II in repressing a revolt in Poland, which improved Prussia's relationship with Russia. It offered a positive contrast to Austria's failure to support Russia during the Crimean War, almost a decade earlier.

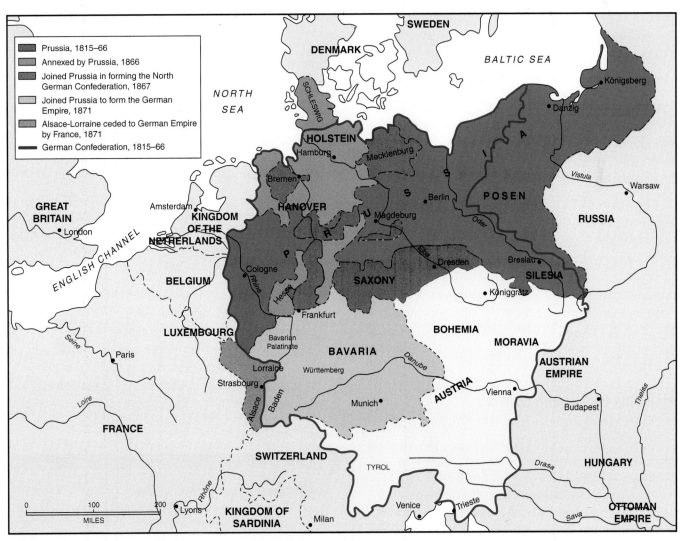

Figure 3.6: A map showing the steps towards the unification of Germany, 1815–71

Prussia and Austria joined forces to wage a swift war against Denmark in January 1864. Denmark was militarily much weaker than the invaders and, in April, lost the fortress of Düppel after a ten-day siege. An armistice was arranged in the hope of finding an agreed solution. Denmark's refusal to consider a compromise, such as the partition of Schleswig, lost it any remaining international sympathy. Bismarck also made sure that Frederick of Augustenburg would not become Duke of Schleswig-Holstein by presenting terms which would have made him a puppet of Prussia, and then blaming him when he turned them down. Fighting resumed in June, leading to a final defeat for Denmark and the surrender of both duchies to Prussia and Austria.

It was now up to Austria and Prussia to decide the long-term future of the duchies. They ignored German nationalist opinion, which wanted to see them both incorporated into the German Confederation under the Duke of Augustenburg. Bismarck knew that Prussia was not yet strong enough for a conflict with Austria, and he could not be sure of international reaction if he tried to take the duchies by force. He therefore concluded the Gastein Convention in August 1865 – a temporary agreement which, in his own words, 'papered over the cracks' between the two victorious powers. It was agreed that Holstein would be administered by Austria, and Schleswig by Prussia. This was a provisional arrangement which gave Bismarck time to decide how to proceed.

Some historians claim that the war against Denmark was proof that Bismarck planned and executed his aims carefully, using Austria as an ally when needed, but turning against it later. In fact, Christian IX instigated the crisis, and Bismarck came under great pressure within Prussia to take decisive action. He embarked on the war without a clear idea of the settlement that would follow, and the terms of the treaty were largely a result of Denmark's refusal to compromise.

Preparing for war with Austria

Unlike the war against Denmark, Bismarck was largely responsible for the Austro-Prussian War of 1866. While more states were admitted to the *Zollverein*, Austria continued to be excluded. Bismarck also made no effort to conceal the disagreements that arose over the government of Schleswig-Holstein, hoping to stir up anti-Austrian feeling in Prussia. Knowing that war with Austria was likely to occur at some point, Bismarck began to seek foreign allies in the hope of isolating his enemy.

Bismarck was sufficiently concerned about which side France might take in an Austro-Prussian conflict that he travelled to France himself to meet with the emperor, **Napoleon III**. The latter was a complex character whose motives are hard to unravel. He aimed to extend French influence in Europe, but also possessed an idealistic sympathy for the aspirations of other nationalities. At Biarritz in October 1865, Napoleon III decided to remain neutral, but, seeing himself as a champion of the newly united Italy, made it a condition that Prussia would hand **Venetia** (at the time governed by Austria) to Italy after the war. The French emperor expected that a war between Austria and Prussia would be prolonged, and he believed that France would benefit by acting as a peacemaker. He wanted an outcome which left neither state as the dominant power in northern Germany. Bismarck's anxiety that France should not ally with Austria led him to make some vague promises about French concessions on the Rhineland, along the border between France and Germany. It is not clear whether he intended to deliberately mislead Napoleon III, but certainly Bismarck made no attempt to concede any land after the war was won.

While Russia would promise to remain neutral in any conflict, Bismarck did succeed in making an alliance with Italy. The Italian army was small, but Bismarck felt that it might still provide a useful distraction during a war, preventing Austria from focusing its entire force on Prussia. In April 1866, he concluded a secret treaty which committed Italy to follow Prussia in going to war with Austria within a three-month period. Italy was prepared to help Prussia in return for gaining Venetia. This meant that Bismarck now had to act without delay in order to benefit from this time-limited commitment.

Most of Europe, including the German states, shared Napoleon III's opinion that the war would be a long one, and public opinion in Prussia was against the conflict. Some believed that Prussia could not win against the strength of Austria; others did not want to fight against the German states that would support Austria. Field-Marshal Moltke was uncertain about the chances of victory and Bismarck himself even expressed doubts about Prussian success.

 KEY TERM

Venetia: An area of northern Italy, including the city of Venice, which was not yet part of the Italian kingdom. Italy, like Germany, was in the process of being unified in the 1860s, and its king, Victor Emmanuel II, was keen to enlarge his new state by acquiring this region.

The Austro-Prussian War, 1866

Surprisingly, when war finally broke out in 1866, the Prussians took only seven weeks to secure a victory. Why did they win the war so quickly and decisively?

NAPOLEON III (1808–73)

Louis Napoleon (Napoleon III) was the nephew of Napoleon (I) Bonaparte, whose achievements he sought to imitate. As a young man, he involved himself in plots to restore his dynasty to power and, in 1848, he was elected president of the Second French Republic. In 1851, he carried out a coup to make himself dictator and the following year he proclaimed himself Emperor of the French. He governed until 1870, when he was toppled by a revolution triggered by his defeat in the Franco-Prussian War. He died in exile in Britain just over two years later.

Austria was a more formidable opponent than Denmark, and there were reasons to expect that it might defeat Prussia. After all, it was generally felt that the Austrians had performed better than the Prussians in the Danish War. Table 3.4 shows that the two sides were fairly evenly matched in terms of numbers of men and weapons. The Austrians had some fundamental weaknesses, however, which these figures do not reveal.

	Austrian forces	Prussian forces
Troop numbers	245 000	254 000
Artillery	650	702

Table 3.4: Relative strengths of the Austrian and Prussian armies in Bohemia (in present-day Czech Republic), 1866

Austria knew that its army was slow to mobilise, so it made the first move to avoid being caught unawares. This enabled its opponents to depict it as the aggressor. It began calling up troops in April in response to news of Italian military movements, and was obliged to continue their mobilisation while talks with Prussia carried on. Fear of a war on two fronts was a major concern for Austria, obliging it to commit 100 000 troops to its southern border, even though in the event, the Italians did not perform well on the battlefield.

In early June, the Austrian government asked the Diet of the German Confederation to review the Schleswig-Holstein question, which Bismarck condemned as a breach of the Gastein Convention. Prussia then sent forces into Holstein, whereupon Austria called on the Confederation for support. When Hanover, Hesse and Saxony sided with Austria, Bismarck invaded them, rapidly overrunning their territory.

The Seven Weeks' War saw just one major decisive battle, at Königgrätz, a fortress on the River Elbe in Bohemia. The battle is sometimes named after the town of Sadová since it was fought between there and Königgrätz. The Prussian army, commanded by Moltke, headed southwards in three sections into Bohemia. Moltke's plan was to use the rail network to move his forces rapidly in the direction of the main Austrian army, and for them to converge on the battlefield. He had five railway lines at his disposal to move his troops, whereas Austria had only one line, from Vienna to Bohemia. The Prussian strategy was a daring concept,

119

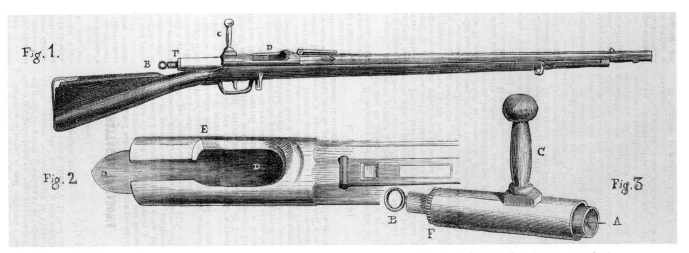

Figure 3.7: A drawing of the Dreyse needle gun used by the Prussian army in the war of 1866, showing its revolutionary loading mechanism

---

ACTIVITY 3.13

Organise your thoughts on the Austro-Prussian War by completing the following table, which encourages you to think about the different characteristics of the two sides.

Reasons for the Prussian victory in the Seven Weeks' War, 1866

	Prussian strengths	Austrian weaknesses
Planning and preparation for war		
Ability to mobilise troops		
Command and control of armies		
Types of weaponry		

---

which depended on good coordination, and the result of Königgrätz hung in the balance until the Prussian Second Army, under Crown Prince Frederick, arrived late in the day.

Another key technological development of the mid-19th century, the electric telegraph, helped Moltke to direct the advance. Training and transport helped the Prussians to victory. They were well prepared and had better officers, and were able to move quickly to take decisive positions on the battlefield. An Austrian general later observed that 'wars now happen so quickly that what is not ready at the outset will not be made ready in time … and a ready army is twice as powerful as a half-ready one.'

Another reason for Austria's defeat was that its forces were led by an indecisive commander, Ludwig Benedek. Instead of concentrating his forces with their back to the River Elbe, he might have been better advised to adopt a more mobile strategy. His best hope was to defeat the Prussian First Army before the other two armies arrived. By failing to take the initiative in this way, Benedek allowed the Prussians to encircle his forces. He was no match for Moltke, whose ability to adapt to changing circumstances, combined with a willingness to delegate decision-making to officers lower down the chain of command, were vital assets. The Austrians lacked an effective command structure and, with the exception of Saxony, were unable to combine the forces of the smaller states with their own. Bavaria, for example, which had 65 000 troops, refused to take the initiative against Prussia.

The Austrian artillery included a large number of guns with rifled barrels. These were of better quality than those used by the Prussians. The latter fought in small units, however, which reduced the damage caused by

the heavy guns. Perhaps the most important advantage the Prussians had was their superior infantry tactics and weapons. Their standard weapon was an early form of bolt-action rifle known as the Dreyse rifle or needle gun – so called because of the shape of the firing pin – which could fire seven shots a minute. This gave the Prussians an advantage over the old-fashioned rifle muskets used by the Austrians, which had to be laboriously reloaded by pushing the ammunition down the muzzle, and could manage only two shots per minute. It also had to be reloaded in a standing position, which exposed the user to enemy fire. The needle gun could be reloaded by a soldier kneeling or even lying down. It was accurate up to 600 metres, whereas the rifle musket's range was closer to 400 metres, and had a devastating effect on the closely packed Austrian ranks.

Outcomes of the Austro-Prussian War: Treaty of Prague and the North German Confederation

The Treaty of Prague, August 1866

The Austrians were quick to seek peace, fearing that prolonged conflict might cause further problems in their multi-ethnic empire. The peace terms were established in the Treaty of Prague, but they were not harsh. Others in the Prussian leadership, including the king, favoured a triumphal entrance into Vienna. Bismarck, however, had no desire to humiliate Austria by seeking concessions other than granting Venetia to Italy. Although defeated, Austria was still a powerful state and Bismarck did not want to make it a permanent enemy of Prussia. He was looking to the future when Prussia might need Austria as an ally. He was also wary of weakening Austria to such an extent that France or Russia might decide to intervene. This was unlikely, but these powers would not want the Habsburg Empire destroyed while it was a useful counterweight to Prussia's growing strength. In any case, Austria's dissolution might create a dangerous power vacuum in southern Europe, where it performed a useful function holding together a collection of disparate national groups. Provided that Austria's power in northern Germany was permanently broken, Bismarck was content. He was willing to leave Austria to focus its priorities on eastern Europe and the Balkans.

The treaty allowed Bismarck to replace the Austrian-dominated German Confederation with the North German Confederation. This was not an association of free states, but a political union in which Prussia simply took over the states north of the River Main: Hesse-Cassel, Nassau, Hanover, the city of Frankfurt and Schleswig-Holstein. Several rulers, including the king of Hanover, were, in effect, deposed, as Bismarck was not prepared to run the risk of these royal families recovering and seeking revenge.

This meant that, from the west bank of the Rhine across to eastern Prussia, there was a continuous swathe of Prussian territory. Saxony retained its king, Johann I, and some limited independence within the Confederation. This was a special concession won by Austria on behalf of its leading German ally.

The North German Confederation

The new Confederation established Prussian power over an additional 4 million people in northern Germany. The king of Prussia had control over the Confederation's foreign policy and decisions about war and peace. The Confederation was to be governed by a Federal Council (*Bundesrat*), representing the states, and a parliament (*Reichstag*), elected by universal male suffrage. While the parliament was supposed to be democratic and was given some powers, the reality was that Prussia dominated the Confederation, under Bismarck's direction. He was appointed Federal Chancellor, a post which was theoretically responsible to the *Reichstag* but in practice answered to the king of Prussia as president of the Confederation. Crucially, the *Reichstag* had no control over military spending, which amounted to 90% of the annual budget. It was a model of government which was deliberately very different from the kind of western parliamentary democracy supported by traditional German liberals.

The independence of the southern German states (Bavaria, Baden and Württemberg) was guaranteed. Bismarck openly stated that he had no plans to incorporate the southern states and unify all of Germany. At this stage, he did not want to provoke a hostile reaction from France by going too far. He might also have felt that the new Confederation needed time to establish itself before Catholic south German states were admitted. Bismarck did not want to risk a dilution of Prussia's traditional culture. Moreover, he was aware that there was strong resistance to Prussia's values, which many southern Germans summarised as 'pay taxes, be a soldier, and keep your mouth shut'. Bismarck did, however, take steps to strengthen the links between north and south. Most importantly, he set up an elected body to represent both parts of the country in matters of trade, the short-lived *Zollparlament* (1868–70), although Prussia retained control through its presidency of the *Zollverein*. The southern states concluded defensive military alliances with Prussia, which would be important when Bismarck went to war with France in 1870. It meant that, if they faced a common threat, their armies and railways would come under Prussian control.

Victory over the hereditary enemy, autocratic Habsburg Austria, also made Bismarck popular with the Prussian liberals. A large number of them formed the National Liberal Party, recognising that 'blood and iron' had achieved partial German unification where their methods had failed. Not all conservative *Junkers* supported the new Confederation, fearing that Prussia's identity would be watered down, but moderate members of their grouping established the Free Conservatives, who supported Bismarck's plans.

In September 1866, Bismarck introduced an **indemnity bill** to legalise his actions in raising taxes without parliamentary approval over the previous four years, and only seven members of the Prussian Diet voted against it. This showed Bismarck at his most politically imaginative: creating an alliance between moderate liberals and flexible conservatives in support of his bold moves, and leaving the hard-liners at both extremes isolated. He had succeeded in placing Prussia at the head of the nationalist movement, and, from now on, many liberals and conservatives saw him as a heroic figure. He had achieved this in part through good fortune. As a royal courtier reminded him after the Battle of Königgrätz, 'You are now a great man. But if the crown prince had arrived too late, you would be the greatest scoundrel in the world.'

Bismarck had justified the trust that had been placed in him by King Wilhelm I – even if reluctantly at first – less than four years earlier. He had done something which old-fashioned Prussian conservatives would never have dared to do, and which the liberals had signally failed to do in 1848–49. He had shown that the forces of German nationalism could be allied to the interests of the Prussian state. Bismarck's domestic opponents were divided and demoralised by his success. Most importantly, the historic struggle for power in northern Germany between Prussia and Austria had been finally settled. The status of the southern German states, however, remained to be decided. Their fate is the subject of the next section.

 KEY TERM

Indemnity bill: A law passed to protect people who might otherwise face penalties for illegal conduct.

ACTIVITY 3.14

From the Constitution of the North German Confederation, 14 June 1867

> [Article] 6. The Federal Council consists of the representatives of the members of the Confederation, amongst whom the votes are divided according to the rules for the full assembly of the late Germanic Confederation, so that Prussia, with the late votes of Hanover, Hesse-Cassel, Holstein, Nassau and Frankfurt, has 17 votes, Saxony 4 … Mecklenburg-Schwerin 2, … Brunswick 2, [all other states one each], Total 43 …
>
> [Article] 11. The Presidency of the Confederation appertains to the Crown of Prussia, which … has the right of representing the Confederation internationally, of declaring war and concluding peace, of entering into alliances and other treaties with foreign states …
>
> [Article] 63. All the land forces of the Confederation form one single army, which in war and peace is under the command of His Majesty the King of Prussia, as federal Commander-in-Chief …
>
> **Source: Kertesz, G.A. (ed.). (1970).** *Documents in the Political History of the European Continent 1815–1939.* **Oxford: Oxford University Press, pp. 151–52**

How does this source reveal the aims of Bismarck in setting up the North German Confederation?

Reflection: Compare your list of aims with another student's list. Did either of you identify any aims that the other did not? If so, discuss how this may have happened. Would including these different aims change how you would answer the questions?

3.4 How and why was the unification of Germany achieved by 1871?

Bismarck's diplomacy towards France

It is not clear that Bismarck actively sought war with France as a long-term objective, but he was prepared to accept it if necessary. He considered that it might even work in Prussia's interests. A conflict with an external foe, which could be depicted as threatening both southern Germany and the North German Confederation, might act as a means of bringing about complete unification.

Relations between Prussia and France deteriorated after the Austro-Prussian War. Napoleon III was under pressure from French public opinion to gain some compensation for enduring this powerful neighbour on his eastern border. He was a weakened ruler by the late 1860s, exposed to domestic criticism as he was cautiously liberalising the French political system. Bismarck turned down Napoleon's attempt to acquire part of the Rhineland, which belonged to Bavaria and Hesse. Instead, he encouraged him to turn his attention to the Duchy of Luxembourg, an independent state whose ruler was the king of the Netherlands. Some of the inhabitants were German-speaking, and a Prussian garrison was stationed there. This meant that German nationalist feeling was aroused when it emerged in March 1867 that the king was willing to transfer the territory to France, provided that he had Prussian approval. Bismarck then deliberately whipped up German public opinion to prevent the deal between France and the Netherlands from going through. Instead, a conference held in London in May 1867 resulted in Luxembourg being declared a neutral state. The Prussian garrison was withdrawn.

It is unlikely that Bismarck was trying to start a war with France at this stage, but he must have been aware that he was provoking Napoleon into possible future aggression. The south German states – still independent at the time – were horrified to discover that Napoleon wanted to take control of Luxembourg, and turned against France. Events in another part of Europe now unexpectedly played into Bismarck's hands.

The Hohenzollern candidature and the outbreak of war

The Spanish succession crisis

In 1868, the Spanish queen, Isabella, was forced to abdicate by politicians who wanted an end to the rule of the Bourbon royal family in their country. They selected Prince Leopold of Hohenzollern-Sigmaringen as their new monarch. Leopold was from a south German state and a Catholic, like the Spanish, but he was also related to the Prussian royal family. Encouraged by Bismarck, Leopold accepted the offer – a move that was certain to incite French anger as a further example of Prussian expansionism. As king of Prussia, Wilhelm I was head of the Hohenzollern family. He was doubtful of the wisdom of Bismarck's policy.

A major international incident occurred in early July 1870, when a document announcing Leopold's acceptance arrived in Madrid at a time when the Spanish parliament was not in session. This was not supposed to happen. Napoleon should not have heard the news until the Spanish had publicly chosen Leopold. The French government concluded that there was a Prussian plot to encircle France and so put Wilhelm under pressure to persuade Leopold to withdraw.

The king sent Bismarck a telegram describing a meeting about the matter he had just had with Benedetti, the French ambassador, at the spa town of Ems. When he received the Ems Telegram (as it is now known), Bismarck saw an opportunity to portray France as the unreasonable party in the negotiations. He changed the original wording of the telegram to make it appear that the French were demanding a humiliating pledge from Prussia never to support any future renewal of Leopold's candidature. He also gave the impression that Wilhelm had abruptly broken off the discussion with the ambassador. Moltke, who was present when Bismarck edited the telegram, instantly grasped the important difference between the two versions. 'Now it has a different ring,' he declared. 'It sounded before like a parley [a negotiation]; now it is like a flourish in answer to a challenge.'

The outbreak of war against France, July 1870

Bismarck then released the telegram in both Germany and France. The result was public outrage in both Prussia and France. Resolving the situation became a matter of national honour. Urged on by public opinion, Napoleon decided on war. It is not clear how far in advance Bismarck had been thinking in terms of war with France, but this was the outcome of his manipulation of the Ems Telegram. War would almost certainly unite the south German states with the North German Confederation against the common enemy, Napoleon's France. In the event, the French played into his hands by behaving so aggressively.

ACTIVITY 3.15

Bismarck's version of the Ems Telegram, 13 July 1870

> After the news of the renunciation of the hereditary Prince von Hohenzollern had been officially communicated to the Imperial Government of France by the Royal Government of Spain, the French Ambassador further demanded of His Majesty the King, at Ems, that he would authorise him to telegraph to Paris that His Majesty the King bound himself for all time never again to give his consent, should the Hohenzollerns renew their candidature. His Majesty the King thereupon decided not to receive the French Ambassador again, and sent the aide-de-camp [an officer who acts as an assistant to a person of high rank] on duty to tell him that His Majesty had nothing further to communicate to the ambassador.
>
> **Source:** Kertesz, G.A. (ed.). (1970). *Documents in the Political History of the European Continent 1815–1939.* Oxford: Oxford University Press, pp. 200–201

Explain in your own words why the Ems Telegram would cause anger and alarm when published in this form. Is the telegram proof that Bismarck intended to go to war with France, and had been planning for this?

Reasons for the Prussian victory in the Franco-Prussian War, 1870–71

French isolation

France's decision to initiate war in July 1870 was a risky decision. Despite attempts to establish alliances, France was relatively isolated. It was seen as the aggressor while Prussia claimed only to be defending itself. Britain refused to offer support, believing that France was not justified in going to war over the Spanish throne. Italy also refused to come to France's aid while French soldiers were still present in its country, defending Rome on behalf of the Pope. Rome was the last area in the peninsula to remain independent of the new Italian state, and its leaders wanted the French to withdraw so that they could take it over.

The old conservative alliance of Russia and Austria, which had maintained the 1815 settlement for a generation, was now dead, and Russia decided to remain neutral after Bismarck signalled a willingness to help secure a revision of the treaty which had ended the Crimean War. Austria had been weakened by its defeat in 1866 and was now focusing on its empire in south-eastern Europe. Holding that together would require all of its depleted energies.

By contrast, the German national movement supported Prussia. The south German states committed their troops to the war, viewing France as a threat to the whole of Germany, and they fought as well as their Prussian allies. Prussia was able to move half a million troops to the French border while their opponents had only 250 000 men concentrated in the Rhineland.

Prussian military superiority

Prussia's rapid mobilisation and effective preparation for war strongly contrasted with the inefficiency exhibited by France. As in 1866, the value of the Prussian general staff system was evident. By contrast, the French leaders lacked effective means of command and control over their forces. Their army reservists had to proceed to depots to collect equipment before moving to the points where they were meant to assemble. They lacked maps of their own country, having only been issued with maps of Germany, as they expected soon to be crossing the border to win a swift victory. Unlike Prussia, whose military combined short-term, universal conscription with intensive training, France relied on long-serving professionals, recruited by annual lottery. Its reserve force, the *Garde Mobile*, undertook only 14 days of training each year. One of the French generals claimed that their army was 'ready to the last gaiter button', but this was an empty boast. They allowed the Prussians to take the initiative, so that most of the war was fought on French territory.

France had some advantages in terms of weaponry. The recently issued *Chassepot* rifle was superior to the Prussian

ACTIVITY 3.16

How useful is this drawing in explaining the Prussian victory over France in the war of 1870–71?

Figure 3.8: Siege of Paris (19.09.–28.01.1871): Emperor Wilhelm I on the rampart of a Prussian artillery position the day after the surrender of the town. 29.01.1871 (*Contemporary wood engraving*)

needle gun, with an effective range of 1400 metres and a more rapid rate of fire. At the Battle of Gravelotte, for example, in August 1870, the Prussians suffered 20 000 casualties, most of them victims of the *Chassepot*, in return for fewer than 8000 French losses. The French also possessed an early kind of machine gun, the *Mitrailleuse*, but their troops had not learned how to deploy it effectively in support of infantry. Their battlefield tactics were faulty.

They concentrated their troops in prepared defensive positions and controlled their rate of fire as the enemy approached. This approach played into the hands of the more mobile Prussians. They also fell victim to Prussia's improved artillery. Moltke had learned from his army's experience at the hands of the Austrians, and had adopted rifled, steel breech-loading field guns, which outclassed the French in terms of range, accuracy and rate of fire.

ACTIVITY 3.17

This painting, produced in 1877, is not accurate in all details. Bismarck did not actually wear white, for example, so why has the artist, Anton von Werner, depicted him like this? What can you learn from the painting about the way in which Germans wanted to regard the achievement of unification?

Figure 3.9: King Wilhelm I of Prussia being proclaimed German Emperor in the Hall of Mirrors in the Palace of Versailles. Bismarck is the central figure in white uniform and Moltke is to his right, raising his hat. Behind them are the leaders of the German states.

125

Reflection: Compare your approach to this question with that of another student. How did you decide on your approach? Would you change your approach to similar questions following your discussion?

These improvements helped the Prussians and their allies to win the decisive battle of Sedan, near the Belgian border, in September 1870. Here a French army of 100 000 men was encircled and shelled into submission by the Prussian artillery. The French lost 17 000 troops while Prussian casualties were closer to 8000. Napoleon III surrendered to Bismarck. The French emperor was in poor health, but felt that he should be present at the battle, even though he had a poor grasp of military matters. He was then forced to abdicate, after news of the defeat prompted a revolution in Paris and the establishment of a republican government.

Meanwhile, France's Marshal Bazaine allowed himself to be confined with 180 000 troops in the border fortress of Metz, instead of proactively seeking to make use of his resources. In short, France's leaders could not make up their minds whether to fight an offensive or a defensive war. Their lack of a clear strategy proved fatal to their prospects.

The war took a different turn with the decision of the new republican government in Paris to hold out against the invaders in the capital city through the winter. In the countryside, the French used guerrilla warfare to harass Prussian forces. The siege of Paris demonstrated the ruthlessness of the Prussians. A combination of starvation, exhaustion and prolonged artillery bombardment finally led to surrender in January 1871. The republic tried to recruit a new army but failed to find enough trained officers, and the ill-disciplined force was soon defeated.

The defeat of France was a tribute to Bismarck's skill as a diplomatic 'chess player'. As in 1866, before embarking on military action, he made sure that his opponent was isolated among the great powers. He also showed skill in manipulating the growing sense of German nationality, using the French threat as a way of binding the south German states to the war effort. He could not have achieved anything, however, without the successes of the Prussian army, whose readiness to fight was a tribute to Moltke's effectiveness as a commander. The experienced chief of the general staff had further improved the army after the clash with Austria four years earlier. Finally, Prussia was fortunate in the French army's lack of preparation, which cancelled out the advantages it possessed in terms of weaponry. The outcome of the war was largely due to superior Prussian planning, combined with Bismarck's willingness to take a calculated risk in pursuit of his objectives.

Creation of the German Empire, 1871

The new Germany

As a result of the war with France, Germany was fully united. This was not, however, entirely a triumph for German

nationalism. Prussia remained the dominant state in the new Germany. It was a *kleindeutsch* solution to the German problem, with Austria excluded from the new Reich.

Some southern states were still reluctant to be part of a 'Greater Germany' and thus come under Prussian control. Bismarck had to make some concessions to persuade them to join the union. Bavaria, the largest southern state, sought special powers to retain a degree of independence, including control over its own armed forces. Bismarck also gave money to its king, Ludwig II, who was heavily in debt and open to bribery. The funds for this came from the confiscated fortune of the king of Hanover, who had been forced to abandon his throne and flee to Austria after unwisely backing the latter in the war of 1866.

It was not only the southern states that were concerned about the unification of their country. The *Junkers* feared that Prussia would have less power and influence in a larger Germany. There was an argument about the exact title that Wilhelm would take. He wanted to be known as 'Emperor of Germany' but was eventually proclaimed 'German Emperor' or Kaiser in January 1871, at a ceremony held in the Hall of Mirrors in the royal palace of Versailles. Bismarck preferred this title because it did not sound as though Prussia was making an unreasonable claim to authority over the south German states, whose cooperation he needed. The choice of venue was symbolic, since the palace had been created by one of the greatest French monarchs, Louis XIV. This was a visible sign of France's humiliation.

The treatment of France

Bismarck took advantage of France's weakness to impose harsh peace terms. The defeated country was required to pay a sum of 5 billion francs as **reparations**, and a German army was posted in northern France until this was paid. The border province of Alsace and the northern part of its neighbour, Lorraine, were conceded to Germany, mainly to give the newly unified state security against the possibility of a French war of revenge. Although the annexed areas were largely German-speaking, they had belonged to France since the 18th century.

 KEY TERM

Reparations: Money that one country has to pay another as compensation for war damage.

The harshness of the settlement contrasted starkly with Bismarck's relatively generous handling of Austria four years earlier. However, it was a way of binding the south German states to the new Reich. The annexed territory was a **buffer zone** between France and the states of Bavaria, Württemberg and Baden. Its acquisition was part of a strategy of labelling France as an aggressor, which must be seen to be punished as part of the peace settlement. Bismarck had decided that, unlike Austria, France could never develop into an ally in the future, and so the relationship must be based purely on superior strength.

This created a lingering resentment on the part of the French. A statue in the centre of Paris, representing the Alsatian city of Strasbourg, was permanently shrouded in black as a reminder to the population of the loss they had suffered. The French desire to avenge the loss of the two provinces was a long-term cause of the tensions which would lead to the First World War.

KEY TERM

Buffer zone: A protective area separating two potentially hostile countries.

The constitution of the new Reich

The new Reich was very different from the national state for which German liberals had struggled in the revolutionary years of 1848–49. This time, the imperial crown was being offered to a Prussian king by his peer group, the princes, rather than by a popular assembly. Unity had been imposed by means of force from above, not achieved from below by the people.

The constitution was modelled on that of the North German Confederation. Prussia had a deciding voice in the *Bundesrat* since it was allocated 17 out of a total of 58 votes, and 14 votes were sufficient to block any new proposals. It also had a majority of the seats in the Reichstag. The king of Prussia was the Kaiser and commander-in-chief of the armed forces. Bismarck was appointed as Imperial

Chancellor and remained the effective decision-maker in Germany until his downfall in 1890. The heads of the government departments, such as the treasury, justice and the interior, were designated as state secretaries who answered to the chancellor, rather than acting as a team of equal ministers. As Prussian foreign minister, Bismarck was also in control of Germany's external policy. On the other hand, the individual states retained a number of powers, for example over direct taxation, education and welfare policies, and their local parliaments had different relationships with the government in each of the states. It was a *Fürstenbund* or confederation of sovereign principalities. The imperial government was granted certain specific, but important powers: over foreign policy, peace and war, and control of the customs system.

Most importantly, the Prussian army dwarfed the military establishments of the other German states. The military exercised a special role in the new Reich. The army budget was not subject to parliamentary control. Under the North German Confederation, it had been set in 1867 at a fixed level for five years. During the Franco-Prussian War, this was extended until 1874 and, in practice, the Reichstag never gained control of military spending. This meant that the power of the Reichstag to evolve as a genuine parliamentary government, and to hold the Kaiser's ministers effectively to account, was always limited. The new Germany reflected the authoritarian, monarchical, military culture of Prussia.

127

KEY CONCEPT

Significance: the role of the individual

Look back on the information in this chapter on the role of Bismarck. How significant do you think his actions were in the move towards German unification? By contrast, how much did that process owe to other factors, such as the economic strength of Prussia, its military strength, or the mistakes and miscalculations of its opponents in the wars of 1864, 1866 and 1870–71? Overall, how important do you consider this individual was relative to the other forces at work?

Exam-style questions

Source analysis questions

Read the four sources and then answer both parts of question 1.

From a report by the British envoy to Bavaria, Sir Henry F. Howard, to the British foreign secretary, Lord Stanley, 3 December 1866

It remains to be remarked that the feeling of uneasiness in Germany is augmented [increased] by the impression that … when France shall have completed Her military preparations, She will seek a war with Germany so as to obtain those compensations for the aggrandisement [increased power] of Prussia, which She has sketched out, but which She has already learnt will only be yielded to superior force. Whether the fears thus entertained in regard to the eventual course of France and to the alliances to which it may give rise will be realized or not, some seventeen or eighteen months hence, their existence produces a feeling of uncertainty as to the future and furnishes a motive for military preparation on the part of Germany.

Source: Report no. 140, December 3, 1866, in National Archives (formerly Public Record Office, Kew), London, FO 9/177, reprinted at germanhistorydocs.ghi-dc.org

From a letter from Bismarck to Wilhelm I, 20 November 1869

In regard to the South German situation I think the line for Prussian policy is set by two diverse aims … the one distant, the other immediate … The distant and by far the greater aim is the national unification of Germany. We can wait for this in security because the lapse of time and the natural development of the nation which makes further progress every year will have their effect. We cannot accelerate it unless out of the way [unexpected] events in Europe, such as some upheaval in France or a war of other great powers among themselves offer us an unsought opportunity to do so … Every recognisable effort of Prussia to determine the decision of the South German Princes will endanger our immediate aim. I consider this to be … to keep Bavaria and Württemberg in such political direction that neither will cooperate with Paris or Vienna … nor find a pretext to break alliances which we have concluded [with them].

Source: Bohme, H. (1971). *The Foundation of the German Empire.* Oxford: Oxford University Press. reprinted Shreeves, W.G. (1984). *Nation Making in Nineteenth Century Europe.* Cheltenham: Nelson Thorne. p. 166

From the speech of the king of Prussia at the opening of the North German Reichstag, 19 July 1870

The [governments of the North German Confederation] have felt that they have done all which honour and dignity permit to maintain for Europe the blessings of peace; and the clearer it appears to all eyes that the sword has been forced into our hand, with greater confidence we turn, supported by the unanimous will of the German governments of the South, as well as of the North, to the love of the Fatherland and willingness for sacrifice of the German people to the summons to protect her honour and independence.

Source: Kertesz, G.A. (ed.). (1970). *Documents in the Political History of the European Continent 1815–1939.* Oxford: Oxford University Press, p. 203

SOURCE D

From Bismarck's memoirs, published in 1898, recalling the evening when he edited the Ems Telegram, 13 July 1870

After I had read out the concentrated edition to my two guests, Moltke remarked: "Now it has a different ring; it sounded before like a parley [a negotiation]; now it is like a flourish in answer to a challenge." I went on to explain: "If in execution of his Majesty's order I at once communicate this text, which contains no alteration in or addition to the telegram, not only to the newspapers, but also by telegraph to all our embassies, it will be known in Paris before midnight, and … will have the effect of a red rag upon the Gallic [French] bull. Fight we must if we do not want to act the part of the vanquished without a battle. Success, however, essentially depends upon the impression which the origination of the war makes upon us and others; it is important that we should be the party attacked …

Source: Hamerow, T. (ed.). (1973). *The Age of Bismarck: Documents and Interpretations.* New York: Harper & Row, pp. 93–95 reprinted at germanhistorydocs.ghi-dc.org

1 a Read Sources C and D. Compare and contrast Sources C and D as evidence of Prussia's responsibility for the outbreak of war with France in 1870.

b Read all of the sources. 'Bismarck planned in advance to complete the process of German unification by means of a war with France.' How far do the sources support this view?

Essay based questions
Answer both parts of the questions below.

2 a Explain why the rulers of the German states survived the revolutions of 1848–49.

b To what extent was Prussia's military strength the most important reason for the unification of Germany?

3 a Explain why revolutions occurred in several German states in 1848.

b 'Prussia's economic growth was the main reason for its dominant role in the process of German unification.' How far do you agree?

Sample answer
Read Sources C and D. Compare and contrast Sources C and D as evidence of Prussia's responsibility for the outbreak of war with France in 1870.

Source C is taken from an address by the Prussian king, Wilhelm I, to the North German Reichstag, the parliament of the North German Confederation. This body had been created as a result of the Austro-Prussian War of 1866, in which Prussia defeated Austria to become the dominant power in northern Germany. The king is speaking to the Reichstag at the point when the war between France and Prussia broke out. Source D is Bismarck's own account of the outbreak of the Franco-Prussian War in his memoirs, published at the end of his life in 1898.

Source C presents the war as defensive on the part of Prussia and the other German states, stating that 'the sword has been forced into our hand' and claiming that they are fighting to protect their 'honour and independence'. Source D also centres on the idea that the Germans fought a defensive war but it puts a quite different twist on this theme. Bismarck admits that he had altered the text of the Ems Telegram, reporting a meeting between the Prussian king and the French ambassador, to provoke a clash between the two countries. He is much more honest than the author of Source C, in stating that it was important for Prussia and the German states to appear as the victim of French aggression.

129

This is a clear explanation of the content of the sources, focusing mainly on the differences between them. The candidate has, quite correctly, used short quotations rather than copying large sections of the text or relating the content at great length. One important point in Source C, which the candidate has not highlighted, is the reference to the South German states; a key feature of the war was the way in which French aggression could be used to encourage southern German opinion to support the North German Confederation – seen by many historians as a way of completing the process of German unification.

The different dates of the two sources are important in explaining the differences between them. Both are primary sources because they are written by participants in the events of 1870, but Source C comes directly from the time whereas Source D is written almost 30 years later. In July 1870 it was important for Prussia to persuade the other German states to join the war, and this was Wilhelm's main purpose. The other German states would not have supported Prussia if they felt it had acted as the aggressor. We cannot be sure, but it may be that the speech was written for him by Bismarck, as his chief minister and the mastermind behind the conflict with France. By the 1890s, however, the war was in the past and it would not affect the course of events for Bismarck to be honest about how he had manipulated the situation. In fact it may be that he wanted to show his cleverness. He quotes Helmuth von Moltke, chief of the Prussian general staff at the time, as recognising the likely effect of his editing of the telegram, which underlines his own brilliance to the reader.

> This is an effective paragraph which begins to analyse why as well as how the two sources differ. It makes good use of contextual knowledge and speculates intelligently about the possible motivation behind the two extracts.

The intended audiences of the sources are also important in understanding why they differ. The immediate audience for Source C would have been the leading politicians of North Germany but it would also have been published abroad and can be interpreted as justifying military action against France, so that other countries felt less inclined to take the French side. Source D's audience is the general public, particularly those interested in recent political history. Politicians write memoirs when they retire partly to make money but also to justify their earlier actions. Neither source will give a completely reliable account of the events of 1870 because they are both written for particular purposes, and will distort reality in order to make their point. However, Source D, as an insider's account written later, is probably more useful as evidence than a public statement made at the time – although we need to make allowances for a retired politician's desire to exaggerate his own role.

> This is an insightful paragraph which considers the issue of provenance and uses outside knowledge to evaluate the sources for usefulness and reliability. The candidate could, however, have commented further on the type of language used in the sources. The way that Source C enlists the cause of German nationalism ('love of the Fatherland' and the 'sacrifice of the German people') in support of Prussian interests is worth noting. It is also relevant to highlight the dubious argument here, that the North German Confederation has done its best to maintain 'the blessings of peace'. This claim could have been examined. In D, Bismarck is careful to state that he was acting in obedience to the king whereas in fact he was exercising considerable independence. His caricature of France as the 'Gallic bull' is a striking use of language. In conclusion, this is a good response which explains and evaluates the sources, and makes some effective use of contextual knowledge – but it could have gone a little further in making greater use of the evidence presented in the sources.

Sample answer

Explain why the rulers of the German states survived the revolutions of 1848–49.

The German princes were taken by surprise by the revolutions which swept across their territories in 1848–49, but within a year they had recovered their power. This was partly because of their own instinct for survival and the support they received from the two most powerful states, Austria and Prussia. However, it was mainly because of the internal weaknesses and divisions of the revolutionaries. In this essay I will explore these different factors, in order to explain why the princes survived the revolutionary upheavals of this period.

> This introduces the key aspects of the explanation quite concisely, so that the reader knows what to expect in the main body of the answer. It also shows awareness of the need to assess the relative importance of different factors. But does the final sentence really add anything? Remember that time is limited. It would have been better to add a sentence to explain what is meant by an 'instinct for survival'.

The princes initially granted the revolutionaries some of their demands, setting up constitutions which limited their own power. This showed their ability to react to circumstances; they knew that they could be swept from power if they tried to use military force at a time when support for the revolutions was strong, in the spring of 1848. But they were waiting for the right time, when the revolutions started to run out of steam, to fight back. Most of the princes had made sure that they kept their armed forces under their control. This meant that when the revolutionaries started to fall victim to internal divisions, the princes were able to step in and recover control.

> This is a valid explanation, and the last sentence links neatly to the next paragraph, which deals with the weaknesses of the revolutionary movement. But it lacks examples to support the points it makes. It could include, for example, the support provided by Prussia to the rulers of Baden, Württemberg and elsewhere in suppressing the uprisings in 1849. On a point of style, the phrase, 'started to run out of steam' is not wrong, but a more formal expression, such as 'began to lose momentum', might create a more 'professional' impression.

It is doubtful that the princes would have recovered their power so easily, if they had been confronted by more united and better organised revolutionary forces. The revolutions of 1848–49 in the German states were undermined by divisions between liberal, middle-class groups and more radical, working-class elements. They were struggling for different objectives and did not see eye to eye with each other. For example, in the Rhineland, better-off middle-class revolutionaries abandoned the revolution because they feared that armed working-class crowds were presenting a threat to their property. This weakened the movement and helped the princes to regain control.

> This is a stronger paragraph because it uses a specific example, events in the Rhineland, to illustrate the point it is making. But a sentence or two to explain the different aims of the two types of revolutionaries would have helped to develop the argument. What were the liberals and radicals seeking?

The weakness of the revolutionary movement was illustrated by the failure of the Frankfurt Parliament, which the liberal nationalists hoped would create a new constitution for Germany as a whole. It was too slow to agree on a form of government and was also divided between those who wanted a smaller Germany, led by Prussia (*Kleindeutschland*) and those who wanted a larger *Grossdeutschland* which would include Austria. The Parliament did not have armed forces of its own and when a crisis occurred in Schleswig-Holstein, which German nationalists wanted to see join the other German-speaking provinces, they had to rely on Prussia for help. In August 1848 the Prussians made their own peace with Denmark, whose king was the ruler of Schleswig-Holstein, when it suited their interests.

> This paragraph concisely highlights the key weaknesses of the Frankfurt Parliament, whose failure was a key reason why the liberal revolutions of 1848 ended in disappointment. It uses appropriate terminology (*Kleindeutsch land/Grossdeutsch land*). It would have been better with a concluding sentence linking to the theme of the essay – the power of the princes. It could have ended, for example: 'This showed that the goals of liberal nationalism could not be realised without the cooperation of the princes, who had shown that they still possessed the vital resource of armed strength, which they would use to serve their own interests.'

131

Finally, the recovery of the two largest states, Austria and Prussia, from the shocks of March 1848 helped the princes to recover. Austria was soon in a position to use its leadership of the German Confederation to its advantage, under a new prime minister, Prince Schwarzenberg. In Prussia the key role was played by King Friedrich Wilhelm IV, who had first seemed to show sympathy for the revolution but, when he felt strong enough, crushed its hopes. This occurred when he turned down the offer of the German imperial crown in April 1849. This showed that he refused to accept the authority of the parliament and he would only receive such a crown if it was offered by his own peer group, the German princes. The fact that the revolutionaries had such high hopes of the king, rather than pushing for the more radical solution of a German republic, shows how unlikely they were to succeed.

> This is another strong paragraph. It would have benefited from more material on the recovery of Austria, but the analysis of Friedrich Wilhelm IV's role is particularly good. The final sentence nicely links the part played by the king with the weaknesses of the revolutionaries.

The princes recovered so rapidly from the upheavals of 1848–49, partly because they were resourceful and they knew when to retaliate. They had never given up their most important powers, even when they had been forced to grant their subjects more freedoms and had introduced constitutions. But the main reason for their survival was the weakness of liberal nationalism, which from the start was not well enough organised or united to succeed.

This conclusion highlights the most important points of the argument, which have been developed in the main body of the essay. But it does not fully show the connections between the different causes. It demonstrates good knowledge of the topic, although, as noted, more examples would have helped – few princes and their states are actually mentioned and, perhaps understandably, the focus is mainly on Prussia. It explains the main factors with relevant supporting information, and there are no factual inaccuracies. It would benefit from a little more detail, and a more fully supported conclusion.

Summary

After working through this chapter, make sure you understand the following key points:

- how the forces of conservatism held back the process of German unification between 1815 and the 1860s

- the roles that liberalism and nationalism played in the unification of Germany

- why the revolutions of 1848–49 failed to produce a united Germany

- the importance of Prussia's growing economic and military strength in the process of unification

- the part played by Otto von Bismarck in making Prussia the dominant power in a united Germany

- the importance of a succession of wars fought by Prussia, against Denmark, Austria and France, in bringing about German unification.

Further reading

Breuilly, J. (2011). Austria, Prussia and the Making of Germany, 1806–71. (Chapters 3 to 7 give a chronological account of the process of unification; Chapter 8 compares Austria's and Prussia's strengths. Chapter 9 is a helpful conclusion.)

Clark, C. (2006). *Iron Kingdom: The Rise and Downfall of Prussia, 1600–1947.* London: Allen Lane/Penguin. (Chapters 12 to 15 provide more advanced material on Prussia in the period 1815–71.)

Feuchtwanger, E. (2001). *Imperial Germany 1850–1918.* London: Routledge. (Chapter 1 covers German nationalism from 1850–62. Chapter 2 deals with the three wars of unification.)

Hawes, J. (2017). *The Shortest History of Germany.* London: Old Street Publishing. (Looking at Germany from before it was Germany until the present day, this is a helpful read to give context to the events in the chapter.)

Stiles, A. and Farmer. A. (2015). *Access to History: The Unification of Germany and the Challenge of Nationalism.* 4th Edition. London: Hodder. (Chapters 1 to 4 discuss the process of German unification from 1789 to 1871.)

Williamson, D.G. (2010). *Bismarck and Germany, 1862–1890.* London: Routledge. (Parts 1 to 3 describe unification, focusing on the role of Bismarck. Part 7 gives an overall assessment of his career and importance.)

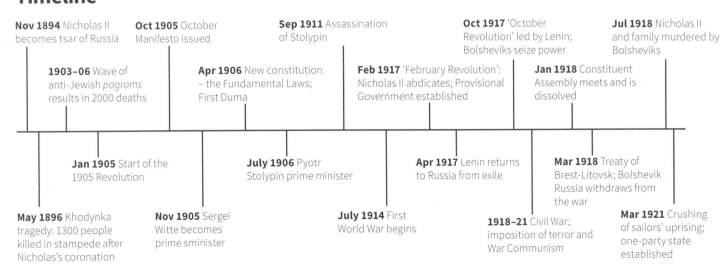

Chapter 4
The Russian Revolution, 1894–1921

Learning objectives

In this chapter you will:

- learn about the causes and outcomes of the revolutions which occurred in Russia in 1905 and 1917
- learn how the Bolsheviks reshaped Russian society and politics after seizing power in 1917
- understand the underlying conditions which promoted revolutionary events
- assess the relative importance of social, economic and political factors in bringing about revolutionary change.

Timeline

Nov 1894 Nicholas II becomes tsar of Russia

Oct 1905 October Manifesto issued

Sep 1911 Assassination of Stolypin

Oct 1917 'October Revolution' led by Lenin; Bolsheviks seize power

Jul 1918 Nicholas II and family murdered by Bolsheviks

1903–06 Wave of anti-Jewish *pogroms* results in 2000 deaths

Apr 1906 New constitution – the Fundamental Laws; First Duma

Feb 1917 'February Revolution': Nicholas II abdicates; Provisional Government established

Jan 1918 Constituent Assembly meets and is dissolved

Jan 1905 Start of the 1905 Revolution

July 1906 Pyotr Stolypin prime minister

Apr 1917 Lenin returns to Russia from exile

Mar 1918 Treaty of Brest-Litovsk; Bolshevik Russia withdraws from the war

May 1896 Khodynka tragedy: 1300 people killed in stampede after Nicholas's coronation

Nov 1905 Sergei Witte becomes prime sminister

July 1914 First World War begins

1918–21 Civil War; imposition of terror and War Communism

Mar 1921 Crushing of sailors' uprising; one-party state established

Note: Dates up to February 1918 are given in the traditional Julian Calendar, which was used in Russia until then. By the end of the 19th century, it was in serious need of adjustment: it was running 13 days behind the newer Gregorian Calendar, which by then was being used in Western Europe.

Before you start

Familiarise yourself with Figure 4.1, showing the extent of the Russian Empire on the eve of the First World War. Consider why it might have been difficult for Russia's rulers to govern an empire as large and diverse as this.

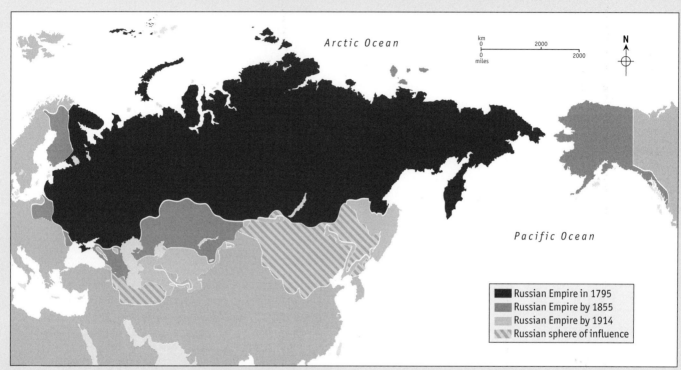

Russian Empire in 1795
Russian Empire by 1855
Russian Empire by 1914
Russian sphere of influence

Figure 4.1: A map showing the expansion of the Russian Empire between 1795 and 1914

4.1 What were the causes and outcomes of the 1905 Revolution up to 1914?

KEY TERMS

Autocrat: A ruler who holds total and supreme power and can make decisions without the approval of any other legal body.

Orthodox Christianity: The official faith of the Russian state, which originated in the eastern part of the Roman Empire; it was independent of any foreign influence and acted as a vital support of the tsarist political system.

At the end of the 19th century, Russia was the largest state in Europe, covering almost 123 million square kilometres and with a population of around 130 million. Compared with the other great powers – Britain, France and Germany – it was economically underdeveloped, and there was a great gulf between the rich and the poor. From 1894 to 1917, the country was ruled by Tsar Nicholas II – an **autocrat** with unlimited power. He belonged to the Romanov dynasty, which had governed Russia since the early 17th century. Nicholas was staunchly opposed to reforms which might have reduced the inequalities that plagued Russian society.

The nature of the tsarist regime: pressures for change and the reaction of Nicholas II to them

A multiracial, multifaith empire

At the end of the 19th century, Russia contained a large number of racial groups. In fact, only 45% of the population were ethnic Russians. The rest comprised Armenians, Germans, Georgians, Poles and Ukrainians, as well as many Asiatic peoples. Each of these groups was proud of its nationality, language, history and religion, and for many years the only force unifying these disparate peoples was loyalty to the tsar. This was sufficient most of the time, but the general attitude towards their ruler changed during the 1890s. In this decade, the tsarist regime alienated the different ethnic groups through a policy of 'Russification' – enforcing the Russian language as well as the **Orthodox Christianity** and laws throughout the land. According to statistics compiled in 1905, almost 70% of the empire's population followed the

Orthodox faith, but there were significant Catholic, Muslim and Jewish minorities. Russia's 5 million Jews endured frequent persecution. They were blamed for Russia's troubles and subjected to periodic **pogroms**. Many fled to Western Europe or the United States. Those who stayed were often drawn into revolutionary activity.

KEY TERMS

Pogroms: Outbreaks of mob violence against Jews, often approved by the authorities.

Emancipation of the serfs: The granting of legal freedom to the serfs – agricultural labourers who belonged to their landlords, or the state, in a condition quite similar to slavery. They were freed in 1861 by Tsar Alexander II, Nicholas's grandfather, but many remained poor and with limited freedom.

The social hierarchy in Russia

The tsar governed with the support of the landowning aristocracy. Unlike in Western European countries, the nobility did not act as a check on the power of the monarchy. They owed their social position largely to military and civil service to the state. There were no truly independent institutions in Russian society. The leaders of the Orthodox Church, which exercised great influence over society, especially in rural areas, were appointed by the tsar.

The vast majority of Russians were peasants. In theory, peasants had been free (that is, they were not bound to a landlord as peasants had been for much of history) since the **emancipation of the serfs** in 1861, but this had brought few changes. They belonged to communes or *mirs* – agricultural cooperatives which organised the distribution of land between households. Peasants had to make 'redemption payments' for the land they received. Most peasants were loyal to the tsar, but disliked the officials who demanded taxes and forced service from them.

The condition of the peasantry was perhaps Russia's most serious problem. Famines were frequent, and, due to poor transport infrastructure, the government could not move food from places where it was plentiful to those where it was lacking. There was widespread poverty, and production levels were low. Peasants were encouraged to move from the west of Russia to Siberia, where land was plentiful but natural conditions were too harsh to support a prosperous agriculture. In 1882, a Land Bank was founded to provide money for local communities and individual peasants to buy land. In 1905, redemption payments were cancelled, but in reality this made little difference to the peasants.

ACTIVITY 4.1

The only national census to take place in tsarist Russia was held in 1897. It gave the following data for different classes as a percentage of the population.

Social class	Percentage of the Russian population
Ruling class (tsar, court and government)	0.5
Upper class (nobility, higher clergy, military officers)	12.0
Middle classes (merchants, factory owners, bankers)	1.5
Working classes (factory workers, small traders)	4.0
Peasants (agricultural workers)	82.0

Table 4.1: Census figures showing different groups in Russia, 1897

Source: Adapted from Lynch, M. (1992). *Reaction and Revolutions: Russia 1881–1924*. London: Hodder & Stoughton, p. 10

What does this data tell you about the nature of Russian society at the end of the 19th century? How much of the population was employed in trade and industry, compared with agriculture? Does the table give you any clues to why a revolutionary situation had developed in Russia by 1905?

Economic structure

Russia should have had enough agricultural resources to feed its population adequately, but several factors stunted the economy:

- Agricultural methods were underdeveloped. Neither the mass of the peasantry nor the landowners were interested in any form of modernisation to improve output.
- Russia did export wheat, and by the end of the 19th century grain exports were second only to those from America. Profits from these sales, however, did not benefit the peasantry. The central government, dominated as it was by landowners, did not impose a fair level of taxation on the Russian ruling class. Instead the government relied heavily on indirect taxes, levied on goods.

By 1900, Russia had caught up with Britain and Germany, the two most advanced industrial countries, in terms of the total length of its rail network. Russia's vast size, however, meant that the railways were still only thinly spread throughout the country. This expanded railway system, along with increased industry, did help Russia to export more wheat, which benefited foreign trade, but the money was not equally shared. The government's revenues were limited by the taxation system: income and land were taxed less than indirect taxes on commodities and food, and this system disadvantaged the peasants and the poor who lived in towns. The system by which taxes were collected was inefficient and corruptible, with most taxes disappearing into the pockets of tax collectors and other middle-men before it could reach the central government. The regime also spent its money unwisely. Funds were allocated generously to the army and to the police, but little was spent on improving the economy. Nicholas II was simply not interested in modernisation or reform, and remained firmly committed to autocracy. The result was that the general Russian populace became increasingly alienated from the government and their landlords, although it seems that most peasants continued to believe in the tsar as an individual.

The tsarist political system

Nicholas II became tsar in 1894, announcing, 'I shall maintain the principle of autocracy just as firmly as did my unforgettable father'. Alexander III, who ruled from 1881 to 1894, had opposed any reforms in Russia, believing they threatened his power and the ancient traditions on which the Romanov dynasty had been built. He considered the innovations being developed in the West as unsuitable for his country. His son Nicholas kept his promise throughout his reign: resisting change however much circumstances within Russia altered. He was disastrously out of touch with the feelings of his subjects. This impression was unfortunately established early in his reign, with his reaction to the 'Khodynka tragedy', which occurred during the festivities of his coronation in May 1896. More than 1300 people were crushed to death, and a similar number injured, when the crowd stampeded as rumours spread that there was insufficient food and drink for them all. The authorities proved unable to control the situation. Although Nicholas shared the sense of shock which followed this event, he was insensitive enough to attend a celebratory ball the same evening.

The tsar was in charge of appointing and dismissing ministers, and there was no parliament to limit his authority. The army put down violent unrest and the secret police (known as the Okhrana) kept political dissidents under observation through a network of informers. The Orthodox Church, and especially its leading

official, Konstantin Pobedonostsev, fully supported the tsar's rule. He regarded anyone with alternative religious sympathies as subversive, and was the determined enemy of all reformers in Russia.

The tsar was personally a kind man, devoted to his wife, Alexandra, and his children. His only son, Alexei, suffered from the blood disorder haemophilia, and it was doubtful that he would survive into adulthood. This situation clearly left uncertainties over the succession to the throne, and played a significant part in the instability of Nicholas's regime.

Nicholas possessed some characteristics which might have made him an amiable and respected local nobleman – although he was also a committed anti-Semite – but he lacked many of the qualities required in an effective ruler. He was isolated at court and uninterested in matters of government; he preferred to go hunting than to attend ministerial meetings. He could be swayed easily by advice, usually from courtiers, who also opposed reforms. His ministers were typically chosen because of their social position rather than for their abilities. These men competed for the attention of the tsar rather than cooperating with each other or offering objective advice. Nicholas focused on the detail of day-to-day administration, and found it hard to delegate even unimportant tasks, which meant that he failed to get to grips with larger issues. In short, he claimed the power of an autocrat without possessing the personality needed for the role.

Nicholas ruled through two central bodies whose members he appointed. They were there to help him govern the country, and they did not restrict the tsar's personal power. The State Council, which consisted of senior advisers to the tsar, had no powers. Most of its members were old men appointed because of their long service to the state rather than for their vigour and skill in managing affairs. They were usually appointed for life by the tsar, but he could dismiss them if he wished. Members thus tended to give him the advice that they knew would be welcomed, rather than what they truly believed to be in Russia's best interests.

The members of the senate were also appointed by the tsar. This body was supposed to oversee the operation of the law, but the system was confused and the powers of the senate were unclear.

There were many local officials whose responsibilities were also uncertain. Russia was made up of 97 administrative regions – far more than was necessary to govern even such a large country. Local councils known as *zemstvos* had been set up following the emancipation of the serfs in 1861. They provided a form of self-government for villages and some larger areas where the Russian population lived, but the system was not adopted in areas populated by ethnic minorities. The limited powers of the *zemstvos* could be overruled by governors and other officials who generally opposed reform. Cities and large towns were governed by appointed rather than elected officials. Overall, Russia was administered much less efficiently than the more modern states in Western Europe.

Witte's reforms

The one forward-thinking Russian statesman at this time was **Sergei Witte**, who believed that the answer to Russia's problems lay in foreign loans and foreign exports. The country was rich in raw materials, but lacked the factories and railways required to produce and export manufactured goods. Building these would require huge sums of money, but Russia did not have the funds for this investment. Wealthy nobles were not interested in industry, dismissing it as undignified.

Industrial growth was needed to enable Russia to compete with the more economically advanced nations of the West, and modernisation was necessary to increase Russia's military strength. Witte was convinced that the power of the state must be used to drive the growth of capitalism. He brought in engineers and managers from Western countries to advise the government on how to go about this.

Witte increased taxes and raised money abroad by giving investors high rates of interest. He imposed tariffs on imports in order to protect Russian industries, and increased the value of the Russian currency, the rouble, by linking it to the **gold standard**. Witte was particularly interested in railways, having served as director of the state rail network before being appointed finance minister. The length of railway lines almost doubled during his term of office, opening up previously inaccessible parts of the country to economic development. The most high-profile development was the Trans-Siberian Railway, which eventually linked Moscow with Vladivostok on Russia's eastern coast, although sections of it remained incomplete in the first decade of the new century. These policies led to impressive increases in industrial growth, with coal production in southern Russia more than trebling. Russia became the world's fourth largest producer of steel and the second largest producer of petroleum. One historian called this the 'great spurt'.

KEY TERM

Gold standard: An international monetary system in which the value of a country's currency was linked directly to a fixed quantity of gold in order to give long-term price stability.

However, Witte's policies also caused problems. Twice as much was spent on repaying the foreign loans as was expended on education. Taxes were increased to repay the loans and this affected the peasants most severely.

Nicholas II gave Witte little support, and he was despised among members of the court and other nobility, who considered his ideas dangerous. They were suspicious of his support for rapid industrialisation, which they feared would destabilise rural society. Many members of the upper class also disliked him for having married a divorced Jewish woman. After falling from office, Witte was recalled briefly as prime minister at a time of crisis after the 1905 Revolution, mostly to negotiate a loan from France. His support for reforms was still unpopular with influential courtiers and he was dismissed as soon as the loan was secured.

So, the positive results of Witte's reforms were that industry and the railways grew. The negative results were that the country's national debt increased and the standard of living of most the population declined. At the turn of the century, these problems were certainly serious, but there was no indication that they would be fatal for Nicholas II. The national situation was no worse than it

137

SERGEI WITTE (1849–1915)

Witte was one of the rare officials in Nicholas II's government who supported reform. As minister of finance from 1892 to 1903, Witte was convinced that rapid industrialisation was the solution to the country's economic problems. Nicholas II never supported Witte's ideas and dismissed him, only to recall him briefly as prime minister after the 1905 Revolution.

had been for many years, and most people believed that the tsarist government could survive as long as it did not have to face a major crisis such as a foreign war.

The rise of opposition

By the end of the 19th century, liberals in Russia were pressing for constitutional political change, and increased civil liberties, similar to those enjoyed in Western European states. They had a power base in the *zemstvos* and, by 1904, had formed an organisation known as the Union of Liberation. They were not very powerful, however, because they drew their support mainly from the relatively small middle class and did not appeal to the peasants. There were no official liberal parties until the outbreak of the 1905 Revolution, when the political climate became a little more favourable to their activities. The main liberal party in 1905 was known as the Kadets, which campaigned for a reformed monarchy, subject to limitations on its power.

The oppressive nature of the tsarist political system meant that opposition tended to be driven underground. Critics of the government could not find legal opportunities to express their views. Consequently they often turned to political violence. It was a common saying among educated foreign observers of Russia in the 19th century that its political system consisted of 'autocracy tempered [moderated] by assassination'. The most significant political killing was the assassination of Tsar Alexander II by bomb-throwing members of a revolutionary society in March 1881, an event which left a profound impression on his grandson, Nicholas II.

One radical political group was the Socialist Revolutionaries, founded in 1901, whose aim was to confiscate and redistribute wealth among the peasants. They had a terrorist wing which carried out a number of political assassinations in the years leading up to the 1905 Revolution, including that of the unpopular minister of the interior, Vyacheslav von Plehve. In the long run, the most important opposition group was the All-Russian Social Democratic Labour Party, founded in 1898. It drew its ideas from the German **socialist** thinker Karl Marx, who argued that the course of history was determined by economic forces. Private property had replaced primitive societies in which there was no private ownership. Capitalism replaced the feudal economy of the Middle Ages, which had been based on the ownership of land by the aristocracy. This gave power to the moneyed middle class, or bourgeoisie. Marx called for a revolution

by the lower classes – whom he called the **proletariat** – to overthrow the capitalist system. He claimed that a dictatorship of the proletariat would lead to a classless society; national boundaries would disappear and state governments that suppressed workers would no longer exist.

KEY TERM

Socialist: A person who wants to create a more equal society, based on cooperation, rather than on the capitalist concept of competition.

Proletariat: The urban, industrial working class. They generally had no savings or property, and their only source of income was their own labour.

The industrial growth of the 1890s made Marxist ideas appealing to many revolutionaries who wanted to transform Russian society. The key figure in the early years was Georgi Plekhanov, who aimed to build a broad alliance of pro-reform, anti-tsarist activists. He was challenged, however, by Vladimir Ilyich Ulyanov, better known as **Lenin**, who argued that only a highly centralised, disciplined revolutionary party could successfully lead a revolution in an autocratic state like Russia. The second congress of the Social Democrats met in London in 1903. Lenin decided to restrict membership of the party to those who were active in the cause of revolution and socialism. This would necessarily be a minority. Lenin wanted a revolution in Russia to defeat

Lenin came from a middle-class family and was regarded as politically dangerous from the age of 17, when his older brother was executed for involvement in an assassination plot against Alexander III. Lenin was first sentenced to exile in Siberia and then lived in Western Europe. He returned to Russia two months after the 1917 February Revolution. He opposed the Provisional Government and played a decisive role in the October Revolution of 1917. He governed Russia from this point until his death in 1924.

VLADIMIR ILYICH LENIN (1870–1924)

tsarism. **Leon Trotsky** and Julius Martov – a Russian politician who was also exiled for his beliefs on reform – disagreed with these steps, believing that revolutionary success depended on a wider, rather than a more restricted, membership. They took the longer-term view of Marxism: that capitalism had to collapse from within before communism could triumph.

The deciding vote at Congress was very close: Lenin's group won by two votes. They took the name **Bolshevik** (a word meaning 'the majority'). Martov's group, to which Trotsky belonged at this stage, the minority, became the Mensheviks. They maintained a separate organisation of their own after this split in the Social Democrat Party.

KEY TERMS

Bolshevik: A member of the more radical faction of the Russian Social Democrat Party, which seized power in the revolution of October 1917. The party was renamed the Russian Communist Party in 1918, but the term Bolshevik will be used throughout this chapter for the sake of simplicity.

LEON TROTSKY (1879–1940)

Trotsky came from a well-to-do Jewish family in Ukraine. As a young man, he sided with the Menshevik faction of the Social Democrat Party. In the 1905 Revolution, he organised workers in St Petersburg. He was sentenced to internal exile, but escaped abroad. In 1917, he joined the Bolsheviks and played a key role in their seizure of power and later in the organisation of the Red Army. After Lenin died in 1924, Trotsky lost a power struggle with Stalin. He was expelled from the party and exiled from Russia. He was assassinated in Mexico in 1940 by an agent sent by Stalin.

ACTIVITY 4.2

You are now in a position to make an assessment of how strong and secure the tsarist system was at the start of the 20th century. To do this, review the information you have learned so far, then copy and complete the following table. An example in each column has been given for you. Aim to find about three more in each column. Then try to answer the following question: On balance, do you think that the tsarist system in Russia was bound to fail by the beginning of the 20th century?

The tsarist system was strong and stable at the beginning of the 20th century	It faced serious threats
The tsarist system could rely on the army and secret police to suppress opposition.	This had the effect of driving opposition underground, potentially making it more violent and dangerous.

The war with Japan and its consequences for Russia

By 1900, China was extremely weak – suffering from internal conflict and poor government. Both Japan and Russia saw the possibility of expanding their influence in Manchuria, eastern China, and Korea. Port Arthur in Manchuria offered Russia an ice-free harbour, which would be useful because its other ports were either in the Arctic north or on the Black Sea, with difficult access to other oceans. Japan suggested that Russia could take control of Manchuria if Japan itself could have Korea. These negotiations broke down, however, and war broke out in 1904, after Japan attacked Port Arthur.

In the course of the Russo-Japanese War, the poor quality of the Russian navy was demonstrated when ships had to be sent from the Baltic in the west to confront the Japanese navy. The fleet suffered a devastating defeat at the Battle of Tsushima in May 1905, after taking eight months to arrive. In a stunning victory for the Japanese, two-thirds of the Russian fleet was destroyed, demoralising the surviving Russian sailors. The Russian army, larger than the Japanese but inferior in quality, failed to prevent

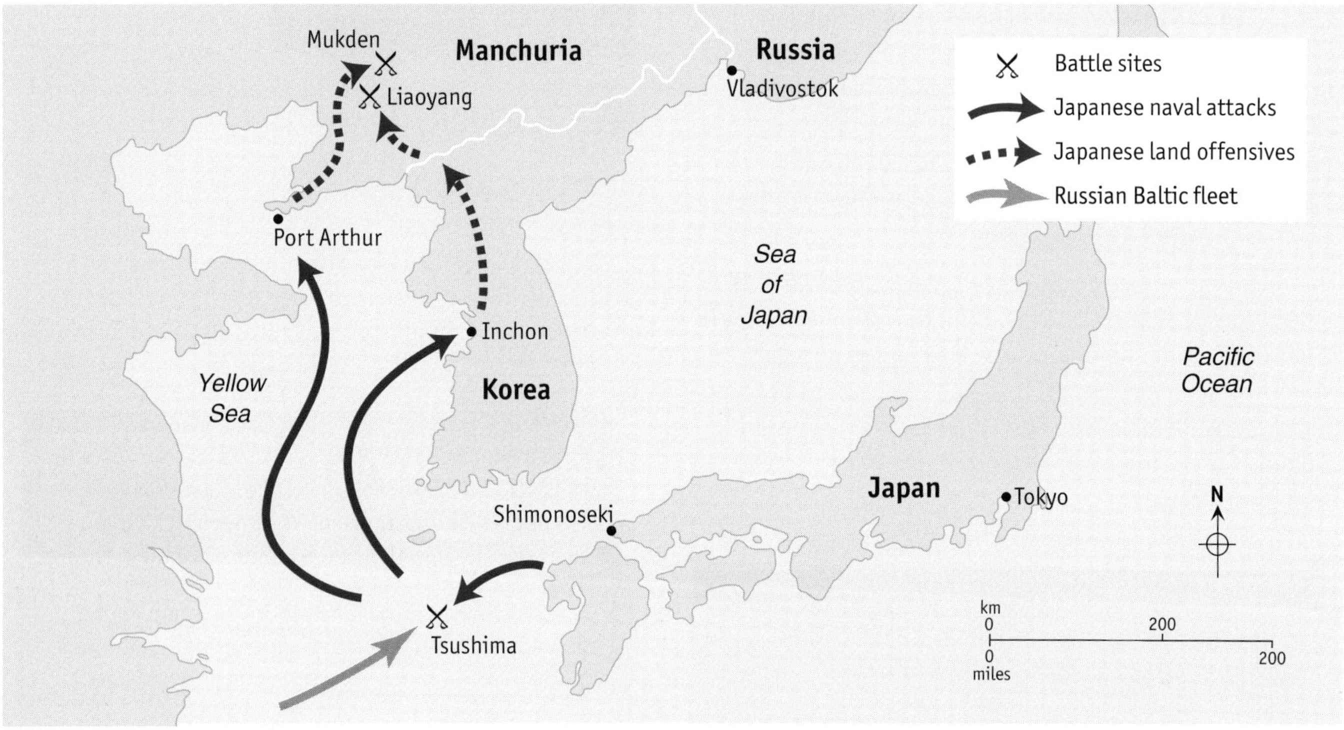
Mukden
Manchuria
Liaoyang
Russia
Vladivostok
Battle sites
Japanese naval attacks
Japanese land offensives
Russian Baltic fleet
Port Arthur
Sea
of
Japan
Inchon
Yellow
Sea
Korea
Pacific
Ocean
Japan
Tokyo
Shimonoseki
N
Tsushima
km
0
200
0
200
miles

Figure 4.2: A map showing the progress of the Russo-Japanese War, 1904–05

the capture of Mukden, the capital of Manchuria. With the Trans-Siberian railway not yet complete, the Russian government struggled to transport troops and equipment from western Russia to the battle zone. Ultimately, Russia had to agree a humiliating peace in the Treaty of Portsmouth, arranged by the United States, in 1905. Japan was left as the dominant power in Korea and Manchuria.

There were several significant consequences of this war:

- Japan began to be regarded as a more modern and efficient state – the first in Asia to defeat a European country.
- Russia's weaknesses were revealed. It turned its international interests from the east to the Balkans, with consequences that eventually led to the First World War.
- Internally, the defeat was a serious blow to the prestige of the tsarist government. The Russo-Japanese war was a cause of the 1905 Revolution.

Key events of the 1905 Revolution: 'Bloody Sunday', wider risings and the October manifesto

The 1905 Revolution

The Russian Revolution of 1905 was not a sudden event; rather it was the culmination of years of discontent caused by several factors. These were primarily economic in nature, and the disturbances which led to revolution were largely unplanned. Mishandling of the crisis by the authorities made it more serious. These were the main causes of the Revolution:

- The poor economic condition of the peasantry, who had seen little improvement in their lives following emancipation. They continued to struggle with redemption payments. The peasants had also borne the brunt of tax increases, imposed to pay for Witte's policies of industrialisation, and they disliked compulsory military service.
- An economic recession in the early years of the 20th century, which resulted in high rates of unemployment. As more people moved to towns and cities, especially St Petersburg and Moscow, overcrowding caused living conditions to worsen. The proletariat lived in squalid housing and unhealthy environments. There was very little medical care and standards of education were very low. Workers had virtually no employment rights. Trade unions were banned and the police cracked down on protests. Real wages declined in this period by an estimated 20%.
- Growing nationalist unrest among racial groups such as the Finns, Baltic peoples, Armenians and Georgians, who resented the policy of Russification.

- Other groups within the empire who wanted a more democratic form of government. Although no legal political parties were allowed, members of the educated middle classes wanted change, and some demanded socialism.
- The autocratic nature of Nicholas II's rule. It distanced him from the population and made the situation worse. Supporters of political reform were confronted by the repressive apparatus of the tsarist police state.
- Defeat in the Russo-Japanese War, which contributed to the impression that tsarist government was incompetent and vulnerable to challenges by hostile foreign powers. It fuelled criticism by liberals who wanted a reformed, more efficient monarchy.

Although revolutionary groups existed in Russia, they were not mainly responsible for the 1905 Revolution. The Bolsheviks and the Mensheviks were caught unawares. However, when unrest broke out, Trotsky and other Mensheviks and radicals tried to promote strikes and other workers' actions. Workers' committees known as **soviets** were set up in factories. In fact, in terms of the 1905 Revolution, Lenin was the right man in the wrong place. He was in exile and returned to Russia 11 months after Bloody Sunday – too late to play an effective role in the revolution.

KEY TERM

Soviets: Workers' councils, which first appeared in industrial cities in 1905. They were to play an important part in the October 1917 Revolution.

Bloody Sunday

In January 1905, a priest named Father Gapon led a non-violent march to the tsar's Winter Palace in St Petersburg, to petition him for an assembly elected by universal suffrage. The crowd also called for basic civil liberties, land reform, fairer taxes and a voice for workers in the running of factories. They were dispersed violently by Cossack soldiers. An estimated 130 people were killed and hundreds more injured. The incident became known as 'Bloody Sunday'. Up to this point, many workers had distinguished between the tsar, whom they described as their 'little father', and the unfeeling, unpopular state bureaucracy. They believed that the tsar did not know of their terrible conditions. Many of the marchers had carried images of Nicholas. Now he was widely blamed for the repression even though he was not present at the time. The marchers were unarmed and they had not intended

to behave in a revolutionary manner, but their harsh treatment stimulated other popular outbreaks.

ACTIVITY 4.3

From the petition of the crowd on Bloody Sunday, January 1905

> Sire, here are many thousands of us, and all are human beings only in appearance. In reality in us, as in all Russian people, there is not recognised any human right, not even the right of speaking, thinking, meeting, discussing our needs … We have been enslaved … under the auspices of YOUR officials … We are seeking here the last salvation. Do not refuse assistance to Your people … Give their destiny into their own hands. Cast away from them the intolerable oppression of officials. Destroy the wall between Yourself and Your people, and let them rule the country together with Yourself.
>
> **Adapted from Kertesz, G.A. (ed.). (1970). *Documents in the Political History of the European Continent 1815–1939*. Oxford: Oxford University Press, p. 298**

What does this extract suggest about the intentions of the marchers? Does its language indicate a desire to overthrow the tsarist system of government, or just to make it work more fairly?

Other disturbances in 1905

Strikes began in Moscow and rapidly spread to other cities as industrial workers organised themselves into trade unions. An estimated 800 000 workers went on strike. The formation of workers' soviets in St Petersburg and Moscow was an important development. They demanded improved conditions for workers and became a focus for wider political agitation. Sailors on the battleship *Potemkin* mutinied, and the government feared more unrest among sailors and soldiers. Middle-class liberals, organised as the Kadets (or the Constitutional Democrats) wanted the tsar's powers to be limited by an elected assembly. They attempted to form a 'Union of Unions', linking up with workers and peasants to demand further political change. Peasants refused to pay rent and attacked the property of the aristocracy, burning 3000 manors in the summer of 1905.

However, the revolutionaries were largely disorganised, with no central coordination, and protests were geographically scattered across the empire. Few determined revolutionaries were involved in the protests. Fortunately for the tsar, the army remained loyal to him at this point.

ACTIVITY 4.4

How reliable do you think this painting is? What would you need to know about the artist and the circumstances in which the painting was made in order to assess it?

Figure 4.3: A painting by Ivan Vladimirov showing the 'Bloody Sunday' shooting of workers in front of the Winter Palace, St Petersburg, 9 January 1905

The October Manifesto, 1905

As unrest continued, Nicholas II was reluctantly persuaded to make concessions to the masses. He did this on the advice of Witte, who was now prime minister. The October Manifesto promised free speech, voting rights for those who had previously been denied an opportunity to participate in politics, and an elected assembly called the Duma (from *dumat*, which means 'to think'). Its agreement would be needed before any laws could be passed. Although Nicholas II initially promised greater liberties and said that the Duma would have the power to act to ensure these liberties were upheld, he did not allow the Duma to elect government ministers or hold them to account, and he claimed the right to discharge the Duma.

Reaction to the October Manifesto was divided. Many of the rebels felt that their voices had been heard,

and that the landowners would have to accept their demands, and moderate liberals, who became known as 'Octobrists', were pacified by the introduction of the Duma. They were drawn mainly from the landowning and business classes, and had been alarmed by the violence of working-class protests. They were relieved to have order restored. In November, peasant unrest was calmed by an announcement that redemption payments would be phased out. A minority of extreme revolutionaries, however – including the Bolsheviks – felt that the Manifesto did not go far enough in addressing the grievances of the Russian people. There was some armed resistance, but the tsar's soldiers suppressed this, bringing an end to the soviets. It seemed for a time that stability would return to Russia.

The reassertion of tsarist authority: the Dumas and Stolypin's reforms

The Fundamental Laws, 1906

Nicholas II's insincerity in presenting the October Manifesto soon became apparent. He proved unwilling to enforce the reforms that he had promised and, in April 1906, issued the Fundamental Laws, which asserted his full autocratic powers. The first statement of the Fundamental Laws was that 'supreme autocratic power belongs to the tsar'. This denied the hopes of those who saw the Duma as a means of bringing more representative government to Russia. The tsar could introduce laws and could veto those passed by the Duma. Furthermore, the elected Duma was to be balanced by the State Council, most of whose members would be appointed by the tsar. Ministers too were still appointed by the tsar, who also controlled military and foreign affairs. The Duma had no way of enforcing its decisions. The police and the army continued to harass real or imagined critics of the tsarist regime: it is estimated that 15 000 people were killed and 70 000 arrested within a year.

ACTIVITY 4.5

From the Fundamental Laws of the Russian Empire, 23 April 1906

> 8 The initiative in all branches of legislation belongs to the Tsar. Solely on his initiative may the Fundamental Laws of the Empire be subjected to a revision in the Council of the Empire and the Imperial Duma.
>
> 9 The Tsar approves of the laws, and without his approval no law can come into existence.
>
> 10 All governmental powers in their widest extent throughout the whole Russian Empire are vested in the Tsar.
>
> Source: Kertesz, G.A. (ed.). (1970). *Documents in the Political History of the European Continent 1815–1939.* Oxford: Oxford University Press, p. 305

How does this extract conflict with the October Manifesto? How would you expect the reformers in Russia to react to this document?

Some historians have argued that Nicholas II missed an opportunity in 1906 to carry through the reforms that would have made Russia a more modern and stable country. However, autocratic rulers rarely prove willing to surrender any of their power, and Nicholas II

was particularly reactionary. It soon became apparent that the reforms were mostly cosmetic. The factors that had caused the 1905 Revolution remained largely unresolved even after Nicholas had put down the revolt and attempted to implement reforms. His treatment of the Duma in 1906–14 was to show his contempt for representative government, and his refusal to provide effective leadership laid the foundations for future troubles.

Stolypin's reforms

Nicholas II took a positive step in 1906 when he appointed **Pyotr Stolypin** as minister of the interior and, later, as prime minister. Stolypin saw agriculture as the primary problem and wanted to work towards improving the peasants' situation. In many ways, his work complemented that of Witte, whose focus had been on industrial growth, although the two men did not work together in government. Some historians consider that if Nicholas had given his full backing to them, as his two most talented ministers, they could possibly have averted revolution.

Stolypin also believed in strict law and order, however, and he ruthlessly repressed any peasant uprisings. 'Stolypin's Necktie' (death by hanging) was used widely to punish rebels after the 1905 Revolution.

Although Stolypin sought reform, he was not a democrat. His first objective was to restore order and only after doing so did he embark on a policy of social and economic reform. He believed that the most beneficial

Stolypin came from a noble family and was politically conservative, but, unlike many of his class, he demonstrated an awareness of the hardships that most Russians faced. He made his reputation by his tough handling of disturbances as a provincial governor in 1905. As prime minister, Stolypin aimed to counter unrest by undertaking reforms that could vastly improve life for the peasants in Russia.

PYOTR STOLYPIN (1862–1911)

change would be to encourage the growth of a wealthy peasant class, or *kulaks*, saying that Russia should 'bet on the strong'. By this he meant that, if peasants became property owners, they would have a stake in maintaining the current system and would be less likely to support revolutionary change.

The *mirs* oversaw the work of peasants and were generally restrictive. They directed what land a peasant could work and which crops could be grown, limiting the ability of an ambitious peasant to make improvements. Stolypin wanted to make peasants independent of the *mirs*. This would allow them to put together their individual strips of land and therefore work them more efficiently. Stolypin also recognised that the high level of redemption payments for peasants' plots of land was a reason why they had taken part in the 1905 Revolution. The high price of land, combined with rural overpopulation and a series of poor harvests, had worsened conditions in the countryside. Many peasants feared that the government would repossess the land holdings of those who could no longer afford their redemption payments.

The Peasant Land Bank, which had been founded in 1882, lent peasants money to buy their land. Those who had little or poor land were encouraged to move to unfarmed land in the east. Many peasants took advantage of these developments, as a result of which Russia began to experience regional changes. In places such as Ukraine and Crimea in the south, where the land was fertile, peasants had an incentive to secure their own land. In the harsh north and east, there was no such incentive. Agricultural production increased in the most favourable regions, making the *kulaks* more prosperous. It also benefited the government and those who exported wheat.

Exact figures are difficult to calculate, but output might have increased by 14% between 1900 and 1914, and the income of some landowners and *kulaks* rose by as much as 80%. Some historians believe, however, that most of the increase was the result of a series of naturally good harvests rather than Stolypin's reforms, and point out that many Russians did not benefit from these policies.

Agriculture was improving by the outbreak of war but the attempt to create a new, independent class of peasant proprietors had not developed very far. Stolypin said that his policy would need 20 years to see results. In 1906–14 only 15% of peasant households were consolidated into farms. Peasants were suspicious of change and did not want to risk leaving the security of the communes. They even questioned the authorities' attempts to measure the land in readiness for enclosure, fearing that they would not

get a fair share. They were especially resistant in central Russia, where peasant support for revolution would be strongest in 1917.

Stolypin was assassinated in September 1911 at the Kiev Opera. He was already losing the favour of the tsar, and it is possible that agents of the state were behind his murder. In the Duma, he had built a good working relationship with the Octobrists, who supported his policies, but his successors as prime minister, Vladimir Kokovtsov (1911–14) and Ivan Goremykin (1914–16), lacked his drive and commitment to reform.

The frustration of political reform: the first Duma, May–July 1906

Although the Duma was an elected body, like many other constituent national assemblies in the world at that time, it represented only a section of the adult population. The **franchise** was not universal: it applied only to male citizens over the age of 25. They did not vote directly for their own representatives but for committees known as electoral colleges, which selected members of the Duma. Crucially for its political influence, its powers were limited to control of a small part of the budget. Accordingly, Nicholas II was increasingly able to ignore its debates and resolutions. The Social Democrats and Socialist Revolutionaries boycotted the elections. The Kadets won 153 of the 448 seats, and proceeded to demand more powers for the Duma. This was unacceptable to the tsar, who dissolved it barely two months later. The Kadets assembled at Vyborg in Finland in protest, and appealed to the Russian people not to pay taxes or submit to military service. This led to scattered outbreaks of resistance, which the government was easily able to crush.

KEY TERM

Franchise (or suffrage): The right to vote.

The second Duma, February–June 1907

The second Duma met for a few months, from February to June 1907. The Kadets had been damaged by their earlier failure, and, in the elections, the more radical Social Democrats and Social Revolutionaries were successful, winning more than a hundred seats between them. This led to deep divisions within the Duma over land reform and the government's law and order policies. The tsar was not prepared to see the Duma become a forum for opposition, and once again it was dissolved. He persisted in calling elections, however, in the belief that an appearance of parliamentary government made his regime more acceptable to Britain and France, with whom he was building closer relationships in order to counter the rise of Germany.

The third Duma, November 1907–June 1912

Stolypin ensured that the franchise was changed to give greater representation to landowners and urban property owners. This enabled the third Duma to last longer than its predecessors. With right-wing parties now controlling 287 of the 443 seats, its relationship with the government was more harmonious and there was progress on land reform, military reorganisation and the introduction of national insurance for workers. It was denounced by radicals, however, as a 'Duma of lords and lackeys', regarded as too subordinate to the government. Even the liberals were uneasy with the way in which the Fundamental Laws had been manipulated to bring about the change in the electoral law.

The fourth Duma, November 1912–August 1914

Divisions between socialists and Octobrists hampered the fourth Duma's chances of success. It was suspended on the outbreak of the First World War. Soviet-era historians tended to see the third and fourth Dumas in particular as part of a worthless experiment in fake democracy – as docile puppets of the tsarist regime. This was because Marxist writers were committed to dismissing all reforms undertaken before the Bolshevik seizure of power. Since the end of communist rule, and the decline in the influence of Marxist historical thinking, more historians have been willing to appreciate the Dumas' attempts to criticise the government and their successes in passing legislation. It is impossible to judge whether, given more time, the Dumas might have developed more power and influence in the state. What is certain is that, for as long as the tsar and his ministers controlled the electoral system, the Dumas could not acquire sustained popular support nor give representative voice to the Russian people's wishes.

The extent of opposition to tsarist rule

How secure were the foundations of the tsarist regime?

In 1913, there were elaborate ceremonies in St Petersburg and Moscow to mark the 300th anniversary of the Romanov dynasty. Nicholas II showed himself in public for the first time since the 1905 Revolution, along with his family, and embarked on an extended tour of Russia. The central theme of the celebrations was the personal rule of the tsar and his mystical sense of union with his people. At the end of the commemorative events, Nicholas was convinced that his rule was more secure than ever, but it was really an elaborate propaganda exercise which concealed the unrest that lay just below the surface of Russian society. The members of the Duma were offended to be seated at the rear of the congregation at the service of thanksgiving in St Petersburg. The festivities did not enhance the image of the tsarina, who appeared strained and left a number of events early. The reason was her concern for the health of her son, Alexei, but she appeared aloof and haughty.

Meanwhile, Nicholas retained the loyalty of Russia's historic institutions. The state officials and the Church remained solidly behind his rule. As we have seen, he survived the upheavals of 1905 because he could rely on the loyalty of the army, although many soldiers were reluctant to fire on peasants and workers, since they came from poor families themselves. On the eve of the First World War, the Russian army was larger than any other European force, but its unity was based on brutal discipline and an insistence on regulation and display, dubbed 'paradomania' by some observers. It had not been modernised in terms of weaponry or tactics. The 1905 *Potemkin* mutiny had shown that the loyalty of the imperial navy could not be taken for granted.

The tsarist regime's resort to repression in the immediate aftermath of 1905 helped to preserve its power in the short run, but this did not give it increased security for the longer term. It benefited from upper- and middle-class fears of revolutionary extremism, without successfully tackling the fundamental problems which had caused the uprisings. The rural gentry and other property owners became more conservative in their attitudes after witnessing the violence of the revolution. The nobles successfully opposed Stolypin's planned reforms of local government, which would have increased peasant representation on the *zemstvos* and challenged traditional aristocratic domination of the countryside. Even those who had shown liberal sympathies at the start of the

ACTIVITY 4.6

How useful is this photograph as evidence of popular support for the tsarist regime?

Figure 4.4: The tsar and his family at the 300th anniversary celebrations of the Romanov dynasty in Moscow, 1913

revolution, such as the leaders of the Kadets, rallied to the regime because they feared working-class violence, not because they wanted genuine political reform. Their leader, Pavel Milyukov, later encouraged patriotic support for the government on the outbreak of war.

The regime also promoted a sense of Russian nationality in the years prior to the First World War. The tsar approved an extreme right-wing grouping called the Union of the Russian People, which organised the paramilitary 'Black Hundreds' – violent gangs who terrorised supporters of democracy. Their most

prominent victims were Jews. At this time, anti-Semitism was widespread in Russia. Conservatives highlighted the presence of Jews in left-wing and revolutionary political parties, regarding them as a threat to social stability and order. They used popular prejudice against the Jews to rally 'patriotic' Russians behind the tsar and his government, with the cooperation of the police. Divisive tactics like these were a worrying development in a country which was supposedly evolving towards parliamentary government. Support for the tsar relied heavily on a backward-looking vision of Russia.

How strong was the opposition?

Industrialisation brought a level of prosperity to Russia, but it also created problems for an authoritarian and inefficient government. Between 1909 and 1914, strikes became more common, as workers demanded increased wages and improved housing and working conditions. Violent repression by the authorities only encouraged further protests. Shop workers and railway employees went on strike; university students staged protests; even sailors in the navy began to demonstrate dissatisfaction with their situation. One significant example of violence against strikers during this period was the massacre in the Lena gold mine in Siberia in 1912. During the strike, 270 miners were killed and almost as many were wounded by tsarist soldiers. An upsurge in industrial militancy did not, of course, mean that another revolution was inevitable. The period immediately prior to the First World War saw increases in strikes in Britain and the USA, for example, where such an outcome was avoided. It did, however, contribute to an atmosphere of growing confrontation in Russia.

Unrest also simmered within the peasantry. Some who had bought their land found they could not keep up their repayments, and arrears to the Peasant Land Bank increased. Many peasants started to feel that their conditions were worse than they had been before the reforms. In the midst of this discontent, radical philosophies such as Marxism began to develop and gain popularity. The police and the army could keep radicals under control, but they could not eliminate them altogether. The exile of Lenin and other revolutionaries kept them out of the clutches of tsarism, but allowed them to continue their work abroad, where they gained increasing support. Radicals in internal exile in remote parts of Siberia still managed to spread their ideas and keep in contact with others. Censorship was evaded and illegal newspapers, pamphlets and books were distributed widely.

However, the Bolsheviks had been weakened following extensive infiltration by the *Okhrana.* Even the leader of the Bolshevik group in the fourth Duma, Roman Malinovsky, turned out to be a police spy, although Lenin refused to believe this at first.

Although the workers, peasants and liberals had initially been united at the start of the 1905 Revolution, they had different interests and did not work together for a common goal. The regime had effectively bought off the moderate liberals by offering mild political reforms. This would never be enough for the socialist opposition, who sought a fundamental transformation of Russian society, but they were unable to push seriously for this until the war changed the situation. The Duma voluntarily dissolved itself on the outbreak of war so that party politics would not prove a distraction at a time of national emergency.

ACTIVITY 4.7

In your opinion, how strong was the likelihood of revolution in Russia in 1914? Make sure you justify your opinion by setting out arguments based on evidence. Review what you have read so far and create a table like the one below. This will help you to marshal the evidence for and against the claim that Russia stood on the brink of revolution by the time war broke out.

	Evidence that the tsarist regime faced challenges by 1914	Evidence that the regime was still secure in 1914
Strength of Russia's traditional institutions		
Success of the Dumas		
State of the Russian economy		
Success of Stolypin's reforms of agriculture		
Levels of public support		
Strength of opposition		

On balance, which side of the argument do you agree with? Look back at the information you have gathered so far, and supplement this with material from other sources. A useful resource is the website of historian Orlando Figes, whose book, A People's Tragedy: The Russian Revolution 1891–1924 (Jonathan Cape, 1996), is a classic study: www.orlandofiges.info/

Reflection: In making your judgment, how far do you think you have been influenced by hindsight – in other words, by the knowledge that revolution did occur just three years later? Would you change your answer if you did not know this?

This appearance of national unity was deceptive. The regime did not really want to undertake serious reform. The tsar had failed to support those isolated ministers, such as Witte and Stolypin, who tried to steer Russia along this path. 1905 had severely damaged the tsar's image in the eyes of the people. It was fear of the state, much more than loyalty and affection for him as an individual, that now preserved stability.

Historians interpret the period from 1906 to 1914 in Russia in different ways. Traditional Soviet historians and some others believed that the fall of tsarism and the triumph of the Bolsheviks were inevitable according to Marxist theories. Most modern historians, however, do not subscribe to this view. They believe that, during this time, the tsar ruled over a fragile society. Internal tensions destabilised the state, and the war caused the decrepit structure to collapse. Some historians claim that Russia was mostly stable, with an improving economy and a government that controlled dissent. They believe the monarchy could have survived if it had not been for the catastrophe of the First World War.

4.2 What were the causes and immediate outcomes of the February Revolution in 1917?

Political, social and economic effects of the First World War, impact of military defeats

Russia claimed that it did not go to war in 1914 to win territory, but rather to protect Serbia – a small state with a population of fellow Slavs – from what Russians believed to be the unreasonable and warlike demands of Austria-Hungary. These intentions seemed honourable to the Russian people, as their country had a long history of tension with Austria-Hungary. The latter was allied to Germany, whose leader was Kaiser Wilhelm II, the tsar's cousin. In spite of these family ties, Russia feared Germany as the main threat to its security. In turn Austria-Hungary believed that Russia was using Serbia to extend its influence in the Balkans and to benefit from the possible future break-up of the Austro-Hungarian Empire. The July 1914 crisis, which led to the outbreak of war, was triggered by the assassination of the heir to the Austrian throne, Archduke Franz Ferdinand, on a state visit to Bosnia. Austria-Hungary blamed Serbia for the killing, and presented its government with an ultimatum. Germany declared war on Russia after the latter went to the aid of Serbia. This meant that Russia was now at war with both Austria-Hungary and Germany – an unwise decision for a country with such major weaknesses.

Russia's wartime weaknesses

The Russian population initially rallied around the tsar as a symbol of national unity. Germany was unpopular and there was an upsurge of patriotic feeling. In the Duma, all except the five Bolsheviks declared their support for the war. Lenin, who had fled to neutral Switzerland, was depressed by the failure of the working class to start a revolution. He was an isolated figure at the start of the war. Events soon began to turn against the tsarist regime, however. Its inability to manage the pressures of war was to lead to its downfall.

The Russian military had made some improvements by the start of the conflict. Defeat by Japan in 1904–05 had encouraged the government to address the deficiencies in the Russian army and navy, and considerable sums of money had been spent both enlarging and improving the armed forces. In 1914, the Russian army was larger than Germany's, and it mobilised more swiftly than expected, invading eastern Germany. The kaiser's army had invaded Belgium and France and was therefore fighting a war on two fronts. However, Russian military planning was deficient in important respects. Large numbers of soldiers and weapons were kept in strongpoints behind the front lines. It was clear that the increased expenditure on the military had not made the army capable of fighting a modern war. It still relied on its cavalry, which was ineffective against modern weapons like machine guns and caused problems because horses required large quantities of food and transport – both of which were more urgently needed elsewhere. Brave cavalry charges resulted in wholesale slaughter. Most commanders relied on bayonets, which meant that large numbers of soldiers were lost to gunfire before they could reach the enemy. Methods of modern warfare had not yet been instilled in the Russian army.

The course of the war

The conflict began badly for Russia, and despite some early victories against the Austro-Hungarian army, and a success against Turkey, it soon became clear that Russia would not be able to defeat Germany in an offensive war. Defeat at Tannenberg in August 1914 showed the superiority of German forces in terms of weaponry, tactics and speed. They also enjoyed better military intelligence, intercepting radio messages which told them where the Russian forces were. Around 70 000 Russian soldiers were killed or injured at Tannenberg, and a further 92 000 captured. The Russian commanders found that they needed to resort to defensive tactics, for which the troops were not well trained.

Study this table of casualties for the major combatant countries in the First World War. What does it tell you about Russia's capacity to cope with the stresses of war?

Country	Number mobilised	Dead	Wounded	Missing/prisoners of war
Russia	12 000 000	1 700 000	4 950 000	2 500 000
France	8 410 000	1 357 800	4 266 000	537 000
Britain and empire	8 904 467	908 371	2 090 212	191 652
Germany	11 000 000	1 773 700	4 216 058	1 152 800
Austria-Hungary	7 800 000	1 200 000	3 620 000	2 200 000
USA (1917–18)	4 355 000	116 516	204 002	4500

Table 4.2: Troop losses to the major combatant countries in the First World War

Source: Adapted from britannica.com

The human cost of the war steadily mounted for Russia, as well as its cost in resources. The peasant majority of ordinary soldiers were short of clothes, food, weapons and ammunition. Guns and shells were piled up, unable to reach the front lines due to the inefficient system of transport and the vast distances to be travelled. Weak army generals did not modify their tactics of throwing masses of badly equipped soldiers against steady gunfire.

Military losses had a drastic impact on the civilian population. They directly caused an enormous displacement of population, with half a million peasant households forced to abandon their farms in 1914–16. Their movement eastwards, away from the German armies, also caused further disruption to society. Attempts by the authorities to maintain popular support tended to have the reverse effect, by drawing attention to the hardships faced by the people. The propaganda put out by the state entirely failed to match the public mood.

Economic chaos and the home front

Russia possessed industries, the railway system had been enlarged and, in peacetime, the harvests were sufficient to feed the population. Its major problem during the First World War was a lack of organisation. The needs of the military were given priority on the railways, at the expense of the civilian population. The system could not transport food and supplies from areas of plenty to where there was

need. As the network failed to cope with the pressures placed upon it, food rotted in depots instead of being moved to the towns and cities where it was needed. The movement of raw materials to manufacturing centres was also disrupted. Labour supply was another problem, as workers and peasants were drafted into the army, placing additional burdens on those who remained in the factories and on farms.

Local government tried to support the war effort in the urban and rural areas respectively with two new organisations, the Union of Towns and the Union of Zemstvos. Their purpose was to offer relief to refugees and orphans, and to help with the provision of medical aid and provisions for the army. They were united in a single organisation known as Zemgor from the spring of 1915. The unions had a certain amount of success in organising hospitals and relieving suffering. They never enjoyed consistent support from central government, however, and they were not equipped to cope with the scale of the economic and social crisis facing the country.

The fundamental problem was that Russia was not prepared for a long war. The conflict cost 15 times more than the Russo-Japanese War, and the government resorted to large-scale borrowing and printing money in order to finance it. This led to runaway inflation. Average incomes doubled in 1914–16, yet the price of fuel and foodstuffs quadrupled. Rising prices affected the lower classes in towns and the countryside. As peasants ceased to get a good price for their produce, they hoarded it, making the food shortages in urban centres worse. Strikes spread in major cities such as Moscow and St Petersburg (now renamed Petrograd as the capital city's original name was of German origin).

Unrest was not confined to the lower classes. Courtiers and generals expressed dissatisfaction with the conduct of the war. The Duma had been suspended on the outbreak of war, but was recalled in July 1915 as pressure mounted on the regime for a change of direction. Its members were not revolutionaries, but they wanted a more efficient tsarist government. However, the tsar rejected their calls for a new government of national unity. He continued to reshuffle his government, appointing few – if – any competent ministers. The liberals and moderate conservatives in the Duma, supported from the outside by the Social Revolutionaries, formed a '**progressive bloc**', which increasingly became a focus for criticism of the regime. The Duma was suspended after less than two months and not recalled until February 1916.

KEY TERM

Progressive bloc: A group consisting of 236 of the Duma's 442 members, made up of Octobrists, Kadets, moderate nationalists and others, which called for a 'ministry of confidence' and an extension of civil liberties.

ACTIVITY 4.9

Hold a group discussion to assess how far the failure of the Russian war effort was the fault of:

- the weakness of the tsar and his regime
- the weaknesses of the Russian army
- the underlying problems of the Russian economy.

Each student should make the case for one of these factors. Remember that you must supply evidence to support your argument.

Nicholas II as a war leader: implications of his personal leadership of the war effort

The tsar at the front

In response to the persistent military failures, in August 1915, Nicholas II decided to go to the front to take personal charge of his armies. This was a fatal mistake: the tsar had no military skill or training, and his presence inspired neither army generals nor common soldiers. His absence from court left a power vacuum in Russia. His new position as leader of the military also meant that he was regarded as personally responsible for defeats. This was unfair, since he took few important decisions and his role was largely a ceremonial one, consisting of attending parades and visiting field hospitals. Perhaps most serious of all, at his headquarters in Mogilev, 600 km south of Petrograd, Nicholas was remote from developments in Petrograd, and he did not appreciate what was happening there.

ACTIVITY 4.10

What features of this cartoon make it clear that it was produced by opponents of the tsarist system?

Figure 4.5: An undated cartoon showing Rasputin (centre) with the tsar and tsarina

Meanwhile, although there were some successes, the overall military situation continued to deteriorate. In June 1916, General Brusilov made some headway against the Austro-Hungarian army in western Ukraine, but when the Germans sent support, Russian forces were pushed back, sustaining almost a million casualties. After this, Russia was never able to mount an effective attack on its enemies.

This inability to reverse the tide of defeat led to growing criticism of the regime from the Duma, after it met again in November 1916. The liberal leader, Pavel Milyukov, delivered a speech in which he repeatedly asked of the government's actions, 'Is this stupidity or treason?' The speech signalled an increasing willingness on the part of progressive politicians to offer open opposition to the regime.

The tsarina and Rasputin

The tsarina, Alexandra, was left in charge of the government in the absence of her husband, but she was incapable of exercising power effectively. Born a German princess, she was viewed with suspicion, and some even accused her of being a German spy. As a woman, she found she had little power or influence over traditionally minded ministers.

One significant factor in the decline of the tsar's reputation was his association with **Grigori Rasputin**. A self-professed healer, Rasputin seemed able to calm the young tsarevich, Alexei, during his frequent periods of illness, and this made him a great favourite of the tsar's wife in particular. However, Rasputin's lowly origins and lack of education meant he was despised by members of the royal court, and many grew concerned over the influence he seemed to have on the tsar and tsarina. Alexandra defended Rasputin fiercely: courtiers who were appalled at his crude manners fell out of favour; critical ministers were dismissed.

Before the First World War, Rasputin's unpopularity was confined to the court and higher circles of government. However, once Alexandra was left in control of the country, she sought Rasputin's advice on many matters. This brought him to the attention of the wider public, with whom he proved equally unpopular. Rasputin was murdered in December 1916 – not by political radicals striking a blow against the monarchy, but by a group of conservative courtiers who wanted to save the tsar's reputation.

GRIGORI RASPUTIN (1869–1916)

Rasputin came from Siberia. He was illiterate and had a reputation as a drunkard, a womaniser and a petty criminal. He spent a few months in a monastery, but had too little education to become a monk. He described himself as a holy man and healer. Rasputin arrived in St Petersburg in 1903, and came to the attention of the royal family, who hoped he could heal their son. He was murdered by a courtier in 1916.

The February Revolution and the abdication of Nicholas II
The collapse of the Russian war effort

Traditional Russian Marxists argued that the fall of the Romanov regime and the triumph of the Bolsheviks were inevitable because of the backward state of Russia and the efficiency of Lenin and his followers. However, most historians now argue against this. They emphasise the importance of the war as an immediate cause of the fall of Nicholas II in February 1917.

151

Industrial workers had two main grievances in the early months of 1917: food shortages and a desire for an end to the war, which was dragging on without prospect of victory. On 18 February, workers at the Putilov steel works, the most important and most politically active factory in Petrograd, went on strike. They were followed by other workers and, on 23 February, by thousands of women demonstrating in the streets on International Women's Day. The police and troops could not be counted on to suppress the disturbances; many had sympathy for the protestors.

Meanwhile, many front-line soldiers began to abandon the war effort. Conditions at the front were unbearable and stories spread of hardships at home. Soldiers drifted back to their homes in large numbers, afraid that their families would die if they did not return to help them. The returning soldiers became a focal point of dissatisfaction in the major cities. Sergei Khabalov, the governor of Petrograd, proclaimed martial law and ordered his soldiers to restore order. The soldiers refused and opened fire on officers instead. Even the Cossacks – once the most loyal of the Romanovs' soldiers – turned against Nicholas.

The tsar was over 600 km away from Petrograd, at his military headquarters, and was out of touch with the developing crisis. Radical Duma members formed a provisional committee. At the same time, the Petrograd Soviet of soldiers, sailors and workers was established. Two quite different steps had thus been taken towards an alternative government. This immediately posed the question of whether the two bodies would merge, cooperate or come into conflict.

The abdication of the tsar

Nicholas decided to return to Petrograd in the mistaken belief that his presence would calm the situation. On the way, troops forced his train to divert to Pskov, 160 km from the capital. Here he was met by army leaders and members of the Duma who persuaded him to give up the throne for his own safety. They included Mikhail Rodzianko, president of the Duma and hitherto a loyalist, who had tried in vain a few days earlier to warn the tsar that he needed to appoint a government which had popular support. On 2 March 1917, having run out of choices, Nicholas decided that **abdication** was his last remaining option. Feeling that his son was too young and unwell to assume such responsibility, instead he nominated his brother, Grand Duke Michael, as his successor in the hope of preserving the monarchy, but Michael was not willing to accept the throne in these circumstances. The monarchy was instead replaced by the Duma committee which declared itself the Provisional Government.

KEY TERM

Abdication: The act of giving up a public office, in this case the Russian imperial crown.

The Bolsheviks played no real part in the downfall of the tsar. Most of the key figures were out of the country and were taken by surprise by events in Petrograd. In December 1916, Lenin had told fellow Bolsheviks, in exile with him in Switzerland, that he did not expect to live to see the revolution.

The regime collapsed because those who might have been expected to defend it, in particular the senior military figures, failed to do so. Their assessment of the disturbances in Petrograd was that the situation was hopeless by late February and that Nicholas must step down. The tsar himself had by this stage lost the will to resist the tide of events. His

own personality played a large part in his downfall. He was unable to empathise with his people's suffering during the war and was too distant from their daily struggle for survival. He lacked the drive and imagination to provide effective leadership at a time of supreme crisis.

The deeper reason for the end of the tsarist system was the way in which prolonging the war tested Russia's economy, transport system, political institutions and armed forces to the point of destruction. Growing casualties and food shortages sapped the morale of the population and undermined support for the war. By taking personal command of his forces, the tsar had identified himself with military failures. This made his own political survival virtually impossible.

ACTIVITY 4.11

From a telegram sent to Tsar Nicholas II by Mikhail Rodzianko, president of the Duma, 26 February 1917

> The situation is serious. The capital is in a state of anarchy. The Government is paralysed; the transport service is broken down; the food and fuel supplies are completely disorganised. Discontent is general and on the increase. There is wild shooting on the streets; troops are firing at each other. It is urgent that someone enjoying the confidence of the country be entrusted with the formation of a new Government. There must be no delay.
>
> Source: Kertesz, G.A. (ed.). (1970). *Documents in the Political History of the European Continent 1815–1939.* Oxford: Oxford University Press, p. 362

Find out more about the background and views of Mikhail Rodzianko. What was his purpose in writing like this to Nicholas? Was he trying to save the monarchy or bring it down?

The formation and purpose of the Provisional Government

The new government

After the abdication of the tsar, the Provisional Government tried to restore stability and to continue the war. It was to prove unable to fulfil these objectives and in the October Revolution was swept away following the seizure of power by Lenin's Bolshevik Party.

Kerensky trained as a lawyer and was a democratic socialist in the wartime Duma. He became the second prime minister in the Provisional

Kerensky reviewing his troops as minister of war

Government in July 1917. He was a popular leader and tried to hold together the different factions. However, he made the fatal error of deciding to continue the war, which the country could no longer sustain. In addition, he postponed land reforms, a long-standing goal for which the peasantry would wait no longer. Meanwhile, the economy deteriorated further. After the October Revolution, Kerensky moved to Western Europe and then to the United States, where he taught at university, dying there in 1970.

The Provisional Government consisted mainly of liberals with a small number of socialists, but no members of the Bolshevik Party. In its eight months of existence it had two prime ministers. The first was a liberal aristocrat, Prince Georgy Lvov. He was a moderate reformer who had acted as a spokesman for rural interests for many years, and he headed the Union of Zemstvos. As prime minister, he was not a strong figure. He believed in the ability of the people to govern themselves, naively assuming that peaceful democratic change could be achieved in the midst of a great war. Lvov was increasingly overshadowed by **Alexander Kerensky**, a leading member of the Social Revolutionary Party, who served as minister of justice and minister of war before succeeding Lvov as prime minister in July 1917.

The Provisional Government and the Petrograd Soviet

The Provisional Government had two serious weaknesses from the start. First, it had developed from a committee of the Duma, itself an institution whose popular credibility had been seriously undermined by government domination and manipulation of the electoral system. Second, it was obliged to share power with the Petrograd Soviet, which claimed to speak for workers and soldiers. Its example was followed in the formation of soviets in other towns and cities.

The Petrograd Soviet was not actually hostile to the Provisional Government and was not initially dominated by the Bolsheviks. The two bodies cooperated on a number of reforms, including an amnesty for political prisoners, the introduction of universal voting rights, the abolition of capital punishment and recognition of trade unions. However, the existence of the Petrograd Soviet potentially presented a challenge to the government's authority. In 'Order Number 1', issued at the beginning of March, it stated that it would obey the orders of the **Military Commission of the State Duma** only if they did not clash with its own decrees. This meant that the government did not possess unqualified control over the army, which was to prove a significant issue. In effect, the government had to accept the existence of a 'dual authority'. This, together with the government's failure to redistribute land to the peasants – the rural population's most important demand – and its attempt to continue an unpopular war, condemned it to eventual disaster.

KEY TERM

Military Commission of the State Duma: A body created by the Duma, at the time of the February Revolution, to manage the army.

153

How useful is this source as evidence of the involvement of ordinary Russians in the events of February 1917?

Figure 4.6: A women's demonstration in Petrograd in February 1917. The banners, though patriotic in tone, express demands forcefully. One reads: Feed the children of the defenders of the motherland', and another: 'Supplement the ration of soldiers' families, defenders of freedom and the people's peace'.

Reflection: Discuss your response to the photograph with another student. How did you each decide on its usefulness as a source?

4.3 How and why did the Bolsheviks gain power in October 1917?

Crises of the Provisional Government

The Provisional Government faced a number of problems in seeking to establish its authority. Russia was internally unstable, and the Provisional Government lacked the strength to restore order. Popular uprisings and army unrest were not uncommon in Europe at this time, but the emergence of the soviets in the cities, countryside and

the army posed a particularly acute challenge. The soviets were not highly organised, but they were sufficiently coordinated to represent a major threat.

Food distribution was still a problem, and peasants demanded that land was redistributed. After the fall of the tsar, the peasants had expected that they would acquire the estates of the nobles and the Church, and when this did not happen they seized land anyway. The government lost support in the countryside by its failure to deal with the problem. Its leading members were property owners who were not keen to legalise this kind of behaviour. The distribution of food was also extremely difficult to achieve in the midst of a wartime emergency. A further problem was posed by Lenin's return to Russia in April 1917. The Bolsheviks, who did not have a worked-out policy of their own towards the peasants, adopted the ideas of the Socialist Revolutionaries (SRs) on land redistribution. This meant that they recognised the land seizures on the basis of 'revolutionary legality'. This was an opportunistic, tactical move by the Bolsheviks, which improved their previously weak support in the countryside, where historically the SRs had been dominant.

The government and the war

It was the continuation of the war, however, that became the most important reason why the Provisional Government eventually failed. It believed that continuing to fight was a matter of both honour and national survival – and indeed Russia was pressed to remain in the war by its allies, who provided vital financial aid. The government hoped that war might appeal to Russian nationalism and unite the country, but instead the loyalty of the soldiers continued to decline. Heavy casualties reinforced a growing sense of war weariness and troops were open to the agitation of Bolsheviks, who encouraged them to disobey their officers and abandon the war effort. In April, the foreign minister, Pavel Milyukov, leader of the Kadets, provoked street demonstrations by declaring that the government intended to fight on to achieve victory. He was forced out at the beginning of May and Prince Lvov attempted to broaden the base of the government by including moderate socialists. The war minister, Alexander Guchkov, was replaced by Kerensky. The soviets became more critical of the government, however, as it failed either to bring about major democratic reforms or to end the war. These events weakened the government by separating it further from the soviets. After a disastrous offensive against Germany in June 1917, in which up to 60 000 troops were lost, it became clear that the army was in no condition to fight, and demands to make peace increased. The failure of the offensive damaged Kerensky's own reputation since he had personally ordered it to go ahead.

The July Days

Sailors at Kronstadt, the naval base close to Petrograd, established their own government in defiance of the Provisional Government. This was followed between 3 and 6 July by numerous demonstrations by workers and soldiers in Petrograd. It is not clear who instigated these disturbances. The Bolsheviks later claimed that they were started by the SRs and Mensheviks. The latter, on the other hand, argued that the Bolsheviks had been responsible but had tried to distance themselves from a failed attempt.

The rising was poorly organised and the participants were divided. The Provisional Government gathered enough soldiers to put down disorder, and Lenin had to leave the centre of action, fleeing to Finland. The episode showed that the Provisional Government – now led by Kerensky as prime minister – still possessed some authority. It branded Lenin as a German agent, closed down the Bolsheviks' newspaper, *Pravda*, and dispersed the party's members.

The Kornilov Affair

It was the Kornilov Affair that restored Lenin's fortunes. Lavr Kornilov, the commander-in-chief of the army, was a conservative army officer who favoured strong action against the Bolsheviks. He was concerned by the worsening war situation, with the Germans now approaching Petrograd, and he believed that he must take action to restore internal stability. In August, he attempted to march on Petrograd at the head of a troop of soldiers known as the 'Savage Division' because of its particularly warlike reputation. It is uncertain how far Kerensky approved of the plan and how far Kornilov acted

Figure 4.7: General Kornilov inspecting his troops. From looking at the photograph, can you suggest what the purpose of the photograph may have been?

independently, but the scheme failed. Kerensky quickly accused Kornilov of attempting a takeover to establish a military dictatorship, and dismissed him from his post. He also called for support from the workers to resist the army. The Bolsheviks now reappeared and gained credit by leading resistance among the workers and soviets. In fact the attempted takeover collapsed because rail workers refused to transport Kornilov and his men to Petrograd, and he was then arrested.

The affair demonstrated the weakness of the Provisional Government. Kerensky had lost the favour of the right by turning against Kornilov, but he had also alienated the left, who suspected him of initially being involved in counter-revolutionary plotting. The episode also further undermined military discipline, with soldiers deserting and turning to the soviets. By the end of August, the Bolsheviks had a majority on the Petrograd Soviet and, soon after, they gained control of the Moscow Soviet. These events convinced Lenin, who returned to Russia on 7 October, that the time was right for a second revolution.

Lenin's leadership of the Bolsheviks

Lenin's political skills

One of Lenin's greatest strengths was his ability to be both idealistic and practical, and his government of Russia after 1917 showed a willingness to compromise when necessary. His adaptation of Marxism gave rise to a new political philosophy that became known as 'Marxism-Leninism'. Lenin had for decades aimed to incite a revolution that would bring down the tsarist autocracy, but, ironically, he did not tolerate any challenges to his own leadership. He was a skilled orator – a fact that contributed to his success in 1917 – but more importantly in developing the Bolshevik movement, he was also a talented writer and a profound political thinker.

Lenin reached two decisions that shaped the future of Russia. First, he appreciated the importance of organisation and discipline within a revolutionary party. The disorganised and fragmented radical groups had achieved very little and spent a great deal of time quarrelling among themselves. Second, he recognised the value of the industrial working classes in securing the success of any revolution. He believed that the peasantry would not be able to mount a united challenge to the tsarist regime. The proletariat worked in factories and lived in towns. As far as Lenin was concerned, it was more likely that they could be shaped into an effective revolutionary weapon.

Lenin's return to Russia

At the start of 1917, the exiled Lenin could not influence events in Russia. In order to return to Petrograd he would have to travel through Germany. This would not normally be possible in wartime conditions. Lenin now had a stroke of luck that he could not have calculated. His isolation in Switzerland ended when the Germans, intending to weaken Russia by stirring up disorder, transported him in a train to the Russian frontier. It consisted of one carriage and was known as the 'sealed train' because the Germans did not inspect the passengers' passports and belongings, and it made as few stops as possible.

Lenin was afterwards accused by his enemies of being a German agent, and it was true that the Bolsheviks had received financial support from the Germans. However, the reason for their cooperation was simply that Lenin's aims coincided with theirs. He wanted Russia to withdraw from the war so that he could embark on the transformation of the country into a socialist society. They wanted him to further their military objectives by undermining the Russian war effort.

Lenin arrived at Petrograd's Finland Station on 3 April, the most important among a number of opposition politicians who were now returning to Russia from exile. As he had spent so much of his life abroad, he did not know Russia and its people well, and he could not automatically assume the leadership of the Bolshevik Party in the country without challenge. Nonetheless, he lost no time in setting out his own strategy for revolution. He condemned the 'dual authority' approach on the grounds that the Provisional Government was a 'parliamentary-bourgeois republic' which was nothing more than a front for capitalism. True socialists should not cooperate with it but should seek its overthrow.

In calling for a second revolution, Lenin was departing from traditional Marxist teaching, which argued that society had to pass through a bourgeois capitalist phase before the proletariat could come to power. He justified this on the grounds that the Russian middle classes were incapable of carrying out a revolution, and that the war had transformed the situation, making widespread socialist revolution likely across Europe. Lenin quickly realised the potential power of the soviets. He saw them as an alternative to the Provisional Government, using the slogan 'All power to the soviets'. His aim was for the Bolshevik Party to take control of the soviets – which did come about during the following few months – and to use them as a springboard to power.

This did not mean that Lenin had a fully worked out plan for the seizure of power. His 'April Theses', in which he set out his call for a second revolution and withdrawal from the war, did not seem realistic at the time to most socialists. His absolute self-belief, however, and single-minded dedication to revolution enabled him to dominate those around him. No one else had Lenin's ruthlessness or his clarity of vision. He knew when to retreat as well as when to take decisive action. He could be brutally harsh towards his opponents, but also immensely persuasive. He understood the importance of propaganda in undermining support for the government and also keeping the workers in a state of readiness for when the time was right to seize control.

Lenin called for 'Peace, Land and Bread'. This slogan had a powerful appeal to the Russian masses. It offered an end to the unpopular war, the transfer of agricultural land from the nobility to the peasants, and food for the hungry. It helped Lenin to win control of the Bolshevik Party.

ACTIVITY 4.13

From Lenin's April Theses, 4 April 1917

> It must be explained to the people that the Soviets of Workers' Deputies are the *only possible* form of revolutionary government, and that therefore our task is, as long as *this* government yields to the influence of the bourgeoisie, to present a patient, systematic and persistent *explanation* of the errors of their tactics …
>
> Not a parliamentary republic – to return to a parliamentary republic from the Soviets of Workers' Deputies would be a retrograde [backwards] step – but a republic of Soviets of Workers', Agricultural Labourers' and Peasants' Deputies throughout the country, from top to bottom.
>
> **Source: Kertesz, G.A. (ed.). (1970). *Documents in the Political History of the European Continent 1815–1939*. Oxford: Oxford University Press, p. 367**

What kind of future is Lenin calling for in this document? Explain carefully the difference between a 'parliamentary republic' and a 'republic of Soviets'.

The role of Trotsky and the Military Revolutionary Committee

Trotsky's reputation

After Lenin's death, Trotsky's great opponent, Joseph Stalin, took power in the course of the 1920s. Trotsky was exiled from the **Soviet Union** and eventually murdered. Trotsky was removed from official Soviet histories and his image was systematically deleted from photographs. He became in effect a 'non-person'. This does not do justice to the part he played in the October 1917 Revolution. Trotsky has been described by historians as the chief organiser of the Bolshevik seizure of power. He was also a brilliant public speaker who knew how to energise audiences, and was widely recognised as having more charisma than Lenin.

KEY TERM

Soviet Union: Shortened form of the Union of Soviet Socialist Republics (USSR), the communist state officially established in 1922 and dissolved in 1991, and comprising Russia and a number of other republics.

It was in some ways surprising that Trotsky was so central to the Bolshevik takeover. Like Lenin, he was abroad when the February Revolution took place and he did not arrive in Russia until May. At that point, he was not a Bolshevik; instead he still belonged to the Menshevik Party. He changed his loyalties during the summer of 1917 as he realised, following the July Days, that only the Bolsheviks could supply the leadership needed to bring about a socialist revolution. He recognised that their increasingly dominant position in the trade unions and factory committees was the key to winning power.

Trotsky and the Petrograd Soviet

Trotsky's main contribution to the revolution lay in his involvement in the Petrograd Soviet, whose chairman he became in September. He organised the Red Guards, an armed workers' group, and took the initiative in the formation of a Military Revolutionary Committee (MRC) of the Petrograd Soviet. These two organisations were supposedly limited to the defence of the Bolsheviks, but their real purpose was to carry out an armed insurrection against the Provisional Government. Trotsky also joined the Bolshevik Party's Central Committee, where he soon became Lenin's most trusted supporter in planning and carrying out the October Revolution. As commissar (minister) for foreign affairs, he was responsible for peace negotiations with Germany in 1917–18, and as war commissar he played a key role in defeating the Bolsheviks' opponents in the Civil War of 1918–20.

The key events of the October Revolution

Why did the Revolution occur?

The short-term causes of the October Revolution in 1917 can be summarised as follows:

- The Provisional Government had no control over events. It was discredited by disobedience from the soviets and by the Kornilov Affair.
- The Russian army was suffering huge losses in the ongoing war, and this made the Provisional Government even more unpopular.
- Kerensky could not deliver other reforms, such as the redistribution of land or a new constitution.

As the German army advanced, Kerensky could not provide enough soldiers to defend key points in the major cities. Rumours began to spread that he was preparing to abandon Petrograd to the Germans. Lenin overruled doubters among the Bolsheviks who believed that Russia was not ready for a revolution. He claimed that he was acting on behalf of the soviets, and demanded that his supporters rise up at this critical juncture. A number of other Bolsheviks on the party's Central Committee wanted to wait until the meeting of the All-Russian Congress of Soviets, which was first scheduled to take place on 20 October and then postponed until the 25th. Lenin did not want to wait for this because it would mean a transfer of power to a coalition, including the Social Revolutionaries and Mensheviks, rather than to the Bolshevik Party on its own. Another looming problem for him was the announcement of elections to a constituent assembly in November. This body was meant to be the first fully democratic all-Russian parliament. It would have the **legitimacy** which the Provisional Government, as a self-appointed authority, lacked. Lenin did not know how well the Bolsheviks would perform in the elections to the constituent assembly, so he was determined to seize power before it met. Lenin did not automatically sway the Central Committee to support his viewpoint; he had to struggle to win the argument with his colleagues.

KEY TERM

Legitimacy: Legal entitlement (to govern).

The seizure of power in Petrograd

The uprising itself was triggered by Kerensky's government, which decided to take pre-emptive action against the Bolsheviks. Kerensky announced that the bulk of the Petrograd garrison was to be transferred to meet the German advance on the northern front. This would have enabled him to remove the most rebellious troops from the capital, thus provoking a poorly planned Bolshevik uprising, which he then expected to crush with ease. The MRC took over the Petrograd garrison on the grounds that a counter-revolution was imminent. Taking swift action, the Bolsheviks gained control of Petrograd and seized the Winter Palace, the former residence of the tsar. It was Lenin who gave the critical direction to carry out the takeover, and he who determined its timing. But it was Trotsky, as leader of the Red Guards, who carried it out.

The revolution lasted from 25 to 27 October. The Bolsheviks claimed that it was a popular action, a revolution of the people. In reality, the Winter Palace was easily taken: few armed men took part and only five people were killed. This was because there was very little resistance from the Provisional Government. Few troops loyal to Kerensky were to be found in the capital by this stage. He had already left Petrograd in a vain attempt to organise forces still loyal to the ideas of the Provisional Government. His ministers either fled or were taken prisoner by the Bolsheviks. Although Soviet myth-making later presented the events of October as a heroic struggle, the truth was that the Bolsheviks had moved into a vacuum created by the weakness of the Provisional Government.

A revolution or a *coup d'état*?

Lenin announced the seizure of the Winter Palace to the delegates at the Congress of Soviets on 27 October. The right-wing SRs and Mensheviks walked out, angry at what they regarded as a takeover by one party rather than an assumption of power by the soviet. This was a mistake – in doing so, they deprived themselves of any influence over the course of events to come. Trotsky savagely denounced them as having passed into the 'dustbin of history', and organised a vote of the remaining delegates in order to give some legitimacy to the Bolshevik government.

Study this drawing made in the 1930s, after the establishment of the Soviet government. What do you think its purpose was?

Figure 4.8: 'The storming of the Winter Palace in Petrograd in October 1917' by Valerian Shcheglov

One of the most important debates about the events of October is whether they amounted to a coup or a popular revolution. The Menshevik analysis was that the February Revolution marked the overthrow of the feudal aristocracy by the bourgeoisie. Following Marx's teaching, they did not believe that Russia had yet reached a stage of economic development where it possessed a sufficiently strong and numerous industrial proletariat. This was why they were prepared to ally themselves temporarily with bourgeois parties until the time was right for the proletarian revolution. Lenin and the Bolsheviks, however, were not prepared to wait. They were focused on seizing power at all costs, and as events after the capture of the Winter Palace quickly showed, they had no intention of sharing it with other parties.

The Bolsheviks owed their success to the superior organisation and determination of the MRC, and the weakness of the Provisional Government. The takeover was the action of a minority, and the kind of mass strikes and demonstrations seen in February were not repeated. Trotsky himself admitted that no more than 30 000 people were actively involved, which equated to only 5% of all the workers and soldiers in Petrograd. One Menshevik politician claimed that only 500 troops would have been needed to take over the Bolshevik headquarters – had they been available. The worst violence in the capital actually occurred after the occupation of the Winter Palace, when Bolsheviks looted the wine cellars then went on a drunken rampage. Outside Petrograd, the Bolsheviks' hold on power was less secure, with fighting in Moscow between their supporters and those who remained loyal to the Provisional Government.

The alternative view is that there was a genuine popular element in the events of 1917. The starting point of this interpretation is the breakdown of central government after the February Revolution. Power was dispersed among many centres, with the election of workers' committees in factories, peasants redistributing land at local level, and groups of soldiers rejecting the authority of their officers. The Petrograd and Moscow soviets, in which the Bolsheviks now had majorities, were increasingly important bodies. National movements in Ukraine and Finland were starting to put their own demands for independence. It can be argued that the Bolsheviks would not have been able to overthrow the Provisional Government had its authority not already been undermined by popular uprisings of this kind. This does not, however, contradict the essential fact that once in power, the Bolsheviks proceeded to work towards a one-party state and to frustrate the democratic impulses which had appeared between the spring and autumn of 1917. Their call for 'all power to the soviets' was a cover for their own desire for power.

KEY CONCEPT

Cause and consequence

The reasons for the October Revolution are one of the most important questions in modern Russian history. In looking at the origins of any major event, you need to be able to distinguish between long-term and short-term causes, and between the actions of individuals and the part played by wider circumstances. Do not think of causes in separate 'boxes', but be aware of the interrelationships between them. Consider the following possible reasons for the Bolshevik takeover in October 1917:

- the weaknesses of the Provisional Government and its inability to win the loyalty of the population
- discontent at the continuation of the war, food shortages and other hardships
- the breakdown of discipline in the army
- the effectiveness of the Bolsheviks' planning and their ruthlessness in taking advantage of opportunities
- the contributions of Lenin and Trotsky.

Organise your thoughts by making notes on each of these areas. Then look for the connections between them. Which factors do you think are the most important, and why?

ACTIVITY 4.15

From the Proclamation of the Military Revolutionary Committee of the Petrograd Soviet on the success of the Revolution, 25 October 1917

To the Citizens of Russia!

The Provisional Government has been deposed. State power has passed into the hands of the organ of the Petrograd Soviet of Workers' and Soldiers' Deputies – the Revolutionary Military Committee, which heads the Petrograd proletariat and garrison.

The cause for which the people have fought, namely, the immediate offer of a democratic peace, the abolition of landlord ownership, workers' control over production, and the establishment of Soviet Power – this cause has been secured.

Long live the revolution of workers, soldiers, and peasants!

Source: Kertesz, G.A. (ed.). (1970). *Documents in the Political History of the European Continent 1815–1939*. Oxford: Oxford University Press, p. 376

Does this source support the view that October 1917 in Russia was either a coup or a popular revolution? Refer to the content of the source in support of your answer.

Reflection: Compare your approach to this question with that of another student. Did you use different approaches to selecting content from the source to use in your answer? Would you use some of these approaches in your own work following your discussion?

●●● THINK LIKE A HISTORIAN

Look at two different sources on the downfall of a political leader or government in recent times. How does your study of the collapse of the tsarist regime and the Provisional Government help you to understand the failure of other kinds of government?

4.4 How were the Bolsheviks able to consolidate their power up to 1921?

Bolshevik reforms and the establishment of a dictatorship

The aftermath of the October Revolution

The most immediate task for Lenin and his followers after the fall of the Provisional Government was to secure the survival of their barely established regime. They desperately needed a period of stability that would allow them to begin creating a socialist state. Yet the country was still at war with Germany and at the same time the Bolsheviks faced a range of internal opponents. In Petrograd, civil servants and bank clerks went on strike, paralysing the institutions of government until the Bolsheviks forced them to obey. Fighting continued in Moscow, and the Bolsheviks' hold on rural areas was even less secure. The railway workers' union, Vikzhel, threatened to cut off vital supplies to Petrograd unless the Bolsheviks agreed to form a government with the Mensheviks and SRs. This obliged Lenin to authorise talks with the other parties, but he broke these off in early November when he felt strong enough to do so. He remained true to the concept of 'democratic centralism': the view that only the Bolshevik Party represented the workers, and that multi-party electoral politics was a deception which would merely preserve the power of the bourgeoisie.

The main governmental body was the **Council of People's Commissars (Sovnarkom)**, chaired by Lenin, which declared that it had the right to pass laws independently of the Petrograd Soviet. Alongside this was the Central Committee of the Bolshevik Party, the body that had directed the October Revolution under Lenin's leadership. It was the highest authority within the party between its annual congresses. From 1919, it appointed a five-member body, the Politburo, which became the real centre of power in the Soviet Union.

The new government's first acts were attempts to pass into law elements of the Bolshevik slogan, 'Peace, Land and Bread'. The 'Decree on Land' urged the break-up of large estates and the transfer of land to the peasants, something which was already happening unofficially in the countryside. This had the effect of accelerating the breakdown of military discipline, as soldiers abandoned their posts to return home to secure land. The 'Decree on Peace' stated that Russia aimed to withdraw from the war without '**payment of indemnities or annexations**'. This was an appeal to the war-weary soldiers still fighting at the front. The 'Decree on Workers' Control' recognised the takeover of factories by workers' committees.

KEY TERMS

Council of People's Commissars (Sovnarkom): The supreme government body, created in October 1917. Commissars acted as ministers, in charge of the various government departments.

Payment of indemnities or annexations: The payment of money or the handover of areas of land as part of a peace settlement.

The Red Terror and the police state

Other measures indicated that the Bolsheviks intended to construct a police state. The opposition press was banned and members of other parties were arrested. The Left SRs were admitted to the Sovnarkom for opportunistic reasons: they had broken away from the Social Revolutionaries to accept the October Revolution, and their links to the peasants made them useful.

The functions of the MRC were transferred early in December 1917 to a new body, the Cheka, a secret police force modelled on the tsarist Okhrana. Its leader, the Polish-born Felix Dzerzhinsky, was a completely ruthless individual who instructed the organisation's members to undertake a 'battle to the death' against supporters of counter-revolution. This was the beginning of the terror – the use of force to crush any form of opposition to the Bolshevik state. At least 8500 died in the first year of the terror (1918–19), while innumerable others were arrested, imprisoned and tortured. The targets of the terror were indiscriminate: not just supporters of the tsarist regime and other political opponents but also priests, better-off peasants, those who hoarded grain or sold other goods for profit, and, indeed, anyone who came under suspicion on account of their bourgeois background or appearance. The confiscation of property, under the slogan 'Loot the looters', accompanied physical abuse and murder. One of the most violent episodes was the killing of the former tsar and his family in July 1918. The family had been kept under house arrest since the revolution and in their final months were moved to Ekaterinburg in Siberia. They were summarily shot, without trial, on the orders of local Bolsheviks and with the approval of the government, in a cellar of the house in which they were being detained.

161

The dissolution of the Constituent Assembly, January 1918

Elections to the Constituent Assembly were held in November 1917, using the secret ballot and with all Russian citizens over the age of 20 allowed to vote. The Bolsheviks did well in Petrograd and Moscow, and they were popular with the military, but they polled poorly in rural areas, and overall their share of the vote was only 24%. They won only 175 of the 715 seats. The Socialist Revolutionaries emerged as the largest party with 40% of the vote and a total of 370 seats. The breakaway Left SRs, who were still allied to the Bolsheviks, gained just 40 seats.

The Constituent Assembly met for only one day, 5 January 1918. The Socialist Revolutionaries refused to approve a Bolshevik decree declaring Russia a 'soviet republic' and tried to substitute their own policies. Lenin's solution to this challenge to the Bolsheviks was simple. He had the Assembly dissolved by Red Guards, an action which met with almost no resistance. The workers seemed content to allow government to remain in the hands of the soviets.

This was the end of the most democratically elected body in Russian history to be convened up to that point. Nothing like it would be possible again for 75 years, until after the collapse of the Soviet Union. The dispersal of the Assembly showed beyond doubt the refusal of the Bolsheviks to give up power. It was justified by Lenin as 'a complete and open liquidation of democratic forms for the sake of revolutionary dictatorship'.

The impact of Brest-Litovsk

Conflicting Bolshevik ideas on ending the war

The traditional Bolshevik view of the First World War was that it was an imperialist conflict which could be ended only by socialist revolution in the participating countries. If this did not occur spontaneously, the Bolsheviks were prepared to instigate it by carrying 'revolutionary war' into the rest of Europe. By December 1917, however, there were signs that Lenin was prepared to abandon this as unrealistic. With the Russian armed forces disintegrating, he became convinced that Russia must seek a separate peace with Germany. It was important to end the fighting in order to give space for the establishment of a socialist state in Russia. The Bolsheviks could not expect lenient terms from the victorious Germans, but, by prolonging the conflict, they could end up having to accept even worse conditions. In any case, as a Marxist, Lenin believed that any concessions would be rendered meaningless in the

fullness of time, as revolution would eventually occur across Europe.

This was a controversial viewpoint within the Bolshevik Party. The idea of conceding land to Germany contradicted the 'Decree on Peace', issued the previous October. Many of Lenin's colleagues still favoured the strategy of 'revolutionary war'. Trotsky, who had been appointed commissar for external affairs (the equivalent of foreign minister), was conducting talks with Germany and Austria-Hungary at Brest-Litovsk in Poland. He argued for a policy of 'neither war nor peace'. By this he meant dragging out negotiations as long as possible, in the hope that the enemy's war effort in the west would collapse and be followed by a revolution inside Germany.

Lenin was convinced that this approach would result in more German victories and might cause the collapse of the revolution. In arguing his case, Lenin was clear that he was not abandoning the long-term prospect of European-wide revolution, but that, at the moment, the priority was the defence of socialism in Russia, the only country where it had so far been established. He told his fellow Bolsheviks that 'Germany is only pregnant with revolution', but that 'a completely healthy baby has been born to us: the baby that is the socialist republic'.

What eventually swayed a small majority on the party's Central Committee to support Lenin's position was the increasingly menacing stance of the Germans. They declared in mid-February 1918 that unless the Bolsheviks came to terms, they would invade the heartlands of Russia. With German armies now only 600 km from Petrograd, it was clear that they were capable of carrying out their threats. This would have meant the collapse of the October Revolution.

The treaty of Brest-Litovsk

On 3 March 1918, Russia signed the treaty of Brest-Litovsk. This was a peace overwhelmingly in Germany's favour. It gained an area which was 1 million square kilometres in size, including Poland, Finland, the Baltic provinces and most of the Ukraine – containing half of the old Russian Empire's industry and farmland, and a third of its population. The end of the war in the east also allowed the Germans to transfer half a million men westwards for a huge spring offensive against British and French forces. The Bolsheviks could not be certain that the Germans would not after all launch an assault on the areas of Russia not covered by the treaty. Shortly afterwards, the decision was reluctantly taken to transfer the Russian capital from

Petrograd to a more secure location in Moscow, 700 km to the south-east and further from the border.

The treaty was extremely unpopular within the Russian leadership. Trotsky refused to sign in person and sent a subordinate to take his place at the ceremony. The Left SRs, who envisaged a popular guerrilla war against the invaders, were particularly hostile to it. Lenin's opponents gave way in face of his repeated insistence on party loyalty and his threats to resign if they did not accept his strategy. The course of events, however, justified Lenin's pragmatic approach. The Bolsheviks gained a small breathing-space

before the onset of civil war in Russia later that year. In August 1918, the German position on the Western Front began to collapse, leading to the withdrawal of German troops from the areas they had occupied since Brest-Litovsk. The German surrender in November cancelled out some of the worst features of the treaty, although the Versailles peace conference in 1919 did not restore Poland, Finland or the Baltic states to Russia. More importantly for Lenin, as events started at last to move in his favour, he was able to consolidate his hold over the government as the Left SRs withdrew from it.

Figure 4.9: A map showing western Russia after the Treaty of Brest-Litovsk; areas in black are those conceded to Germany

> **ACTIVITY 4.16**
>
> 'The Treaty of Brest-Litovsk was an apparent failure, but in reality was a major success for Lenin's leadership of Russia.' Draw a table with two columns: on one side, a list of key points in support of the treaty, and, on the other, the reasons why some Bolsheviks were opposed to it.

Reasons for the Bolshevik victory in the civil war, including War Communism

Reds versus Whites

The Bolsheviks were opposed from 1918 to 1920 by a variety of different groups. The conservative counter-revolutionaries were known as the 'Whites', a colour traditionally associated with the monarchy, while the Bolsheviks were the 'Reds'. However, the opposition to the Bolshevik regime was much broader than this. Armed peasant resistance groups were also labelled as Whites by the Bolsheviks, although in fact they had little in common with conservatives who wanted to see the restoration of tsarism. They were also known as the Greens, and their main motivation was anger at Bolshevik seizure of supplies from their communities. Opposition to the Bolsheviks also came from members of national groups, in Ukraine, Georgia and elsewhere, who wanted independence from Russian rule. The SRs tried to stage a takeover of the Moscow Soviet and Fanny Kaplan, an SR activist, made an unsuccessful attempt on Lenin's life in August 1918.

One group with its own agenda was the so-called Czech Legion, an armed force of 35 000 subjects of the Austro-Hungarian Empire. They had joined the Russian side in the war, in a bid to win their independence, and had found themselves stranded in central Russia after the Treaty of Brest-Litovsk. Clashes between the Czech Legion and the Bolsheviks along the Trans-Siberian Railway in May 1918 helped to spark the civil war. The Czechs aimed to reach Vladivostok on the Pacific coast, in order to travel around the world to link up with Western allies and eventually reach home.

There were several White armies. One, led initially by General Kornilov, was based in the Caucasus region of southern Russia. It was led by General Anton Denikin after Kornilov was killed in April 1918. He attempted an attack on Moscow in 1919 before being pushed back to the Crimea. General Pyotr Wrangel led another White army

in the south. Unlike Denikin, he did not favour a frontal assault on Moscow, but attempted to link up with White forces in Siberia.

The army in Siberia was led by Admiral Alexander Kolchak. Known as the 'Supreme Ruler', he organised an expedition into western Russia in March 1919. He too was pushed back. Losing support, Kolchak was betrayed to the Bolsheviks and executed in January 1920. A further army was assembled on the Baltic coast, with British support, under another former tsarist general, Nikolai Yudenich. He came close to taking Petrograd in the autumn of 1919 while Bolshevik forces were occupied elsewhere, but failed to gain control of the railways and was defeated.

The emergence of so many groups indicated how limited Bolshevik control of Russia was outside the party's urban heartlands. By the end of 1920, however, they had secured victory.

Reasons for the Red victory

The Bolsheviks defeated the Whites for several reasons. The first was the internal weaknesses of the Whites. Their armies were scattered geographically, on the margins of the Russian land mass, and they failed to cooperate effectively with each other. A critical mistake was made in spring 1919 when Denikin failed to link up with Kolchak's forces on the River Volga, turning instead towards Ukraine. Had the two White armies combined at this stage, they might conceivably have won. By contrast, as a party with a primarily urban base, the Bolsheviks held on to their strongholds in the industrial west of Russia.

Foreign intervention also played an important part. The Whites depended for supplies on Britain, the USA and France, who occupied Archangel in the White Sea and Murmansk in the Arctic after the Treaty of Brest-Litovsk. They also sent forces to the Baltic, the Black Sea and southern Russia. Meanwhile, Japan, which was allied to the Western powers, occupied Vladivostok. By identifying themselves with foreign intruders, the Whites lost the chance of depicting themselves as champions of the Russian motherland. The allies wanted to punish Russia for withdrawing from the war, and to prevent supplies loaned to its government since 1914 from falling into German hands. They continued the intervention for a time after the end of the First World War because of ideological hostility to the Reds, and because the Bolsheviks had refused to repay the debts incurred by previous Russian governments. The foreign powers' interest diminished, however, and they sent only enough aid to keep the White armies in the field, not enough to give them a real chance of victory. After four years of European war, Britain, France and the USA had little enthusiasm for further conflict. Lacking determined commitment to the cause, they withdrew their troops from Russia in 1919–20.

The Whites failed to win popular support. Both sides in the civil war committed atrocities and resorted to requisitioning food from the peasants, which made them very unpopular. However, the Whites were much less effective than the Reds in exploiting the propaganda value of their opponents' crimes. The Whites were unable to escape from the charge, frequently made by the Bolsheviks, that, if they won the civil war, the land gained by the peasants since 1917 would be restored to the old landowners. Peasant opposition, for example, was crucial to the defeat of Denikin's attempt to take Moscow in the autumn of 1919. Nor did the Whites show

interest in appealing to the national minorities' desire for greater autonomy. This was particularly damaging because their armies were based mainly in areas such as the Caucasus and the Baltic, where there were large non-Russian populations. In the minds of the people, the Whites stood only for a restoration of the tsarist system. As former prime minister Prince Lvov acknowledged: 'We were mistaken to think that the Bolsheviks could be defeated by military force. They can only be defeated by the Russian people. And for that the Whites would need a democratic programme.'

By contrast, the Bolsheviks made the most of their strengths. The Reds were more united and dedicated. As commissar for war, Trotsky was in charge of the Red Army. He and Lenin worked together effectively. Trotsky realised the importance of making the Red Army more professional. He recruited former tsarist officers because they possessed the necessary military skills and experience, even though this was unpopular with

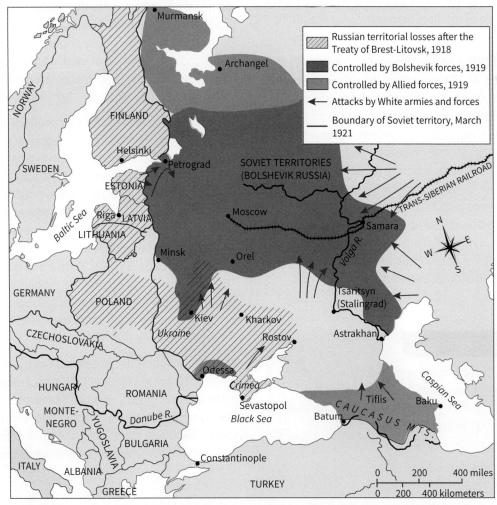

Figure 4.10: A map showing the positions of the Whites' armies during the Russian Civil War

the Bolsheviks. Their loyalty was guaranteed by holding family members hostage. Party workers known as political commissars were attached to each army unit to supervise the officers. There were severe punishments for desertion and disloyalty. Distinctions of rank, which had been abolished after the revolution, were restored. In spite of these measures, Red Army soldiers were never as disciplined as their opponents. Mass conscription, however, enabled the Red Army to increase in size until at its peak, 5 million soldiers were under arms – more than double the number of White troops combined. Control of Petrograd and Moscow meant access to the resources of the country's main arms factories. There was an underlying sense of purpose, generated by a combination of Bolshevik ideology and fear of the Red terror. Propaganda posters, films, and speeches by Trotsky and other leaders helped to win support across the country. Most importantly, the Bolsheviks maintained control of the rail network so that they could move men and supplies rapidly to where they were needed, an asset denied to the Whites. Trotsky conducted his campaigns from an armoured train, giving him the advantage of mobility across the vast distances of Russia.

In the summer of 1918, Lenin authorised a policy which became known as 'War Communism': the nationalisation of large-scale industry, the abolition of private markets and the forcible requisitioning of surplus grain from the peasants. In 1920, it expanded with an attempt to replace money with a system of state rationing. War Communism helped produce the Bolshevik victory by increasing central control over the economy. The tightening of discipline over the workforce enabled the Bolsheviks to produce more arms than their opponents. As we will see, War Communism was unpopular with the people and it generated problems of its own, but, in the short term, it introduced a degree of order into an otherwise chaotic economic situation.

ACTIVITY 4.17

How far do you agree that the Whites lost the civil war because of their own weaknesses and divisions, rather than the strengths of the Reds? Organise your thoughts by making notes on each of the two viewpoints.

Kronstadt and the introduction of the NEP

War Communism and the growth of opposition

Historians do not agree on the reasons for the introduction of War Communism. Some see it as a pragmatic response to the economic problems of the civil war period – the shortage of food and the decline of industrial production. It was an attempt to cope with an emergency situation and was only a temporary diversion from a more moderate policy of state-managed capitalism. Others, however, regard War Communism as the true expression of Marxist ideology, part of a long-term drive towards a fully planned economy.

However it might be interpreted, the reality was that, although the Bolsheviks had an ideological hatred of the market, they were divided over the policy itself. The details of War Communism were improvised and often changed. One important factor was the Bolsheviks' suspicion of the peasants, whom they saw as fundamentally selfish and hostile. Marxist teaching had always stressed the importance of industrial workers and had tended to dismiss those who lived in the countryside as uninterested in a socialist revolution. The Bolsheviks were also worried by the movement of large numbers of urban workers to the country in search of food, whose flight deprived industry of vital manpower. The non-agricultural labour force fell from 3.6 million to 1.5 million in 1917–20.

Whatever the causes of War Communism, its economic consequences were disastrous. Nationalisation of industry did not lead to an improvement in economic growth. By 1920–21, large-scale industrial production had fallen by 82% compared with 1913, the last full year of peace before the First World War. Food shortages worsened as peasants produced only what they needed for their own subsistence, knowing that any surplus would be seized by the authorities. By 1920, Russia was facing famine. The regime maintained that the problems were due to the peasants' concealment of grain, and its officials introduced increasingly harsh measures in a bid to make them give up what they were hiding.

There were hundreds of peasant revolts, the most serious of which began in Tarnbov, 350 km south-east of Moscow, in the autumn of 1920. It was suppressed following the deployment of Red Army troops, who resorted to brutal tactics, including the use of poison gas. Officially, the government described such uprisings as the work of 'bandits', but it became impossible to sustain this line as opposition to government policies spread beyond the peasantry. Starving industrial workers went on strike. There was also growing anger about the increasingly centralised power of the party. A 'Workers' Opposition' movement arose in 1920 to protest at the subordination of trade unions to the authority of the party. Workers' meetings called for a restoration of freedom to trade and of civil liberties.

The Kronstadt uprising, February–March 1921

Matters came to a head in February 1921 with an uprising of sailors at the Kronstadt naval base, on an island outside Petrograd. Joined by urban workers, they formed a revolutionary committee which put a series of demands to the government. The sailors had once been described by Trotsky as the 'pride and glory of the revolution'. They had taken part in the July Days and the crushing of the Kornilov coup in 1917. A shot fired by the cruiser *Aurora* in October 1917 had signalled the start of the Bolshevik takeover. Now the sailors were arguing that the Bolsheviks had betrayed the socialist ideals for which they had fought. The party had accumulated an excessive amount of power and denied ordinary workers essential freedoms.

Under the direction of Trotsky, 60 000 Red Army troops, backed by Cheka units, assaulted Kronstadt in March, advancing across the frozen sea that surrounded the base to do battle with the 15 000 defenders. After a siege of two weeks, the base fell and the survivors were treated mercilessly.

The tenth Party Congress and the NEP, March 1921

In spite of the brutal nature of the repression, it was clear that the regime would have to moderate its policy of War Communism. At the tenth Party Congress, which opened while the uprising was being put down, Lenin declared that the events at Kronstadt had 'lit up reality like a flash of lightning'. Food requisitioning was replaced by a **tax in kind** and, once they had paid this, peasants were now allowed to sell their surplus grain on the market. This was the foundation of the New Economic Policy (NEP) – a recognition by Lenin that the party needed to reach a settlement with the peasantry. This did not mean that the government had given up on long-term plans to take the peasants' landholdings into state ownership, but this was certainly to be delayed. The NEP was a controversial move back towards the market economy, with a new class of merchants and profiteers known as the 'Nepmen' emerging to make money from the new opportunities. Such capitalist activity had been illegal since the Bolsheviks took power. Lenin insisted that it was necessary to take this step, since these uprisings faced by the government were 'far more dangerous than all the

167

Figure 4.11: This photograph shows Red Army troops loyal to the Bolsheviks advancing across the frozen Gulf of Finland to suppress the 1921 Kronstadt uprising.

Cambridge International AS Level History Modern Europe, 1750–1921

Denikins, Yudeniches and Kolchaks put together'. It was the only way to deal with the desperate food situation and to avert the collapse of the Russian economy. He described it as 'a peasant Brest-Litovsk' – comparing it with the unpopular treaty with the Germans, which he had defended as taking one step backwards to take two steps forward. Lenin depicted the NEP as a compromise between socialism and capitalism. The 'commanding heights' of the economy, including large-scale industry and banking, remained in the hands of the state. A central planning agency, known as Gosplan, was tasked with giving advice on the long-term development of industry.

At the same time, Lenin made it clear that the political control of the party would not be relaxed. He secured a vote condemning the Workers' Opposition and banned **factionalism** within the party. The Central Committee would be the supreme body in the party and the country. Russia was now officially a one-party state. This was the logical outcome of the policies followed by the Bolsheviks towards all forms of opposition since the October Revolution.

KEY TERMS

Tax in kind: A tax paid in goods or services rather than in money.

Factionalism: Arguments between small groups within a larger organisation such as, in this case, a political party.

ACTIVITY 4.18

From the demands of the Kronstadt sailors, 1 March 1921

1 In view of the fact that the present Soviets do not represent the will of the workers and peasants, immediately to re-elect the Soviets by secret voting …

3 Freedom of meetings, trade unions and peasant associations …

5 To liberate all political prisoners of Socialist Parties, and also all workers, peasants, soldiers and sailors who have been imprisoned in connection with working class and peasant movements …

11 To grant the peasant full right to do what he sees fit with his land and to possess cattle, which he must maintain and manage with his own strength, but without employing hired labour …

Source: Kertesz, G.A. (ed.). (1970). *Documents in the Political History of the European Continent 1815–1939*. Oxford: Oxford University Press, pp. 435–36

The government tried to depict the Kronstadt rebels as agents of the White counter-revolution.Using this extract from the sailors' demands, what do you think were the real reasons for the uprising? Refer closely to the extract in your answer.

THINK LIKE A HISTORIAN

We have seen that in his pursuit of power, Lenin was prepared to be pragmatic: to modify his ideas in order to achieve his goals. List some examples of this characteristic shown in this chapter. Can you think of other examples of political leaders who have succeeded because they possess this willingness to change in response to circumstances, or unsuccessful ones who have failed because they have been too inflexible?

Reflection: Compare your list of reasons and supporting evidence from the extract with a partner. Have you used different parts of the extract to support similar reasons? Discuss your approach to how you decided which parts of the extract to use. Would you change how you choose supporting evidence from sources following your discussion?

168

Exam-style questions

Source analysis questions

Read the sources and then answer both parts of question 1.

SOURCE A

From the October Manifesto, issued by Tsar Nicholas II, 17 October 1905

In commanding the responsible authorities to take measures to stop disorders, lawlessness, and violence, and to protect peaceful citizens in the quiet performance of their duties, We [i.e. the tsar] have found it necessary to unite the activities of the Supreme Government, so as to ensure the successful carrying out of the general measures laid down by Us for the peaceful life of the State.

We lay upon the Government the execution of Our unchangeable will:

To grant to the population the inviolable right of free citizenship, based on the principles of freedom of person, conscience, speech, assembly and union.

… to include in the participation of the work of the Duma those classes of the population that have been until now entirely deprived of the right to vote …

To establish as an unbreakable rule that no law shall go into force without its confirmation by the State Duma …

Source: Kertesz, G.A. (ed.). (1970). *Documents in the Political History of the European Continent 1815–1939*. Oxford: Oxford University Press, pp. 301–302

SOURCE B

From the Manifesto to better the conditions … of the peasant population, issued by the tsar, 3 November 1905

The only way to better permanently the welfare of the peasant is by peaceful and legal means … we have decided:

To reduce by half, from January 1, 1906, and to discontinue altogether after January 1, 1907, payments due from peasants for land which before emancipation belonged to large landowners, State and Crown.

To make it easier for the Peasant Land Bank, by increasing its resources and by offering better terms for loans, to help the peasant with little land to buy more …

Source: Kertesz, G.A. (ed.). (1970). *Documents in the Political History of the European Continent 1815–1939*. Oxford: Oxford University Press, p. 302

SOURCE C

From the Fundamental Laws of the Russian Empire, 23 April 1906

The supreme autocratic power is vested in the Tsar of All the Russias. It is God's command that his authority should be obeyed not only through fear but for conscience' sake …

7 The Tsar exercises the legislative power in conjunction with the Council of the Empire and the Imperial Duma.

9 The Tsar approves of the laws, and without his approval no law can come into existence.

10 All governmental powers in their widest extent throughout the whole Russian Empire are vested in the Tsar.

72 No one can be prosecuted for an offence except according to the process established by law.

78 Russian subjects are entitled to meet peaceably and without arms for such purposes as are not contrary to law.

Source: Kertesz, G.A. (ed.). (1970). *Documents in the Political History of the European Continent 1815–1939*. Oxford: Oxford University Press, pp. 305–306

SOURCE D

From the announcement of the dissolution of the First Duma, 21 July 1906

A cruel disappointment has befallen Our expectations. The representatives of the nation, instead of applying themselves to the work of productive legislation, have strayed into spheres beyond their competence … and have been making comments upon the imperfections of the Fundamental Laws, which can only be modified by Our imperial will. In short, the representatives of the nation have undertaken really illegal acts, such as the appeal by the Duma to the nation.

The peasants, disturbed by such behaviour, and seeing no hope of the improvement of their lot, have resorted in a number of districts to open looting and the destruction of other people's property, and to disobedience of the law … We shall not permit arbitrary or illegal acts, and We shall impose Our imperial will on the disobedient by all the power of the State.

Source: Adapted from Kertesz, G.A. (ed.). (1970). *Documents in the Political History of the European Continent 1815–1939*. Oxford: Oxford University Press, pp. 306–307

1 **a** Read Sources A and C. Compare and contrast Sources A and C as evidence of the tsarist government's response to the revolution of 1905.

  b Read all the sources. 'The tsarist regime in Russia had no intention of addressing the problems which caused the revolution of 1905.' How far do the sources support this view?

Essay based questions

Answer both parts of the questions below.

2 **a** Explain why the Bolsheviks were successful in consolidating their power between 1917 and 1921.

  b 'The tsar's weak leadership in the First World War was the most important reason for his downfall.' How far do you agree?

3   a   Explain why the White forces were defeated in the Russian Civil War.

     b   To what extent was the downfall of the tsarist system in 1917 caused by Russia's economic weakness?

Sample answer

'The tsar's weak leadership in the First World War was the most important reason for his downfall.' How far do you agree?

Tsar Nicholas II was not trained as a general and he was not really suited to the role of wartime leader. He had a limited grasp of what was needed to bring about victory in war. A major error was his decision to take command of the Russian armies in person in August 1915, replacing his cousin who had been commander-in-chief up to this point. He hoped that this would reverse Russia's poor military performance during the first year of the war, but it turned out to be a serious mistake. However, there were other reasons for his downfall in the February 1917 Revolution. The Russian economy was failing under the strain of the war. The population was suffering from food shortages and the morale of the army collapsed in 1916–17.

> This opening paragraph has two main strengths. It focuses immediately on the factor highlighted in the question. It also indicates that the answer will provide some balance, as other factors are referred to.

The war had been going badly for the Russians since the start of the fighting in August 1914. The army had been defeated by the more effective German commanders when they invaded Germany, at the Battle of Tannenberg, and they had won few battles since then. The Russians were not properly equipped for a war of this kind. Soldiers lacked training and good weapons, and they were short of food and basic supplies. One of the main problems was that the rail network was not adequate when it came to moving troops and supplies, as well as taking vitally needed food to the cities. Soldiers started to desert the army in 1916, as they became concerned about the problems facing them. They were demoralised by the defeats and heavy casualties and they wanted to go home to help their starving families. The tsar was unable to cope with these problems because he lacked the ability to be an effective leader.

> This is an accurate summary of the deteriorating situation in Russia, but it does not fulfil the expectations raised in the introduction because it does not link the tsar to the problems described.

The tsar's decision to lead his armies in 1915 was one of his worst mistakes because the government in Petrograd was left in the hands of his wife, Alexandra. She was unpopular with the Russian people because of her German background and her reliance on Rasputin, a strange holy man who had great influence at court. The monarchy lost the respect of the people as rumours spread about Rasputin's relationship with the tsarina and other ladies in the royal circle. Another way in which this was damaging was that Rasputin influenced the appointment and dismissal of ministers, something he was not qualified to do. The level of leadership in Petrograd was poor. Rasputin was murdered in late 1916 by supporters of the monarchy, who were disturbed by the damage he was doing to it, but by then it was too late to reverse it.

> This is a stronger paragraph because it makes a direct link between an important aspect of the tsar's faulty leadership – his personal command of the armies – and the problems of government. This offers some focused explanation of what went wrong for the Russian war effort.

There were deeper reasons why the tsar fell from power. The root cause of the crisis was the fact that the Russian economy was not equal to the task of supporting a long war. Although average incomes actually rose during the first two years of the war, prices rose by a much larger factor. This was because the government used borrowing to finance the war, causing the value of money to fall. The food crisis became worse as peasants hoarded grain rather than selling it, because they could not get a fair price for it. Combined with the breakdown of the transport system, this led to food shortages in the cities, leading to protests and strikes by early 1917. A strike in the Putilov steel works, the most important factory in Petrograd, was a major blow. This in turn further weakened the war effort.

The poor suffered most from the collapsing home front, and it was their anger which led to the breakdown of order in Petrograd. However, the country's elites were also becoming critical of the government. When the Duma was recalled in 1916, liberals and moderate conservatives joined together in the 'Progressive Front' to demand a change of direction. It was the military and civilian leaders, for example Mikhail Rodzianko, who in the end advised

Nicholas to abdicate in March 1917 to protect his personal safety, and in the hope that this would allow the monarchy to continue under a new tsar. The police and army, on whose support the regime relied, could not by this stage be depended upon to put down hostile crowds in Petrograd. They had sympathy for those who were protesting and failed to exert themselves to defend the tsarist system.

> Here the essay introduces some balance: these two paragraphs help to meet the requirement to show 'how far' one factor was the most important. It is a little brief, however: we are not told much about the reasons why the Progressive Front was critical of the government, and the jump to the abdication is sudden. The essay states that the elites played an important role in the final crisis of the monarchy, but does not fully explain this point.

The tsar was partly responsible for his own failure. He had always been distant from his people's everyday living conditions, and his decision to attempt to run the war from his military headquarters, 600 km from Petrograd, made this problem worse. He did not understand the situation which had developed in his capital city and believed that he could calm the situation there by returning. Nicholas was on his way there when some of his generals and leading politicians intercepted his train and advised him to abdicate. He gave way with little persuasion required, suggesting that he had never really measured up to the role of tsar. His personality was poorly suited to governing his empire and this was especially so in the midst of war. However, there were long-term reasons for the fall of the monarchy. The state of the Russian economy and army, and the fact that the country could not meet the demands of war on this scale, were the underlying causes of the tsar's fall.

> The conclusion has some important strengths. The revolution is linked to the quality of the tsar's leadership, and there are some insights into his personality and poor qualifications for government. The relative significance of different factors is considered, and the judgement is consistent with the line taken earlier in the essay, pointing towards deeper reasons for the tsar's fall. However, this would be improved still further if the judgement were fully supported. The key prompt in the question, about the tsar's war leadership, is not developed sufficiently in the body of the essay. For example, the fact that by taking command in person, the tsar was unintentionally associating himself with military failure, is not covered. The point about his isolation from political affairs at his headquarters is not addressed until near the end of the essay.

Summary

After working through this chapter, make sure you understand the following key points:

- the reasons for the 1905 Revolution, and the tsarist regime's response to it

- the strengths and weaknesses of the tsarist government at the outbreak of the First World War

- the long-term and short-term causes of the February 1917 Revolution and the role of the First World War in forcing these events

- the reasons for the downfall of the Provisional Government and Lenin's success in bringing the Bolsheviks to power

- how the Bolsheviks consolidated their hold on power between 1917 and 1921.

Further reading

Bromley, J. (2002). *Russia 1848–1917.* London: Heinemann. (Chapters 3 to 5 of the AS section give a narrative of Russia from 1881 to 1917, while the A2 section explores themes in greater depth.)

Culpin, C. (2012). *The Russian revolution 1894–1924.* London: Hodder. (Chapters 1 and 2 introduce the topic, while Chapters 3 to 7 pose key questions about the 1905 Revolution, Russia in 1914, the 1917 Revolutions and the Civil War.)

Figes, O. (2014). *Revolutionary Russia 1891–1991.* London: Pelican. (Chapters 1 to 7 provide a stimulating overview of the period 1891–1921.)

Lynch, M. (2015). *Access to History: Reaction and Revolution: Russia 1894–1924.* London: Hodder. (Chapters 1 to 3 cover Russia from 1894 to 1914; Chapter 4 deals with the background to the February Revolution; Chapter 5 explains the Bolshevik takeover; and Chapter 6 the consolidation of power.)

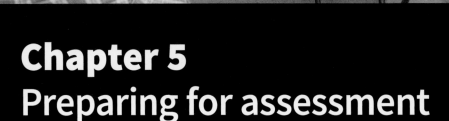

Chapter 5
Preparing for assessment

Learning objectives

In this chapter you will:

- learn about the skills that you will develop by studying AS Level History
- find out what types of question will test your skills and learn what other skills you will need in order to answer them
- understand how your skills and work might be assessed and how you can study and revise most effectively.

5.1 Introduction

In order to achieve success at AS Level History, you will need to develop skills that, perhaps, were less important in courses you might have taken in the past. Generally, pre-AS level assessments require you to demonstrate your knowledge and understanding of certain historical events. Now you will be required to analyse and interpret your knowledge in much greater depth.

This has implications for the way you study History at a higher level. Your teacher will provide the essential background knowledge, help you to develop the various skills you need in order to do well, and suggest the resources that you will need to work with.

It is essential at AS Level, however, that you are prepared to work and research independently and participate in discussion, which is essential for developing your own ideas and judgement. Your teacher cannot tell you what to think or what opinions to have, although they can help you learn how to think and how to form opinions. At AS Level, you will have far more responsibility for developing your own ideas, views and judgments. If you wish to aim for high-level grades at AS Level, you will have to put forward your own views on a subject and explain your reasons for coming to those views. To do this effectively, you need to acquire independent learning skills. In particular, this means reading as widely as possible around a topic so you can gain access to different interpretations of the same issues and events.

History is not a series of universally accepted facts, which once learned, will provide you with a detailed and accurate understanding of the past. Just as historical events were perceived in many different (and often contradictory) ways by people who experienced them at the time, so they have been interpreted in many different (and often contradictory) ways by historians who have studied them subsequently. Historical debates rage all the time, which make it very clear that historians often disagree fundamentally about the reasons for, or the significance of, certain key events.

You need to understand, for example, that there is no right answer to why the revolutions occurred in Russia in 1917. Many great historians have researched this topic in depth and have come to very different conclusions. You will need to learn to reflect on those conclusions and to reach your own judgement. This process of reflection will also give you an insight into the methods historians use to put across their ideas; you will be able to adapt these methods for your own use when answering historical questions.

History may seem to deal primarily with facts, but it is equally about opinions, perceptions, judgements, interpretations and prejudices. Many people in Britain in the 1830s, for example, felt that the government should not interfere in the way in which factories were managed. They believed it should be left to individuals to decide where they worked and how they worked, regardless of age or sex. On the other hand, others felt strongly that there should be regulation, but often for very different reasons some religious, some economic, some social or simply from a sense of genuine compassion. There are just as many diverse opinions from historians on this significant decision.

You will be asked for your opinion or judgement on an issue like this, and will have to make up your own mind. You need to study the evidence, reflect on what kind of evidence it is and then analyse what it proves. This will allow you to form an opinion. When asked for an opinion or judgement, you will need to back up what you offer with reasons and evidence. In this way, historians are like lawyers in court. You are making a case and then proving it. Sometimes your fellow learners and teachers might disagree with your opinion and be able to provide compelling evidence to demonstrate why. Sometimes they might convince you to change your mind. Sometimes you will be able to convince them to change or refine

their opinions. Sometimes you might just agree to differ. It is this ability to see things in different ways, and to have the confidence to use your own knowledge and understanding to make judgements, form opinions and develop arguments, that makes history so interesting and challenging.

5.2 What skills will I develop as I study AS Level History?

It is worth stressing that, alongside your historical knowledge and understanding, a wide range of skills will be assessed in the course of your studies. Most of these will be invaluable to you in both higher education and your working life. They include the ability to:

- acquire in-depth subject knowledge
- learn how to select and use knowledge effectively
- use independent research skills, which are critical for success, at AS Level and beyond
- develop independent thinking skills
- apply knowledge and understanding to new as well as familiar situations
- handle and evaluate different types of information source
- think logically and present ordered and coherent arguments
- make judgements, recommendations and decisions
- present reasoned explanations, understand implications and communicate them clearly and logically
- work effectively under pressure
- communicate well in English
- understand that information learned in one context can be usefully deployed in another.

All of these will be tested in some way in your History assessments. Merely learning a large number of facts will not enable you to achieve your best at AS Level History; you have to demonstrate a range of skills as well. Work on the principle that roughly half the marks awarded are for knowledge and understanding, and half are for your use of the skills listed above.

How can I acquire and demonstrate the most important skills?

It is worth stressing that these skills will form an essential part of the assessment process at AS level. AS level studies are not just about learning facts: you have to develop the skills to use them properly.

Acquiring in-depth subject knowledge

You need to find the most suitable way to acquire the knowledge you need and the most effective way of remembering it, so that you can use it when necessary. Often, it is a combination of reading, noting, listening, writing and discussing that helps to retain knowledge.

Selecting and using that knowledge effectively

Once you have acquired the right amount of subject knowledge, you must learn how to use it effectively. If you are asked a question on one of the many reasons why there was rapid industrialisation in late 18th-century Britain, you should not write about all the reasons for industrialisation, just the one specified.

Using independent research skills

The ability to research for yourself it vital. It would be virtually impossible for any teacher to give you all the information you need. You must be able to effectively use a library and other research sources and tools, such as the internet, to find out things for yourself.

Developing independent thinking skills

You must learn how to think for yourself and be able to challenge ideas. You will be asked for your view on a subject, for example whether canals or railways played a greater role in the industrialisation of Britain. Both transport innovations have a strong claim here, but which do you think played the greater role, and why?

Handling and evaluating different types of information

You need to look at different types of information and assess how accurate and useful they might be. For example, you may need to put yourself in the position of a historian who is writing about Bismarck and the war with France. Many contemporary sources defend his role; others are strongly critical. Some are obviously from biased writers or cartoonists; other writers might have benefited or lost by the decision. Which is the most reliable and useful? Why? This is the sort of skill that might be useful in the present day – for example, if you are deciding which way to vote in an election after you have been presented with arguments from all sides.

Analysing and making judgements

This combination is a vital skill. You will be asked for a judgement on, for example, whether the Directory's rule of France between 1795 and 1799 was successful. First, you will have to work out for yourself what the criteria for success is in this context. Then you will need to consider the grounds on which the Directory might be seen as a success – in the role of the defence counsel, if you like. Next you should consider the grounds on which it might *not* be seen as a success. Finally, in the most difficult part, you will have to weigh up the two sides and come to a conclusion. You must be prepared to give clear reasons to defend your decision.

Explaining

You will need to explain quite complex issues clearly, For example, you could be asked to explain why Trotsky was so important to Bolshevik success, and have ten minutes in which to do it. You will have to briefly explain what Trotsky's role was, then in three or four sentences explain why he was essential to the party's progress. Note that you will need to give sufficient focus to the 'so' word in the question.

5.3 What types of question will test my skills?

There are three broad types of question at AS Level. They will assess your:

- knowledge and understanding, and your skills in communicating them
- analytical, evaluative and communication skills
- ability to read a range of sources, under pressure of time, grasp the essential points they make, contrast and evaluate those sources and reach a judgement on them, demonstrating a range of skills as well as historical knowledge and understanding.

Understanding what a question is asking you to do

There are certain key words that appear in many AS Level History questions. These 'command words' are the instructions that specify what you need to do. They make it clear what is expected from a response in terms of skills, knowledge and understanding.

Source-based questions

Questions based on source extracts might ask, for example:

To what extent do Sources A and C agree *on the extent of Bismarck's responsibility for causing the war with France?*

175

This type of question is looking for a firm *judgement* on the **extent** to which the sources **agree** (and disagree) about Bismarck's role. It is your *understanding* of those two sources that is key, along with your ability to *identify the key points showing agreement and disagreement*. The question is also looking for *source analysis* and *contextual knowledge*.

Note that, in this instance, only the two sources specified should be used.

Compare and contrast *the views in Sources B and D on the role of agriculture in the industrialisation process.*

This type of question is looking for your ability to *identify the similarities and differences* of the views expressed in the two sources about agriculture's involvement in industrialisation. A good response will comment on whether there are more similarities than differences, and why. *Contextual knowledge* and *source evaluation* will also be expected.

Again, only the two sources specified should be used.

'Trotsky's work was the most important reason for Bolshevik success in 1917.' **How far do Sources A to D** *support this view?*

What this task is looking for is a clear *judgement* of **how far** *all four* sources (not just the two specified in the first type of question) do, or do not, support the given view of Trotsky's role. You might find that a useful way of dealing with this type of question is to use the structure outlined below for questions that highlight knowledge and understanding. You need to offer a *balanced argument* in addition to your judgement, and you must make careful use of *all four sources* and demonstrate *contextual* knowledge as well. The supporting paragraphs after your judgement are a good place to do this. Demonstration of *source evaluation* skills will also be required.

To what extent *do Sources A to D support the view that economic problems were the main cause of the French Revolution?*

You can take a similar approach to this type of question as you did with the 'How far …' question about Trotsky above. You need to make a firm *judgement* on *how far* the sources back up the claim that the economy was the main cause of the revolution (not just a vague 'to some extent'). You also need to make a good case for your argument.

It is important to use *all four sources* and *contextual knowledge* when backing up your points. It is appropriate to quote the occasional phrase if you feel it is important to your argument, but avoid copying out large sections of the

documents. Demonstration of *source evaluation skills* will be crucial here.

Other questions that assess knowledge, understanding and analytical skills

Command terms and key words in non-source-based questions might include:

Explain why *the Provisional Government failed.*

This type of question clearly requires an *explanation of why* the Provisional Government in Russia failed in its objectives. It is therefore your *ability to explain something clearly* that is being assessed, as well as your *knowledge and understanding of the reasons* for the Provisional Government's failure. It is assessing your ability to *select and apply your in-depth knowledge effectively*.

'The counter-revolutionary groups in France failed between 1789 and 1799 through poor leadership.' **How far do you agree?**

This type of question requires *analytical* skills, as well as *knowledge and understanding of the reasons* for the shortcomings of the various groups. You need to consider whether it was *just* leadership factors which led to failure, or whether there were other, more important, issues. You need to make a *judgement based on the evidence* you have learned. Your ability to analyse a topic you know a lot about is being assessed, as well as your ability to come to a judgement on **how far** (based on a scale from, for example, 'not at all' to 'completely' leadership was, or was not, responsible).

To what extent *was Russia's entry into the First World War the reason for the downfall of tsarism?*

This type of question is also assessing your *analytical* skills and needs a similar approach to a 'How far' question. There has to be a firm *judgement* on the issue of **extent**. There also has to be evidence in the response to show that you have analysed the implications of entry into the war on the tsar's position, and considered the degree to which it did lead to his downfall (keeping the focus firmly on his **downfall** and not getting sidetracked by a narrative of the war) compared with other factors which might have played an important part. Then you need to come to a *conclusion* based on the evidence.

How successful *were the tsar's reforms after the 1905 Revolution?*

This type of question assesses your *analytical* skills as well as your *knowledge and understanding* of the tsar's attempts to reform Russia. It requires a firm *judgement* on the *degrees* of success, or otherwise, that the tsar had. There needs to be some *reflection* on what the *criteria for success* might be. Would the reforms be considered a success if they just helped the regime to survive longer or if they brought real benefit to the Russian people? You need to show that you know and understand what the tsar did and the impact of those actions. An *examination of the nature and extent of the success* achieved should then lead to a concluding *judgement on the degree of success* attained.

How effective *was the opposition to the Directory?*

A similar approach can be used here to the 'how successful' type of question. Some *reflection* on what **effective** opposition means is expected. Stopping the Directory from achieving its objectives? Slowing it down? Making it more cautious in putting forward the policies it really wanted to? The question requires an *examination of evidence* of how the opposition prevented the Directory from doing what it wanted to, and also where it failed to do so. A good response will come to a *firm judgement based on the evidence*. Avoid vague responses such as 'It had some effect'. Argue your case strongly.

Questions that highlight knowledge and understanding

This type of question assesses your ability to:

- understand a question and its requirements, and to keep a firm focus on that question alone
- recall and select relevant and appropriate factual material, and demonstrate your understanding of a possibly complex topic
- communicate your knowledge and understanding in a clear and effective manner.

An example of a 'knowledge and understanding' question might be: *Explain why Napoleon was able to seize power in 1799.*

A good-quality answer to this type of question will:

- be entirely focused on this question. It should only be on Napoleon and his seizure of power; no reference to any other important event is necessary. You do not need to explain his actions once in power.
- identify three or four relevant points and develop them with supporting detail
- indicate which of those points you feel are the most important and why, and suggest why another factor might be of less importance. This is vital in an 'explain why' type

of question to demonstrate that you have thought about the relative importance of the points you are writing about

- be written in as clear English as possible.

When answering, remember:

- Explain why.
- Answer the question that was asked and do not spend time on Napoleon's later career.
- Do more than merely list facts which might or might not be linked to the question.
- Make specific points and back them up with relevant and accurate detail.

This type of question is testing understanding as well as knowledge. It is not just a case of remembering one relevant point. It is also very important to show that you understand its significance *in context*.

Questions that highlight analysis and evaluation

This type of question assesses your ability to:

- understand the question and its requirements and keep a firm focus on that question alone
- recall and select relevant and appropriate factual material
- analyse and evaluate this material in order to reach a focused, balanced and substantiated judgement
- communicate your knowledge and understanding in a clear and effective manner.

Examples of these questions are:

1 'The revolutions of 1848 in Germany were caused primarily by economic factors.' How far do you agree?

2 How effective were Lenin's economic policies?

Your answer to the first question, on the revolutions in Germany in 1848, should contain a clear judgement or argument:

- It should be entirely focused on this question. It is not asking about why the revolutions failed. It is asking whether you think economic factors were the primary cause of the revolutions, or whether they were among many causes, or if there was another primary cause. Be careful not to write a narrative of the revolutions themselves or spend much time on the background history of Germany, unless you feel it is directly linked to the question. You might have only 30 minutes to write a response, so manage your time carefully. This is an important skill to develop.

177

- Demonstrate that you have thought about causative factors in general. What do you really think led people to take the risks they did in 1848? Did participation in the various revolutionary acts vary between classes? Were people driven by the simple fact that they were hungry, or was idealism more influential? (If, instead, the question was about whether the revolutions were failures, then show that you have thought about what 'failure' implies in the context of Germany in the 1840s and 1850s. What do you think are the criteria for success or failure in this case? Did those men achieve something and did they influence later events? It is that indication that you have really thought for yourself about the implications of *failure* in this context, and what *success* might look like, that marks out a really high-quality analytical essay.)

- Be balanced: show that you have considered both the case for economic factors being the major cause, and the case for other factors. Show that you have thought about a wide range of issues, weighed them all up and come to your own conclusion.

- Include careful analysis: demonstrate that you have weighed up both the case for and the case against the point raised in the question and come to a reasoned judgement. Your response should not simply lay out the case for and against and then leave it to the reader to come to a decision.

- Offer knowledge and understanding by backing up the various points you make with accurate and relevant detail.

Remember:

- Avoid simply stating a case for and one against and leaving it to the reader to decide what the answer is. This is common error.

- Give a clear and developed answer. Make sure that your case is clearly laid out and developed carefully. You have made it quite clear why you think economic factors were the principal factor (or not) and given clear reasons for that. Those reasons should then be followed up in subsequent paragraphs which contain the factual details to back up those points. Good responses usually contain an opening paragraph which sets out the answer clearly and gives the reasoning behind it. Later paragraphs – perhaps three or four of them – deal with the development of the case. In dealing with the case against, the strongest answers clearly explain, with supporting evidence, why you do not think it valid, demonstrating you are aware of alternative views.

- Show you have really thought about 'failure' in this context.

Tips for answering questions that ask 'How far do you agree?'

'The revolutions of 1848 in Germany were caused primarily by economic factors.' How far do you agree?

Try thinking about this in terms of a scale, with 'I completely agree because …' at one end and 'I completely disagree because …' at the other, with 'somewhat' in between:

Completely agree   Somewhat agree   Somewhat disagree   Completely disagree

Depending on where you are on the scale, responses could be similar to the ones below:

1. Economic factors, such as poverty, unemployment and hunger, were the principal causes of the revolutions because without them the vital working-class support would not have been forthcoming. While there were other causative factors, such as … and …, they did not play nearly such an important part as the economic factors.

2. While economic factors did play an important role in causing the revolutions of 1848, the most important cause was the desire by many middle-class people for greater freedom and an end to the rule of autocratic monarchs. This was more important because …

3. Economic factors only played a minor role in causing the revolutions of 1848. The major causes were the desire by many middle-class people for greater political freedom and the wish to unite Germany and end the domination of Austria. In one or two states, there was hunger and unemployment, which did lead to some working-class unrest, but the revolts were always led by middle-class men aiming at political reform or unification.

4. Economic factors rarely played any role in causing the revolutions of 1848. Much more important were … and …, as it was these two factors which …

Opening sections like these demonstrate thinking about the relative importance of causes and not just trying to remember what all the causes were. They show analytical skills and understanding, not just knowledge. Remember that all three are being assessed at AS Level.

A response to the second question, on the effectiveness of Lenin's economic policies, should show the following:

• It should be entirely focused on the effectiveness of those policies. The question does not ask about the reasons for the revolution of 1917, or whether the Provisional Government's policies were unsuccessful. The response needs to be only about how *effective* Lenin's policies were.

• It should demonstrate evidence of thinking about what effective policies might be in the very challenging circumstances of Russia between 1918 and 1921. Would such policies reduce unemployment, end inflation or restore the people's confidence in their leaders? Would they rebuild the Russian economy, feed the people, prevent a return to tsarism, establish socialism? It is important to show that you are thinking analytically.

• It should demonstrate knowledge and understanding by identifying the various policies adopted by Lenin and the Bolsheviks.

• Its should use analytical ability by weighing up the identified policies and commenting on the extent to which you consider them to be effective or otherwise. The focus should be on the effectiveness of each policy, but you should also comment on the overall effectiveness.

Another example of a timed essay-type question might be: *'Louis XVI must take full responsibility for causing the French Revolution.' How far do you agree?* Different students will take different approaches to this type of question, and you will find your own. While you are developing your techniques, you might find the following structure helpful. Even if you choose to organise your essay differently, it is important to note the strengths of this one and apply the same principles in your own writing.

Paragraph	Content
1	This needs to contain a succinct, clear answer to the question. Should Louis take full responsibility for causing the revolution, or not? An answer might be, for example: *He must take most, but not all, responsibility. There were many other causes which were beyond his control. The reasons why he should take most responsibility are:* (a) … (b) … (c) … *But there were other factors which played an important part, such as* (d) … *and* (e) … This paragraph does not need not to contain much detail, just broad reasons, and should demonstrate that you are focusing on the question and thinking analytically. Avoid vague introductions or trying to 'set the scene'.
2	This could take point (a) and develop it in detail. Make sure that the objective of the paragraph is clear from the start, for example: *The principal reason why Louis must take much of the responsibility was* … And then bring in three or four accurate and relevant facts to back up your point: the evidence. This section might also explain why you feel this particular issue was the most important point, highlighting an analytical approach.
3	Point (b) could be developed here in a similar way. Again, take care to ensure that the objective of the paragraph is made clear: that you are relating what you write very obviously to your statement that those policies achieved little. There is often a tendency to forget the purpose of the paragraph and simply list the facts. This often leaves the reader asking, 'So?'
4	Again, make the objective clear and add as much comment as you can to explain why this point is of less importance than (a).
5	This is a good place to develop the case 'against' in points (d) and (e), to demonstrate the balance required in this type of response. There is nothing wrong with strong arguments, however, and if you feel there is no case 'against', say so and why. It might nonetheless be a good idea to start this paragraph with, for example: *Defenders of Louis might argue that* … and explain a possible defence of his work, however weak you might think it is.

Paragraph	Content
6	If you have developed your response as suggested above, this paragraph can be quite brief. Avoid repetition, and keep an analytical focus, perhaps emphasising the reasons behind your thinking.
	It is important to have included an introduction as suggested in paragraph 1, not just to indicate a case each way and leave all the analysis and answer to the 'conclusion'. That type of response is likely to contain facts and no analysis or judgement.
	Another failing might be that the case for is very long and detailed, while the case against is much briefer and undeveloped, and yet the brief conclusion is that the case against wins even though all the facts presented point the other way. In this case, there is just not enough analysis to fully answer the question.

Another example to consider is the following essay **'Napoleon remained in power for so long simply because he was a successful general.' How valid is this view?**

One way of approaching this type of question is outlined below.

Paragraph	Content
1	Identify the principal reasons why Napoleon was able to retain power for such a long time, such as his reforms, military successes, effective propaganda. Emphasise your response to the word 'so' in the question. It demonstrates that you are thinking analytically from the start. Including between three and five reasons shows good knowledge and understanding.
2	Take what you think was the most important reason for his hold on power – for example, his retention of what many saw as the main gains of the revolution – and develop this point in detail. Then develop the reasons why you do **not** think his success as a general was the most important reason.
3, 4 and 5	Continue to develop in depth the reasons you have set out in your first paragraph, again making sure that your analytical thinking is clear and you are not merely listing reasons.
6	Avoid repetition. Focus on why you prioritised in the way you did, and show that you have thought very carefully about the factors behind the length of Napoleon's reign as referred to in the question.

Questions that highlight your ability to read, contrast, evaluate and judge a range of sources

Source-based questions are testing your ability to:

- understand a question and its requirements
- understand the content of a source in its historical setting
- analyse and evaluate source content and the sources themselves
- reach a focused and balanced judgement based on evidence
- communicate your argument in a clear and effective manner.

A source-based question might contain, for example, four sources on reasons for the Prussian victory in the Franco-Prussian War and then ask:

1 Compare and contrast the accounts given of the state of the Prussian army in Sources B and D.

2 How far do Sources A to D support the view that the principal reason for Prussian victory in the war was French incompetence?

When answering, remember:

- You do not need to provide a summary of the sources, or copy out large parts of them. You might need, however, to quote just a phrase or two to back up your points.
- Evaluate the sources. You must show clearly that you have really thought about their provenance and validity.
- Include relevant contextual knowledge.

A response to a question such as number 2 above should contain:

- Evidence that you have fully understood all four sources (not just the two specified in the first question!) and grasped their overall arguments. Demonstration of clear comprehension is vital for a high-quality answer.

- Evidence that you have identified the extent to which each source does, or does not, suggest that French incompetence led to Prussian victory, and that all four sources have been considered carefully and used in your response.
- A focused and balanced judgement on the issue of responsibility.
- Contextual awareness – that you have background historical knowledge and understanding, and that you are not just relying on the sources for information.
- Evaluation of all four sources in this specific context (which is likely to differ from that of the first question) and consideration of their validity and provenance.
- A firm, specific judgement. Avoid merely saying, for example, 'The French must take *some* responsibility.' A more appropriate response might be 'While the French government must take some responsibility for Prussian victory, the most important factor was the excellent quality of the Prussian army and its very competent leadership.'

Further guidance on source-based questions

In order to make judgements and form opinions about past events, historians need to gather as much information and evidence as possible. They use a wide variety of sources for this, including written extracts, speeches, photographs, cartoons, posters, film footage, oral records and archaeological finds. Much of the evidence historians find is contradictory, reflecting the many different perspectives and opinions of the people who produced the sources.

Documents and photographs, for example, can be created or altered by those wishing to present the most favourable view of themselves. Historians, therefore, need to analyse their sources very carefully in order to form their own opinions and judgements about the past while avoiding a one-sided or very biased study of an event or person.

Learning how to reflect on and evaluate information before you make up your own mind on a subject – whether this is who you might vote for or which mobile phone you might buy – is an important skill to acquire. The feature 'Think like a historian' used throughout this book should give you an idea about how the skills you develop in this course are useful in other areas of your life.

In much the same way, you will be faced with a variety of different historical sources during your course. You will need to be able to analyse those sources in the light of your own subject knowledge. The key word here is *analyse*. This means going far beyond just a basic *comprehension* of what a source is saying or showing. A mistake to avoid in answering source-based questions is just describing or summarising the source. You need to ask yourself questions about how reliable the source is and why it appears to contradict what some other sources seem to suggest.

Primary sources

A primary source is one that was written, spoken, drawn or photographed at, or very near, the time. It could also be a recollection some years later of an event or person. It is usually the product of someone who was directly involved in the event, or who was, in some sense, an eyewitness to it.

Primary sources tend to reflect the customs and beliefs of their creator, and the time and place from which they come. You should not be critical of the contents of a primary source just because, for example, it does not share your values. Opinions in the UK today about equal rights, for instance, are very different from those held by many people 150 years ago.

A primary source has many advantages to a historian:

- It provides a first-hand, contemporary account.
- It can offer an insight into the author's perceptions and emotions at the time.
- A source created by someone directly involved in an event might give detailed 'inside information' that other people could not possibly know.

Disadvantages of a primary source might be:

- The source only gives the reader the opinions of the person who created it, which might not be typical of opinions at the time.
- A source created by someone directly involved might contain bias – for example, in trying to convince an audience to agree with a particular line of argument.
- Eyewitnesses might not always be completely reliable. They might not have access to the full details of an event, or they might be trying to impose their own opinions on the audience.
- The source might be based on the memory of an event or meeting which happened many years before, or could be over-reliant on the recollections of another person.

Different types of primary source you might be asked to use include:

- a speech
- a private letter
- a diary
- an official document, such as an Act of Parliament, an order from a minister to a civil servant, a report from an ambassador to his foreign secretary, a secret memorandum by an official, a legal judgement
- an autobiography
- a cartoon
- a photograph
- a newspaper report
- an interview.

A note on bias

The word 'bias' is often misused in history essays. A dictionary definition of bias is 'the action of supporting a particular person or thing in an unfair way by allowing personal opinions to influence your judgement'. Bias can be explicit and conscious, for example, politicians seeking election will naturally emphasise the good points about their record, and emphasise the bad points about their opponent's. Bias can also be implicit and unconscious.

A note on hindsight

Hindsight is the ability to look back at an event some time after it has occurred, with a fuller appreciation of the facts, implications and effects. With hindsight, it is easier to understand the reasons why an event took place, its significance and the impact it had. It is vital to remember that people living at the time of the event did not have the advantage of hindsight!

Assessing the reliability of sources

It should now be clear that historians have to be extremely careful when using sources. They cannot afford to accept that everything a source tells them is completely reliable or true. People exaggerate. People tell lies. People might not have seen everything there was to see People have opinions that others do not share. People simply make mistakes.

Imagine you are out walking, lost in your own thoughts, when you suddenly hear a screeching of brakes and a thud

behind you. As you turn in the direction of the sounds, you see a pedestrian fall to the ground, clearly having been hit by a car, which you see driving quickly away. You are the only person around. Your first priority would be to try to assist the pedestrian and call the emergency services. When the police arrive, they see you as a vital eyewitness to the accident, and they naturally want to take a statement from you.

But were you really an eyewitness? Did you see the accident, or just hear it and see the result? You saw the car drive quickly away, but does that mean the driver was speeding or driving dangerously at the time? How might your sense of pity for the pedestrian affect your idea of what actually happened? Could you be certain the pedestrian was not to blame for the accident? Could the pedestrian have stumbled into the path of the car? Deliberately jumped? Could you describe the car in detail, or the driver? How far might your recollection of the event be influenced by your own shock? How and why might the statements of the car driver and the pedestrian differ from your own?

So, what can we do, as historians, to minimise the risk of drawing inaccurate conclusions from sources? There are a number of questions that need to be asked in order to determine how reliable a source is and to evaluate its provenance. These apply to all types of source, not just written ones:

- Who wrote it?
- When was it written?
- What is the context?
- Who was the intended audience?
- Why was it written? What was the author's motive?
- What does it actually say?
- How does it compare with your own subject knowledge and with what other sources say?
- What do you think the author might have left out?

Suppose, for example, that this is the statement given to the police later in the day by the driver of the car involved in the accident: 'I was driving carefully along the road well within the speed limit. Suddenly and without warning, a pedestrian jumped out in front of me from behind a parked lorry. I did not see him until it was far too late and it was impossible for me to stop in time and avoid hitting the pedestrian. In a state of panic, I did not stop. I drove away, in shock, but within minutes I calmed down and realised that I had to go and report the issue to the police. I had my children in the car, so once I had taken them home, I reported the incident to the police.'

- **Who wrote the source?** The driver of the car involved in the accident. Naturally, the driver would clearly not wish to be blamed for the accident, and therefore might have a very good reason for being less than honest.

- **When was it written?** Later on the same day as the accident. By this time, the driver would have recovered from the initial shock and understood that there was probably no option but to report the incident to the police. The driver might well have seen the witness and believed that they had the car's details and description. However, there would have been time for the driver to reflect on the incident and develop a version of events so that the responsibility for the incident could be placed on the pedestrian. Given the shock and what might have happened since, would the driver's memory be accurate?

- **What is the context?** The driver reporting to the police to admit involvement in the accident. The police would take this statement in the event that the case went to court.

- **Who was the intended audience?** Initially the police, but also possibly a counsel who might have to decide whether or not to prosecute the driver, and therefore, a judge and a jury.

- **Why was it written? What was the author's motive?** The statement had to be written as it was the law. It is possible that the driver accepted the need to report their involvement in the accident. It is also possible that the driver, realising that the police would most likely catch up with them, was anxious to report the incident in order to clear their name by laying blame on the pedestrian.

- **What does it actually say?** The driver claims not to have been driving too fast or dangerously, and that the accident was entirely the pedestrian's fault for jumping out suddenly into the road from behind a lorry, without checking for traffic. The driver admits to leaving the scene of the accident out of panic.

- **How might it compare with what other sources say?** The police are in a difficult position here. The driver might well be telling the whole truth and giving a perfectly accurate description. The driver might also have made up the entire story if they were driving too fast or using their phone. Other witnesses might be able to comment on how fast the car was going at the time. There might be some CCTV footage of the accident of variable quality. Mobile phone records can be checked. Marks on the road can be assessed. The driver mentions 'children' in the car. Would they be able to give a version of events, but, if so, would they just support their parent? If the parked lorry which hid the pedestrian from view had been moved,

can an accurate picture of the whole event be made? The pedestrian might be concussed and not have an accurate recollection of events. If the police discover that the pedestrian had a long record of depression, might that not reinforce the possibility that he had 'jumped out' as the driver's statement alleges?

Finding the truth can be a very challenging task.

The following source is a letter from the Austrian ambassador to Prussia to his foreign minister in Vienna in February 1866, just after Austria and Prussia had waged a successful war against Denmark.

> So far the differences between Austria and Prussia have been limited to the Governments of the two countries. Now they have been translated to the field of public opinion. I am clear that Bismarck feels that the time has come to mount a great Prussian action abroad, and if it can be done in no other way, to go to war if he thinks the time is right for it. Such an action has been his ambition from the beginning of his political career. It would deal with his ungoverned and unscrupulous, but daring, wish for great achievement.
>
> If he is successful, especially if it was attained by means of a victorious war, the government in Prussia would more easily master its internal problems. It would be difficult to deal with Prussia's internal problems without the diversion of war. It has been suggested that the king of Prussia might end his domestic problems by a coup d'état, simply assuming total power, which Bismarck may have recommended, but the king refused absolutely. The only means by which Prussia's many domestic problems can be overcome must be sought in an active and successful foreign policy. It is this that guides Bismarck's policy. How far Bismarck has succeeded, or will succeed, in winning over the king of Prussia to his extreme warlike policy is the question on which the whole future depends. A solution using force goes against the grain with the king, but he is very open to persuasion.
>
> **Translation of Vienna, Haus-Hof-und Staatsarchiv, PA III, no 91**

183

All sources need to be viewed critically, not just accepted at face value. To analyse this source effectively, you need to consider the same questions.

- **Who wrote it?** The Austrian ambassador to Prussia. His job was to represent Austria's interests in Prussia and to report back to Vienna all events in Prussia which might affect Austria.

- **When was it written?** In February 1866, after the war against Denmark which had been fought by Prussia with Austria as an ally and before the war between Austria and Prussia later in 1866.

- **What is the context?** There had been a successful outcome of the conflict with Denmark, which both Austria and Prussia had gained from. Prussia had done a great deal better than Austria. There was internal conflict in Prussia, however, which was threatening Bismarck's position, which would also affect his ambitions for Prussian expansion and German unification under Prussia. (Bismarck was known to dislike Austria and wanted to reduce its influence in Germany.)

- **Who was the intended audience?** The foreign minister of Austria and other members of the Austrian government. It is unlikely that it would have been published or given to a wider audience or appear in the press.

- **Why was it written? What was the author's motive?** Ambassadors were expected to give accurate reports based on careful acquisition of evidence. Austria's policy towards Germany would be strongly influenced by this report. It would be in the ambassador's interest to make the report as accurate and reliable as possible.

- **What does the report actually say?** The main point is that there is internal unrest in Prussia and the ambassador thinks that one way of dealing with it is for Bismarck to mount a successful foreign war. It is a warning about Prussia's future intentions.

- **How does it compare with other sources?** We know from other sources that Bismarck wished to limit or destroy Austria's domination of Germany.

- **How reliable is it likely to be?** Ambassadors tended to be educated and experienced men who were paid to report accurately. There might, however, be some pro-Austrian bias as well as personal antagonism against Bismarck.

Questions that ask you to compare and contrast sources

One type of question you might face is 'compare and contrast'. Whenever you compare two or more things, you should draw attention to the similarities and what they have in common. When contrasting, you should draw attention to the differences and points where they disagree.

A high-quality answer will show examples of the following skills:

- *Makes a developed comparison between the two sources, recognising points of similarity and difference.*
- *Uses knowledge to evaluate the sources and shows good contextual awareness.*

You are expected to do a great deal more than just give a summary of the two sources. You have to show that you have reviewed the content of the sources and that you fully comprehend them and can use your knowledge and understanding of them to answer the question. You also have to demonstrate contextual knowledge and show that you are fully aware of the sources' provenance. You must evaluate them very carefully.

The following sources might have a question such as:

Compare and contrast the views in Sources A and B on the causes of the French Revolution.

SOURCE A

Adapted from the memoir of Antoine Barnave, a revolutionary, in prison awaiting execution, 1793

The democratic ideal which was stifled under all European governments while the feudal system remained powerful, has gathered strength and continues to grow. As the arts, trade and the pursuit of luxury make industrious people richer, making the rich landowners poorer and bringing the different classes closer together through money, so science and education bring them closer in their daily lives, and recall men to the basic idea of equality. To these natural causes can be added the influence of royal power: long undermined by the aristocracy, it had called the people to its aid. Conditions in France were ripe for a democratic revolution when the unfortunate Louis XVI ascended the throne.; the governments' actions favoured its explosion.

The two privileged orders which still retained control of the government were ruined through their taste for luxury and had degraded themselves by their way of life.

184

The Third Estate, by contrast, had produced enlightened thinkers and acquired enormous wealth. The people were restrained only by their habit of obedience and limited hope they had of breaking their chains. Government had succeeded in containing this hope, but it still flourished in the heart of the nation. It was already apparent that, amongst the growing generation influenced by the Enlightenment, for royal power to remain it would have required a great tyrant or a great statesman on the throne.

Louis XVI was neither; he was too well intentioned not to try and remedy abuses which had shocked him, but he had neither the character or the talents to control an imperious nation in a situation which cried out for reform. His reign was a succession of feeble attempts at doing good, showing weakness and clear evidence of his failings as a ruler.

http://alphahistory.com/frenchrevoltuion/
antoine-barnave-failures-1793/

SOURCE B

Adapted from *Memoires* by Marquis de Bouillé, a French aristocrat in exile, 1797

The turning point was 1789. It was that year that the Revolution, already apparent in the minds, customs and way of life of the French nation, began to take effect in government. I will describe the principal reasons for this and some of the events to which it led. The most striking of the country's troubles was the chaos of its finances, the result of years of extravagance intensified by the great expense of the American War, which had cost the state over twelve hundred million livres. No one could think of any remedy but a search for fresh funds as the old ones were exhausted.

M de Calonne, minister of finance, had produced a bold and wide ranging plan. This plan changed the whole system of financial administration and attacked all its vices at their root. The worst of these were: the arbitrary system of allocating taxes, the high cost of collection and the abuse of privilege by the richest of taxpayers. The whole weight of public expenditure was borne by the most numerous, but the least wealthy part of the nation which was being crushed by the burden. This plan was submitted to the Assembly of Notables. All the Assembly did was to destroy M de Calonne and he was abandoned by the king. Shortly afterwards the king was unwise enough to make Brienne principal minister. Brienne tried to put through some parts of Calonne's plans, but the *parlements* resisted strongly. Then the troubles began. They broke out first in Brittany, where the government was compelled to bring in armed forces but did not dare use them owing to the reluctance shown by the troops to be used against such people. In Paris, the people's discontent, already raised to the point of rebellion by angry members of the *parlement*, there were riots which had to be put down by force. The upheavals became even more violent in 1788, and then the government made a great mistake: it promised to call the Estates-General. They had not met for almost two hundred years and in the long period of time there had been such great changes in the minds, the way of life, in the character, customs and government of the French nation that their meeting could now only produce upheaval.

alphahistory.com/French revolution/ryalist-causes-of-the-french-revoltuion-1797

- **What information does the source contain?** Both are trying to explain why a revolution occurred in France starting in 1789.
- **Who wrote them?** Source A is by a revolutionary directly involved in the revolution. Source B is by an aristocrat who had fled France.
- **When were they published?** 1793 and 1797. Both are clearly primary sources.

185

→

- **Context?** Source A was published in 1793, after the author's death during the early stages of the Terror. Source B was published in 1797, after the death of the king and the end of the Terror, and during the rule of the Directory.
- **Audience?** In both cases, as many people as possible.
- **Motive?** In both cases, the writers are trying to explain what had happened and why. There might be an element of trying to justify their positions.
- **Contextual/subject knowledge?** In both cases, the information they provide is accurate, if selective.
- **Validity? Provenance?** Both writers were involved in the events in France at the time, although on different sides of the revolutionary divide. While they might have been trying to justify their actions, they both tried to reach similar conclusions. Given that the author of Source B is an aristocrat, it is worth noting that he is critical of both the king and his own class, which adds to the validity of his comments.

A good way of comparing the views contained in these two sources is to devise a simple plan once you have read them carefully, keeping the focus strictly on the causes of the revolution. For example, Source A:

- stresses the growth of democracy – conditions were right for it
- points out that social and economic changes are bringing classes together
- notes that royal powers being undermined by the aristocracy was 'unfortunate'
- emphasises the failings of the First and Second Estates
- raises the point about Enlightenment ideas
- mentions the failings of the king.

Source B talks of:

- France in 'chaos'
- the failure to back Calonne
- the privileges of the nobility
- taxation
- the failings of the Notables
- wider unrest in Brittany, spreading to Paris
- the summoning of the Estates General and the lack of awareness of what had changed since it had last met.

From this plan it is easy to see where the authors disagree and agree.

Figure 5.1: The caption beneath the image translates as, 'The forces of the counter-revolution smashing themselves to pieces against the strength of the USSR'.

Visual sources: posters

Visual sources should be analysed and evaluated in much the same way as written ones. Look at Figure 5.1, a propaganda poster published during the civil war period in Russia. The fortress on the left represents Soviet Russia, and the warship on the right represents the counter-revolutionary forces.

- **What is the message of the poster?** That Russia is secure against the forces of counter-revolution.
- **Who is saying it?** The Bolshevik government, which controlled all the media in Russia at the time.
- **Context?** The civil war period in Russia, probably 1920. The newly established regime was involved in a life-and-death struggle against its many opponents, both inside Russia and externally in its former allies such as France and Britain.
- **Audience?** As wide a readership as possible, making a clear visual message which might appeal to the many illiterate people in Russia at the time.

- **Motives?** To convince the Russian people that the new regime was secure, and that supporting it, and not the counter-revolutionary Whites, was the most sensible course of action.
- **Contextual knowledge?** It demonstrates Bolshevik propaganda techniques well. The Bolsheviks were anxious to secure support from the mass of the Russian people.

Visual sources: photographs

Photographs also need careful analysis and evaluation.

- **What does Figure 5.2 tell us?** It shows a group of armed men charging towards the Winter Palace, apparently being fired on by opposition within it.
- **Who is providing the information?** In the case of photographs, the photographer is often anonymous, as is the case here. Was the photographer employed by the Bolsheviks, who might be anxious to demonstrate the heroism of the Red Guards? It might have been by someone neutral and therefore present a realistic picture of what happened.

Figure 5.2: The storming of the Winter Palace by the Red Guards, October 1917

- **When was it taken?** The Bolshevik government maintained that it was taken during the attack. It was later discovered that the photograph in fact shows a re-enactment staged well after the event.
- **Context?** Part of a propaganda exercise designed to emphasise the heroism of the Red Guards.
- **Audience?** This depends on whether it was published, and where. In this case, it was published as widely as possible, both within Russia and outside as part of a sustained Bolshevik propaganda campaign.
- **Motives of the photographer?** Impossible to say. It could be used to keep a record of what actually happened or for propaganda purposes. The latter is the most likely.
- **Subject knowledge?** There needs to be awareness of the events of 1917, particularly the actual seizure of power in St Petersburg and Moscow, and the later

Bolshevik campaign to gain support and emphasise the bravery of those who risked their lives in the successful revolution.

Like all sources, photographs can be of tremendous value to a historian, but they need to be used with care. Captions can be misleading and the action captured might actually be an re-enactment production. Airbrushing to remove individuals from photographs was common practice in Russia in the 1920s.

Visual sources: cartoons

Cartoons can be difficult to analyse. In most cases, they are drawn and published for two reasons:

- to amuse and entertain
- to make a point and send a message.

Figure 5.3: 'The Abbot today and the Abbot formerly', c.1789, published in a radical anti-clerical pamphlet circulating in France in 1789

To achieve either, or both, of these, cartoons might employ symbolism and a subtle form of humour which might be easily understandable to people at the time, but which is less obvious to us.

Look at Figure 5.3. The clergyman on the left, looking thin and hungry, represented the clergy in France after the confiscation of the Church's wealth, the one on the right, representing the clergy before the confiscation, looks very well fed and prosperous.

- **Who is providing the source?** It was one of many radical pamphlets circulating in France in the revolutionary period.
- **When was it published?** In 1789, but it was possibly in circulation earlier.
- **Context?** The clergy and the Roman Catholic Church in France, the First Estate, were not only very wealthy, but largely exempt from paying any taxes. The bulk of taxation was paid by the Third Estate. The majority of the clergy strongly opposed the demands of the Third Estate for reform after the meeting of the Estates General.
- **What is the message?** The reforms put forward by the National Convention were having an impact, and that the wealth and privilege of the clergy had been destroyed.
- **Audience?** As wide as possible. This type of pamphlet was getting a wide readership all over France and was playing a significant role in driving forward the revolutionary process.
- **Motives of the cartoonist and the editors of the pamphlet?** To maintain the attack on counter-revolutionary forces and emphasise the gains of the revolution.

When you study a cartoon like this, you need to reflect carefully how far your own subject knowledge supports or challenges the views represented.

Cross-referencing between sources

A source should never be used in isolation. It needs to be interpreted in the light of information obtained from other sources, as well as your own knowledge. There are three main reasons why cross-referencing between sources is so important:

- We can only judge how useful and reliable a source is by comparing it with what we already know and what other sources say.
- Reading several sources can help us deal with apparent contradictions and other concerns we might have about the source.

- By using a combination of sources, we can often deduce things that none of the individual sources would lead us to by themselves.

Look at the three sources below. Analyse and evaluate them as: a) different views of Father Gapon in 1905, and b) the causes of the 1905 Revolution.

SOURCE A

The American Ambassador to Russia writing to the US Secretary of State in Washington, 31 January 1905

Sir,

The changes which have come over the internal situation in Russia since my departure early in October mark distinctly the beginning of the end of the old regime and the dawn of a new era …

It is now clear to every impartial observer that the [trust] … of the working men had been worked upon by a group of socialists with Father Gapon, now raised by this press to the position of a demi-god – a sort of Second Saviour – at its head, although he has to his record the violation of a young girl of 12 years of age. My authority for this, and he told me that he spoke with knowledge, is the Austro-Hungarian Ambassador Baron d'Aehrenthal.

The correspondent of the 'Standard', who had an interview with this renegade priest, has told me that he was a thorough-paced revolutionist, and that he had utterly deceived the working men into the belief that his sole purpose was to aid them to better their condition, and secure from their employers concessions on the lines indicated in the appeal to the Emperor, which was drawn up by him. That his own purpose went beyond the mere presentation of this appeal now seems clear, and … there seems little doubt that his real intention was to get possession of the person of the Emperor and hold him as a hostage.

https://Alphahistory/Russianrevolution/us-ambassador-bloody-Sunday-1905/

189

SOURCE B

Father Gapon's eyewitness account, written later in 1905

We were not more than thirty yards from the soldiers, being separated from them only by the bridge over the Tarakanovskii Canal, which here marks the border of the city, when suddenly, without any warning and without a moment's delay, was heard the dry crack of many rifle-shots. I was informed later on that a bugle was blown, but we could not hear it above the singing, and even if we had heard it we should not have known what it meant.

Vasiliev, with whom I was walking hand in hand, suddenly left hold of my arm and sank upon the snow. One of the workmen who carried the banners fell also. Immediately one of the two police officers to whom I had referred shouted out, 'What are you doing? How dare you fire upon the portrait of the Tsar?' This, of course, had no effect, and both he and the other officer were shot down – as I learned afterwards, one was killed and the other dangerously wounded.

I turned rapidly to the crowd and shouted to them to lie down, and I also stretched myself out upon the ground. As we lay thus another volley was fired, and another, and yet

another, till it seemed as though the shooting was continuous. The crowd first kneeled and then lay flat down, hiding their heads from the rain of bullets, while the rear rows of the procession began to run away. The smoke of the fire lay before us like a thin cloud, and I felt it stiflingly in my throat …

A little boy of ten years, who was carrying a church lantern, fell pierced by a bullet, but still held the lantern tightly and tried to rise again, when another shot struck him down. Both the smiths who had guarded me were killed, as well as all those who were carrying the icons and banners; and

all these emblems now lay scattered on the snow. The soldiers were actually shooting into the courtyards of the adjoining houses, where the crowd tried to find refuge and, as I learned afterwards, bullets even struck persons inside, through the windows.

Horror crept into my heart. The thought flashed through my mind, 'And this is the work of our Little Father, the Tsar.' Perhaps this anger saved me, for now I knew in very truth that a new chapter was opened in the book of the history of our people. I stood up, and a little group of workmen gathered round me again. Looking backward, I saw that our line, though still stretching away into the distance, was broken and that many of the people were fleeing. It was in vain that I called to them, and in a moment I stood there, the centre of a few scores of men, trembling with indignation amid the broken ruins of our peaceful movement to help our people.

https://Alphahistory/Russianrevolution/eye-witness-account-of-bloody-Sunday-1905/

SOURCE C

Leon Trotsky writing on Father Gapon and Bloody Sunday when in exile in 1930

The forms taken by the historic events of January 9th could not, of course, have been foreseen by anyone. The priest whom history had so unexpectedly placed for a few days at the head of the working masses imposed the imprint of his personality, his views and his priestly status on the events. The real content of these events was concealed from many eyes by their form. But the inner significance of January 9th goes far beyond the symbolism of the procession to the Winter Palace.

→

Gapon's priestly robe was only a prop in that drama; the protagonist was the proletariat. The proletariat began with a strike, united itself, advanced political demands, came out into the streets, drew to itself the enthusiastic sympathy of the entire population, clashed with the troops and set off the Russian revolution. Gapon did not create the revolutionary energy of the workers of St. Petersburg; he merely released it, to his own surprise. The son of a priest, and then a seminarian and student at the Religious Academy, this agitator, so obviously encouraged by the police, suddenly found himself at the head of a crowd of a hundred thousand men and women. The political situation, his priestly robe, the elemental excitement of the masses which, as yet, had little political consciousness, and the fabulously rapid course of events turned Gapon into a 'leader'.

The liberals persisted for a long time in the belief that the entire secret of the events of January 9th lay in Gapon's personality. It contrasted him with the social democrats as though he were a political leader who knew the secret of controlling the masses. In doing so they forgot that January 9th would not have taken place if Gapon had not encountered several thousand politically conscious workers who had been through the school of socialism. These men immediately formed an iron ring around him, a ring from which he could not have broken loose even if he had wanted to.

But he made no attempt to break loose. Hypnotized by his own success, he let himself be carried by the waves. But although, on the very next day after Bloody Sunday, we ascribed to Gapon a wholly subordinate political role, we all undoubtedly overestimated his personality. With his halo of holy anger, with a pastor's curses on his lips, he seemed from afar almost to be a Biblical figure. It seemed as though powerful revolutionary passions had been awakened in the breast of this young priest employed at a Petersburg transit prison.

https://Alpha history/Russianrevolution/Trotsky-on-the-1905-revolution/

There is a contradiction between the information provided by the three sources.

- Source A is highly critical of Gapon, his background and his motives. Ambassadors should, in principle, be impartial and informed observers, but this appears to be an exception. It is notable that he has not been back in Russia for long, and he clearly does not like socialists. Where does he get his information from about the 12-year-old girl? It is hearsay. He suggests that Gapon is intending to seize the emperor. Is there any evidence of this elsewhere?

- Source B is written by Father Gapon himself sometime in the months after the march. He was, of course, there and playing a leading role. There is no indication that he is exaggerating his role and he writes much about the bravery of others and the way in which the tsar's troops fired on a defenceless crowd. There appears to be no evidence of the sort of motives attributed to him by either Sources A or C. He comes across as a simple, brave man trying to make a point with his 'icons and banners'. There is plenty of evidence elsewhere to support what he says, but we should consider the possibility of him trying to downplay radical ideas or personal ambitions, or show himself to be braver than he actually was.

- Source C was written by Trotsky, a leading revolutionary, some years after the event. He was out of Russia in January 1905, but returned the following month to St Petersburg. He puts forward a very different image of Father Gapon, calling him an 'agitator' who became a leader 'by accident'. Trotsky is trying to fit Gapon and his march into his interpretation of events in Russia in the years before the revolution, in which Trotsky played a leading part.

By linking these three sources with our background subject knowledge, we can conclude that Gapon was seen in a very different light by different people, and many different motives can be attributed to him and his movement.

A summary on dealing with source-based questions

- Show that you have fully grasped what the source is saying. Try highlighting the key points. Remember that the key point can often be in the last sentence.
- Demonstrate that you have thought about its provenance and reliability. You must not just accept what

the source is saying. Think about what the author might have left out. You need to test a source's reliability by:

- comparing what it says with what other sources say and with your own subject knowledge
- looking carefully at who created it, when, why and for what purpose or audience.
- establishing if there are any reasons to doubt the reliability of the source

- Interpret. What can be learned from the source, taking into account your judgement on how reliable the source is?
- Keep objective. Always look at a source objectively and with an open mind.
- Never make assumptions. For example, don't assume that a source must be biased because it was written by a certain person from a certain place at a certain time. These points might establish a motive for bias, but do not necessarily prove that a text is biased.
- Never make sweeping or unsupported assertions. A statement such as 'Source A is biased...' *must* be accompanied by evidence that you know exactly what bias is as well as evidence and examples to demonstrate in what way it is biased, together with reasons to explain why it is biased.
- Compare sources. If you are asked to compare and contrast two sources, make sure you analyse both sources carefully before you start to write your answer. Draw up a simple plan.
- Evaluate the sources clearly.
- Draw conclusions: what can you learn from your analysis of the sources? How does it enhance your knowledge and understanding of a topic or event?
- Include contextual knowledge.

5.4 How might my skills and work be assessed?

Revision techniques

Too often, students think that the purpose of revision is to get information into their brain in preparation for an assessment. It is seen as a process where facts are learned. If you have followed the course appropriately, however, and made sensibly laid-out notes as you have gone along, all the information you need is already there. The human brain, like a computer, does not forget what it has experienced. The key purpose of revision is not to put information into the brain, but to ensure that you can retrieve it when it is required.

Revision needs to be an ongoing process throughout the course, not just in the days or weeks before an exam. The focus of your revision should be identifying the key points, on, for example, why there was unrest in Britain after 1815. Once you have those key points clear, the supporting detail will come back to you. The notes you make during the course therefore are very important, and it is vital that they are presented effectively.

Copying lists of facts from a book can be a pointless exercise. You need to think about what you are writing, comprehend it and learn to analyse it. Make your notes in such a way that you are answering a simple question. For example: 'What were the most important causes of the 1905 Revolution in Russia?' Don't just write a list of the causes. Prioritise them with reasons. This will prompt you to study all the various things that happened in Russia in the build-up to the events of 1905. You will think about which issues were the most important and why. Once you have identified the key points, make sure there are two or three relevant factors which show that you understand why they were key points. Doing this will then help you deal with a variety of questions, such as: 'Explain why there was a revolution in Russia in 1905' and 'To what extent was the 1905 Revolution caused by the failings of the tsar?'

Quality revision and plenty of practice in attempting questions under timed conditions is vital. If you feel you have not done enough at school, you could ask your teacher to provide some questions so you can practise on your own under timed conditions.

Exam preparation

This section offers a few general points about how you could approach an examination. Some might seem obvious, but it is worth remembering that, under pressure, we are all capable of making mistakes. It is useful to be aware of potential pitfalls.

The syllabus will include details of what you need to know during your course and for the exams. You should be aware of:

- What topics the questions can be about. This will be covered during your course.
- What form the questions can take. Your teacher can help you understand the types of task you are likely to face, and the syllabus will give details of wording. The different types of question in this book should also help you become more familiar with exam-style questions.

192

- How long you will have to answer an assessment paper.
- Which parts of a question paper you can ignore. Some papers might have separate sections for those who have studied International History and for those who have studied US History.
- The equipment you will need for writing and what you may or may not bring into an exam room. There are very strict rules on mobile phones, for example, and smart watches. Check if you are allowed to bring water in.

Rubric

- All examination papers contain **rubric**. This provides you with essential information about how long a timed assessment will last, how many questions you have to answer and from what sections, and so on. It is surprising how many students make rubric errors each year, by attempting too many questions, for example, or questions from inappropriate sections of a paper These basic errors can really damage your chances of success.

KEY TERM

Rubric: This is the set of rules and instructions you must follow in an exam. They will usually tell you how long the exam will last, where to put your answers, how many questions to answer and from which sections.

Question selection

Sometimes, you will be required to answer all the questions in a paper. However, if you have an opportunity to choose, for example, two out of three questions, this advice might be useful:

- Read all parts of all questions before you make your selection.
- Avoid choosing a question just because it is about a *topic* you feel confident about. This is not necessarily a guarantee that you understand what the question is asking and you can answer it effectively.
- Select by task – what the question is asking you to do – rather than by the basic subject matter. A question might ask, for example, 'To what extent was mass immigration the major cause of rapid industrialisation in the late 19th century?' You might know about the mass immigration, but might not have revised all the other vital factors which contributed to rapid industrialisation. Be careful.
- If questions consist of more than one part, make sure that you can answer all parts. Avoid attempting a

question because you are confident about the topic in part (a) if you know very little about part (b).
- Decide the order in which you are going to attempt the questions. Perhaps you should not leave the question you feel most confident about until last if you are worried about running out of time.

Timing

It is a good idea to work out in advance how long you have to complete each question or part of a question. Make a note of it and make every effort to keep to that timing.

Practising answering questions under timed conditions is something you can do on your own as part of your revision Take care not to make the mistake of spending too much time on a question which you know a great deal about and leave yourself insufficient time for a question which might carry twice as many marks.

If you run out of time, you will not be able to answer all the questions fully. If you have spent too long on your first question with its two parts, there might be a case for attempting the second part of the next question if it carries more marks.

Planning

There is nearly always the temptation in an exam to just get started rather than spending time on planning. Without planning, however, there is very real risk of including irrelevant information, or not fully explaining the relevance of information.

A useful plan for an 'Explain why …' question might be three or four bullet points identifying the main reasons for the event, in order of importance, with a couple of supporting facts for each. Effective plans for the longer essay-type questions, such as 'To what extent …', could be set out in 'case for' and 'case against' columns or as a mind-map, which has a focus on thinking out an answer. A plain list of facts will not be much help as a plan. Use the plan to clarify your ideas on what the question is asking.

How much information should be included in a response?

This is not a straightforward question to answer. An important factor to remember at AS Level is that about 50% of marks are allocated to your knowledge and understanding of a topic, and about 50% to the skills used in applying them. In the source-based sample questions provided in this book, you can see that it is important to bring in contextual knowledge to back up your source evaluation and the points you are making. You might find that including a couple of factual points, such as 'The tsar was writing this in 1906, as part of his aim to prevent more unrest' is a suitable approach for the first part of a source-based question. For a second part, where you should develop a case, the points you make need to be backed up by clear references to the sources, and then by at least two factual points.

For questions in papers where there are no sources, the factual information plays a more significant role. However, this information should provide support to your arguments, rather than dominating your response. In an 'explain why' type of question, it is most important to identify the reasons why something happened, and then back up each of those reasons with two or three items of information. In essay-type questions, you should think in terms of bringing three or four factual items to support your points. Look on facts as the evidence of your knowledge and understanding.

How much should I write?

There is no requirement to write a specific number of words in a response, nor to fill a certain number of pages. Aim to keep your focus on writing a relevant response to the question set and making sure that you are aware of the assessment criteria for the type of question you are dealing with. Don't worry if another student seems to be writing more than you are.

Past papers

Previous exam papers can be very helpful. They will give an idea of what types of question have been assessed in the past and provide plenty of opportunities for practise. If you use past papers, it is important to attempt the questions under the appropriate timed conditions. It should be stressed, however, that, while tackling past papers is very good practice, attempting to memorise answers is very poor preparation. Students who produce ready-made answers are likely to be answering a question they expected, not the one they are actually being asked.

The syllabus

The syllabus provides:

- details of the options to be studied at AS level
- how many options have to be taken

- how long each examination is
- what proportion of the overall marks are allocated to each paper
- the assessment objectives and the relationship between them and the different papers you take. It might say, for example, that:
  - 30% of the total marks at AS Level are awarded for Assessment Objective (AO) 1(a), which is knowledge and understanding in Paper 2
  - 30% of the marks are awarded for AO2(a), which is analysis and evaluation in Paper 2
- details of each of the papers, what form the questions take and how many questions there are in each paper; if there are sources, it will be clear how many there will be, what type of sources might be used and the maximum number of words in an extract, so you will know how much you will have to read
- the key questions; these indicate broad areas of history for study; all questions set in the exam will fit into one of the key questions. To use the International syllabus as an example, if a key question is 'Why was there a rapid growth of industrialisation after 1780?', then one of the AS Level exam questions might be something like, 'To what extent was improved transport the principal cause of the rapid industrialisation in the late 18th century?'
- key content; this suggests some of the areas which should be studied, but these are not all the areas to study for a key question; the fact that you are studying something which is not specified in the key content does not mean it will not be examined.

There are decisions to be made by your teachers when it comes to AS Level History. There might be a choice of areas of study – for example, between European history and American history. The choice might depend on the teachers' expertise and the range of resources available in your school. There may also be a choice of how many topics to study. Your teachers will decide whether to study all three topics, in order to give you a choice of question in the exam, or just study two, in order to focus on them and so build up additional knowledge and understanding.

There are real benefits to having the syllabus available in helping you know what to expect during your course and in the assessments.

Mark schemes

Mark schemes accompany the question papers and make it clear how your work will be assessed. They are in two parts. The first is a generic mark scheme, which lays out what is required from a response in general terms. This will specify the elements that make up a high-quality work, such as developed analysis, balance or source evaluation. The second part indicates the type of factual support expected and the principal points in a 'compare and contrast' question.

The mark scheme helps you to see what a good-quality answer looks like and you can use this to reflect on your own work and consider how it might be improved. The mark scheme makes it clear that just learning facts is not enough, you need to demonstrate a range of skills as well.

Assessment objectives

Assessment objectives cover the skills to be tested in the exams. The assessment objectives (AO) for AS Level History are:

- AO1: Recall, select and deploy historical knowledge appropriately and effectively.
- AO2: Demonstrate an understanding of the past through explanation, analysis and a substantiated judgement of: key concepts causation, consequence, continuity, change and significance within an historical context, the relationships between key features and characteristics of the periods studied.
- AO3: Analyse, evaluate and interpret a range of appropriate source material.
- AO4: Analyse and evaluate how aspects of the past have been interpreted and represented.

Index